The Long Road to Grace
Confessions of a Slow Learner

Merlin Nichols

TEACH Services, Inc.
PUBLISHING
www.TEACHServices.com • (800) 367-1844

World rights reserved. This book or any portion thereof may not be copied or reproduced in any form or manner whatever, except as provided by law, without the written permission of the publisher, except by a reviewer who may quote brief passages in a review.

The author assumes full responsibility for the accuracy of all facts and quotations as cited in this book. The opinions expressed in this book are the author's personal views and interpretations, and do not necessarily reflect those of the publisher.

This book is provided with the understanding that the publisher is not engaged in giving spiritual, legal, medical, or other professional advice. If authoritative advice is needed, the reader should seek the counsel of a competent professional.

Copyright © 2015 Merlin Nichols

Copyright © 2015 TEACH Services, Inc.

ISBN-13: 978-1-4796-0351-0 (Paperback)

ISBN-13: 978-1-4796-0352-7 (ePub)

ISBN-13: 978-1-4796-0353-4 (Mobi)

Library of Congress Control Number: 2015901970

All scripture quotations, unless otherwise indicated, are taken from the Holy Bible, New International Version®, NIV®. Copyright © 1973, 1978, 1984, 2011 by Biblica, Inc.™ Used by permission of Zondervan. All rights reserved worldwide.

Scripture quotations marked NIV84 are taken from the Holy Bible, New International Version®, NIV®. Copyright © 1973, 1978, 1984, by Biblica, Inc.™ Used by permission of Zondervan. All rights reserved worldwide.

Scripture quotations marked KJV are taken from the King James Version. Public domain.

Scripture quotations marked NKJV™ are taken from the New King James Version®. Copyright © 1982 by Thomas Nelson, Inc. Used by permission. All rights reserved.

Published by

TEACH Services, Inc.
PUBLISHING
www.TEACHServices.com • (800) 367-1844

Contents

Foreword 5

Prologue 7

Introduction 9

1. From the Shoulders of a Giant 15

2. The Dead Become One 41

3. A Mystery That Reveals 64

4. United We Grow 95

5. Focusing the Light 128

6. In Submitting Conquer 156

Epilogue 177

To Mirja
who has been my constant friend,
counsellor, critic, and wife for 52 years.

Life with you has been good.

Foreword

My wife and I have known Merlin Nichols over the last half century or so. We knew him first as a school teacher, and later we worked together for several years on the board of Canadian University College. We saw him as earnest, dedicated, thoughtful, concerned, and discerning. I remember that when he spoke on the board, we all listened. Did we see the real person? You'll have to decide.

Following his stint on the board, we lost contact for several years until one day we received a phone call requesting that we read a manuscript he had written on Ephesians. Having never read anything he had written, we were not prepared for our delight in the literary excellence, clarity of thought, and down-to-earth applications we experienced in our read.

You will be delighted, too, as you join the author "on the shoulders of Paul." Written in a "Merlin" style, this is a book that will appeal to people of any level of education as it compels the reader to search his own soul for those long-hidden secrets.

The author's focus is on spiritually energizing us ordinary people as we travel this earthly road through grace to glory. Writing from personal experience, his special concern is for those who, perhaps unconsciously, are relying on their church pedigree rather than on a personal relationship with Jesus to see them through.

Never known for fishing in murky theological waters, the author has produced a work that is theologically spot on as it deals with issues of every-day life. He has succeeded in transferring the enthusiasm of the apostle Paul to us ordinary readers who frequently struggle with maintaining a living faith as we navigate the mazes of this world.

As you ride through Ephesians with the author on the shoulders of Paul, you will find yourself asking many questions: Squeezed between time and the frustrations of life, how can I find my personal high road that Paul challenges me to travel? Is my reputation as a Christian a façade or a reality? Do I have the true joy of a daily relationship with my Creator? Can I praise God for sins forgiven and the power to live for Jesus? Do I understand true righteousness by faith? Am I not yet tired enough of the futility of my self-generated attempts at holy living? Will the cares of this life or even plain and ordinary lethargy ultimately do me in spiritually?

Is there hope? Find out what this book offers to us regular folk as we travel through life. Confessions will excite you, encourage you, energize you, and humble you. You will be challenged by the author's personal journey as you, too, reflect on your life from the shoulders of Paul. The author lowers you to the depths of your soul as he reinterprets Paul's Ephesians in the context of our modern lives. You will not be left in despair but will be elevated to the mountain peaks of joyful freedom as you experience the power of the Holy Spirit changing your focus and your life.

In this book the author relates his own experiences as a failing Christian who finally comes to full trust, confidence, and life in Jesus. It is the story of a journey from failure in self to victory in Jesus. It is a story that inspires hope as we learn to trust in the forgiveness given in Jesus and in the power of the Holy Spirit to lead us to ultimate victory.

The Long Road to Grace

While the author leads us through Ephesians in the context of our normal lives and daily experiences, this story is really about Jesus, you, and me.

Yes, I was surprised to be asked to review this manuscript, but accepting the assignment led me to a deeper appreciation of the meaning of Ephesians for my own life.

If you are not satisfied with where you are with God today, and be wary of spiritual satisfaction, then this read is for you. Go ahead. Turn that page.

Bob and Myrna Tetz
West Kelowna, British Columbia
June 2014

Prologue

This is my personal story. Perhaps it is your story, too. I had believed in Jesus all my life, but He wasn't the Jesus who jumped into the swamp to save me. He was a Jesus who, though possibly willing to help me out a bit if I did my best first, always insisted that my best was never good enough, nor could it be. When I became good enough to pray, He might listen to me and give me a hand up. For decades I simply could not achieve that elusive, good-enough state of existence. It was always tantalizingly out of reach. I felt as if I was about to be swallowed by quicksand. With a history of sweating out my own salvation—and failing—my fiftieth year was upon me, and my prospects of salvation remained just a faint hope.

I am amazed now that I could have held church office, preached to the saints, contributed to the cause, and performed other acts worthy of the faithful while remaining in a state of spiritual death. Spiritual death linked with church membership is dark, cold, and terribly discouraging, because those in death are aware of their continuing failure to perform, cannot see the way out, and are reluctant or embarrassed to ask for help. They are also delusional, convinced that all will be well with their souls—someday—when they get their acts together, or so they hope. But the act never comes together. And it cannot come together because the only One who can bring it together is out in the cold knocking, unheard, unseen.

Where were all the guardians of the faithful who should have recognized my desperate condition and dispatched search and rescue to my aid? Were they out there in their own private, cold swamps just as I was? Were they just as dead in sin as I was? Did they need the reviving draft of the Holy Spirit as much as I did? Was it that I was just too spiritually atrophied to grasp a helping hand stretched out to me?

We all love a story. I am about to tell you mine. There is a thread of life that links us together from Montgomery to Melbourne, from Denver to Dawson Creek, from Calgary to Cape Town, from Athens to Anchorage, all around the world. The thread of life passes through ancient Ephesus. All threads of life tie us to Ephesus. The metaphors we use will be different, but the thread is the same. Our stories will be different—and yet they, too, will be the same.

I am telling you my story from the shoulders of the apostle Paul as he brings the gospel of grace through Ephesus to us in the twenty-first century. You can do the same; I welcome you to join me on Paul's shoulders and look at life, hope, and forgiveness from his perspective. Your eyes will be opened, your mind expanded, your soul refreshed.

Jesus did, indeed, send His Spirit to revive my soul. You are reading the story of my rescue from a deeply delusional experience, the story of my spiritual resurrection from deadness in sin, and the story of God's grace for this little part of the dying race. It is the story of what God is able, willing, eager, and ready to do for each one of His self-deceived children, for you as well as for me! There is no more need to play hide-and-seek with God. Let Him find you, revive you, restore you, and bring you into grace with its assurance of glory.

Story time! Listen up!

Introduction

Most of us who read the Bible do so without the benefit of personal knowledge of the original languages. Nor do most of us have a profound grasp of the various historical, social, or political contexts in which it was written. If we want to be informed by the linguistic and historical backgrounds, we are at the mercy of the scholars, who tend to intimidate us with wordy technicalities as they, too, struggle to understand or attempt to maintain their theological and historical positions. Archaeological discoveries do shed some light on the Scriptures, but there are still some limitations as understanding of the evidence is always subject to the biases of the scholars interpreting the dusty works of antiquity.

I have a deep respect for scholars and appreciate the windows into the past that they have opened. In fact, I refer to their expertise almost daily. For quick reference, and with some exceptions, the helps in study Bibles are frequently quite insightful—except when they attempt to explain away prophecy (I've noticed the predominant scholarly concept of prophecy is that prophecy, in the sense of predicting the future, does not happen). I recognize the humanity of the scholars with their frailties and foibles; however, we are deeply indebted to them for making the Scriptures available to us ordinary people in the languages that we have at our command. Sixteenth-century Erasmus of Rotterdam, in spite of his failure to take a stand on the side of reform, was one of the most influential scholars of early modern times. By providing an accurate and readable translation of the Scriptures from the original languages, he supported the work of Luther, Tyndale, Melanchthon, and others as they rendered the holy texts into the languages of the people.

Thankfully, we ordinary people are not entirely disadvantaged. In fact, we are far from disadvantaged. We, along with all sincere searchers for truth, scholars included, have free access to the Holy Spirit, who inspired the prophetic outbursts, instructions, and praises we are now studying (2 Peter 1:21). Under His guidance we may focus our Creator-endowed intelligence on understanding and applying the modern renditions of prophecy, poetry, history, and literature that we call the Holy Bible. In the twenty-first century, we are benefiting from the work of many minds over the centuries. The multiple translations available now make it possible for us ordinary students of Scripture to read, compare versions, and apply the messages from God to ourselves.

Applying God's message is my purpose in writing. I am seeking to personally engage the mind of Paul as he records the message of God's grace to the Ephesians, then relate that message in the context of the mindsets of today, whether those reading are truck drivers, school teachers, tire techs, cowboys, Indians, bus drivers, or other ordinary folk like myself. If you happen to be an accountant, a merchant prince, or even a nobody, don't feel you are left out. You're all in. Peruse these pages and graze them for what they are worth. If they provoke your fertile mind to get out of its rut, shake off its lethargy, stretch its limits, and discover grace in Scripture for yourself, this purpose is served well.

I have been looking into Paul's Ephesians for several years and marveling at the robust spirituality and depth of insight I encounter in its 123 verses. As if written by a rock climber, choosing each word like a handhold with meticulous care, yet pausing to contemplate the surrounding peaks and gorges, it inspires confidence. Don't even think of traveling alone when exploring Ephesians. Take with you your Holy Spirit guide. Paul challenges the mind with concepts that rake

If you want to go far hang on to your Guide.

the heavens and plumb the deeps. His spiritual horizons, spreading wide like an untracked valley just now glimpsed for the first time from a mountain ridge, beckon the traveler to adventure into the magnificence of God's grace.

I found that I must be prepared to extend my wings and soar like the eagle, which is simply another way of saying I must wait on the Lord (Isa. 40:31). Spreading wings is the act of faith that allows the gracious Spirit of God to carry us to heights and distances otherwise not even touchable by the imagination. The alternative is to remain earthbound, stolid, uncomprehending, unmoved, and ungraced. As with eagle's wings, glossy pinions won't get us anywhere if they are kept prettily folded while we gaze over grand vistas that call for exploration. The sight of the heights and breadths of grace in Ephesians will motivate us to unfold our wings to catch the invisible wind of the gracious Spirit.

Never having acquired the courage to strap on a pair of wings and dash down the slope into thin air, I have had to admire the hang gliders from the solid earth as they silently maneuver their flimsy crafts on the invisible wind. With my personal experience in the sky limited to jumping out of airplanes with a canopy of fabric packed to deploy on demand over my head, I am more familiar with the relentless attraction of the earth. In my experience, God's grace is like that canopy, preventing my deadly impact on unforgiving soil. In soaring through Ephesians, we should expect to be humbled and awed repeatedly by encounters with divine grace in every paragraph or, from the eagles' or hang gliders' perspective, we will find grace on every mountain peak, in every plummeting gorge, and across every wide-spreading valley.

During our winters I take my Bible to the furnace room each morning where I read until the wood furnace fires up and the heat drives me out to cooler rooms. For several months I have been focusing on reading aloud the letter to the Ephesians each day and have even come to the point where I think I could memorize it entirely—well, why not? Don't be nearly so skeptical. Other people have memorized longer pieces, if not greater works. In my solitary oral reading, I endeavor to express the emotion that I sense in the written text. Expressing the feeling as well as vocalizing the words helps me to appreciate the sentiments that fired Paul's thoughts as he traced those marks on sheep skin and parchment many lifetimes ago.

So many writings that could have satisfied our curiosity about the past, stimulated our imaginations, and directed our investigations of the works of our Father God have been lost through ignorance, greed, avarice, war, and even apathy. Whole libraries have been wantonly burned, their writings now secrets to all but the Almighty. Other libraries have been rediscovered only recently. Their treasures are still shrouded in mystery, reburied in political or professional rivalries, after lying hidden in the dust for centuries. Shameful! Antiquity still is largely a mystery to us. Oh, yes, we have a few ideas, but they are really more like speculations about the relatively few artifacts and writings from the distant past that we have studied. Sadly, these artifacts are interpreted by a worldview that ignores the Creator God, our Father.

In 1900 a mineral-encrusted device was found in a Roman shipwreck off the coast of the Greek island Antikythera. The wreck, with its load of ancient wealth and breath-taking artifacts of a civilization long dead, had lain undetected beneath the blue waters of the Mediterranean for maybe 2,200 years, the rhymes of the ancient mariners as they sang their sea ditties from port to port not even a distant echo. The device found, now called the Antikythera mechanism, lay largely neglected again for more than half a century, this time in a Greek museum. Many years were required to develop the capacity to probe its secrets that are only now being studied.

This intricate mechanism does not fit within our modern worldview as seen through the lens of Darwin, Lyell, and their disciples. Will we shut our eyes or will we modify our worldview to accommodate the modern-type technology that obviously was familiar to the ancients long before the time of Jesus? It makes one wonder if we should read Cicero in a different light. It is entirely plausible that he was at least familiar with the Antikythera mechanism, even if he didn't use it in his daily routines. Could it be that there are other artifacts from forgotten civilizations, still interpreted as cult objects or mere curiosities, that are in fact, mechanical-electrical-technological devices that we do not recognize because we have lost the knowledge that the ancients possessed?

My point? Our omnipotent Father has preserved the Holy Scriptures as written documents. Obviously He considers them to be crucial for our spiritual development and our grace life with Him. While these were preserved, other documents and devices from antiquity, marvelous, inspiring, and useful as they may have been, have been allowed to return to dust, ashes, and mineral-encrusted relics on the bottom of the seas. The flaky artifacts of long-forgotten civilizations that we have found terrify us because we cannot at the same time believe what our eyes see and what Darwin and Lyell told us we should see.

In Ephesians we encounter a God-preserved document of grace from an ancient era that He obviously considers important; He preserved it intact through 2,000 years of ignorance, apathy, upheaval, destruction, neglect, and mayhem. What do you suppose are His feelings when we despise or merely neglect so great a work of spiritual energy and so powerful a source of grace as Paul's Ephesians? What do you suppose are His feelings when we focus our energies on weak and beggarly artifacts of modern depravity or even on the countless artifacts of enlightened ingenuity?

When our work on earth is done, we will have to explain to our Father God the reasons for the choices we made with the things and the time at our disposal. Was the choice time based? Was it because I was listening to the gracious Spirit of God and responding to Him? Was the choice in response to the depraved instincts and urgings of my old nature? Did I succumb to the gentle but unrelenting pressure of my peers (adults are not immune to peer pressure)? All choices have incremental results and eternal ramifications. It was the great leader of the Israelites, Joshua, who urged his followers to choose in the only time they had, today, and not put off that choice until tomorrow (Josh. 24:15). I think Paul would have concurred heartily with Joshua.

What about the setting in which the church at Ephesus was born, nurtured, grew up, and eventually died? The ancient city of Ephesus is well-known to us moderns, and its ruins annually attract thousands of visitors to marvel at the wonders of antiquity. My wife, Mirja (pronounced Mir-ya), and I recently enjoyed a Revelation Cruise in which we walked the stone-paved streets that Paul walked, deep in thought or conversation; we felt the cooling shade of the same stones that sheltered Paul's head from the blazing Asian sun; we paused to encounter descendants of the people to whom Paul gave the gospel those many centuries ago; we stood where he stood as, with salty tears, he said farewell to the church in Ephesus. Our encounter with Paul's past brought hot and sweaty tangibility to his life.

The culture of the city in which Paul spent about ten percent of his ministry was, in Paul's time, already rich in the traditions of many nations and many generations. Ephesus was founded in the tenth century before Christ on the stones of previous civilizations. For a millennium before Paul arrived, conquerors, traders, priests, artisans, clerks, laborers, camp followers, and scholars had rubbed shoulders, shattered swords, and left their spawn in Ephesus. The city reflected the cosmopolitan nature of a busy commercial center and seaport where, according to legend, a god had fallen down from heaven and taken up residence in one of its magnificent temples.

The temple of Artemis (the god who fell) is said to have been among the largest buildings of ancient times. As one of the ancient world's seven wonders, it was situated in this greatest of Asia's cities with 500,000 devotees readily available to bow in awe or dread of fertile Artemis—and spend their money for silver shrines and images of Artemis in the shops of the silversmiths. You must remember Demetrius, the silversmith-merchant and leader of the guild of silversmiths. Demetrius and his guild profited enormously by playing on the superstition and fear of the masses, but because of the preaching of Paul, the guild's profits would soon take a serious hit.

Ephesus was at its peak of prosperity, influence, and decadence when the apostle Paul, taking the road through the interior of Asia (Acts 19:1), arrived with the gospel of grace in this stronghold of the gods. Shortly thereafter, he entered the office of Tyrannus, a local businessman and owner of a lecture hall. They agreed on the terms of the lease, and for two years and three months Paul, speaking boldly and arguing persuasively about the kingdom of God, held daily discussions in the lecture hall between 11:00 a.m. and 4:00 p.m.

It seems that in actual day-by-day routines of work, politics, school, or play, Paul's era was not very far removed from our own. Paul's teaching had results. A strong church, saved by grace and motivated and empowered by its first love of God, reached out to surrounding cities even before Paul moved on to other fields. So effective was his teaching in Ephesus that the guild of the silversmiths, to prevent further loss to their lucrative trade in toy silver gods and shrines, raised a riot to drive Paul out of town. Actually, Paul had been preparing to leave about then for other fields of ministry, and the riot coincided with his departure.

Paul met the leaders of the Ephesus church some months later when he stopped at Miletus on his way to Jerusalem. This was Paul's last face-to-face encounter with the believers in Ephesus. His letter to the Ephesians, likely written from prison in Rome perhaps four years later, is his last known communication with this congregation of believers. The only additional information we have on the church in Ephesus is found in John's Revelation. We learn from John, writing thirty years after Paul's departure, that the church in the city of Artemis was still hard working, persevering, continuing clear on doctrine, remaining righteously intolerant of wicked behavior, and bravely enduring hardship for God without growing weary. But something had gone wrong.

Love, growing cold, had quietly abandoned the hearts of the believers. The Head of the church was clearly dissatisfied with this state of the heart of the Ephesians. He had some pointed and unmistakable direction for the errant congregation (Rev. 2:1–7). Did they heed? Did they tune their ears to the message from heaven? Had they lost their ears (Rev. 2:7)? We don't know, but now we must go back to Paul's letter to hear directly from Paul the message of grace that he wished them to live and share. And this is also our message to live and to share; there really is no other viable option. Let's not be slow to receive it. Let's take every opportunity to share it whether the time is right or wrong, whether we feel like it or not. I would suggest that if you receive an impression, however fleeting, to share God's grace with someone, that urge is prompted by the Holy Spirit, and you will do well to heed it.

A few years ago I was chatting with a member of my teaching staff about Ephesians, and I mentioned that I would like to do a study of the letter from the perspective of the untutored Bible reader. This is that study, and it has actually become the story of my life. I feel as if I am riding through grace on Paul's shoulders, seeing my life through his eyes. As a retired lumber piler, tree faller, choker setter, janitor, farmer, building contractor, truck driver, school teacher, college administrator (I finally found my niche), and now mayor of my home town, I am attempting to cross many of your trails as you, too, travel in grace. Climb on Paul's shoulders and examine your world from a higher perspective. Let this story of my experience in grace bring you in touch with your own story.

Riding through Grace on Paul's shoulders – what a ride!

All quotations printed in italics at the beginning of each section, and at times repeated in the chapter, are my own paraphrases of the passage. I have endeavored to maintain the sense and meaning of the translations I use, and occasionally I have drawn from other sources for clarification. For your own clarity of doctrine, pleased do not depend on a paraphrase; instead, always refer to some modern translation of which there are many. This study of Ephesians is intended to stimulate your thinking. It is not to be dogmatic about doctrine—though it should be very clear where I stand on any point. Please do not use my paraphrases and comments to establish a doctrine. Unless otherwise noted, biblical passages within the text also are my own paraphrases. Scripture allusions as well as all direct quotations from the Bible and other sources are italicized and referenced, so quotations marks are not always used. Direct quotations are from the NIV unless otherwise indicated.

I trust that my style, rather than confusing you, will stimulate you to check the reference from your favorite translation of Holy Scripture. I have endeavored throughout to be true to the Word of God, so please examine in the light of the Bible any statement in this story that concerns you. If my interpretation strays from the clear biblical meaning, well, then, you know which trail to follow.

Enjoy!

Chapter 1
From the Shoulders of a Giant

**Hi Folks, the Name's Paul,
and I Belong to Jesus Christ**

From Paul (I belong to Jesus Christ and was sent by Him to you as an apostle), to all you saints in Ephesus, you believers in Christ who by the decision of our Father God are in His Son, Jesus Christ; to you who remain faithful to your position in Christ Jesus: grace and peace to you from our Father, God, and from His Son, our Lord, Jesus Christ. (Eph. 1:1, 2)

Hey! Bus Drivers, Astronauts, Hair Dressers, Everyone—The church in Ephesus was very dear to the heart of Paul. While duty called him to other fields after building this body of believers, he could say with confidence that he had never hesitated to proclaim to them the whole Word of God with humility and tears (Acts 20:19). Oh, that we all would hold nothing back (Acts 20:27). Only then would we would feel something akin to the raw emotion of Paul and follow his example in living and sharing the gospel! It was with a clear conscience that Paul dedicated the leaders of the Ephesus congregation to God and commanded them to carry on their duties faithfully. By the seaside in Miletus, he prayed with these church leaders, committing them to the care and direction of our Father, then took his ship to a grand destiny through Jerusalem to Rome—and beyond.

Who were the leaders in Ephesus? Were they theologians? Were they scholars? No. Paul was the theologian and scholar, yet he dignified the work that the rest of us do every day by supplying with the artisan skill of his own hands the needs of himself and his assistants (Acts 20:34). You see, Paul, unlike many itinerant preachers who were too important in their own eyes to work for their own support, actually supported himself and his associates. In this he was a living metaphor of God's grace. Paul was a tradesman before he was a scholar, a tent maker before he was a theologian, and he never allowed the skill of his hands to be eclipsed by the fame of his scholarship and preaching.

The church leaders for whom he prayed at Miletus were the skilled tradesmen, the artisans, and the workers of Ephesus: builders, merchants, owners of ships and caravans, laborers, city workers, teachers, longshoremen, all of them. Whatever we are, they were. Paul's charge to the leaders of Ephesus is his charge and command to us: *Keep watch over yourselves and the congregations in which you serve by the command of the Holy Spirit. Keep your own lives always in harmony with God's Spirit and guard the believers with your lives. I commit you now to God and His grace. You need nothing else. Follow my example* (Acts 20:17–37; 1 Cor. 11:1). Our journey through Paul's Ephesians will show us how to keep watch and guard one another under the gentle, persistent supervision of God's Spirit.

When I look around the congregation with which I worship and work, I see ordinary people as they are in their ordinary lives: truck drivers, school teachers, farmers, administrators, welders, dental assistants, pipe fitters, merchants, contractors, mechanics, electricians, students, husbands, wives, singles, homemakers, children, and many others. However, I don't see many scholars or theologians—just people with the common skills needed by the community in every age and every place. Paul's charge to the leaders of the church in Ephesus is his charge to us: go with the Spirit of God and the capabilities with which you have been endowed and lead the church in your home town; reach out to your friends and neighbors whether the time is right or wrong, but first be sure to tend to the safety of your own souls. If you fly with a commercial airline, you will be familiar with this rule: if the cabin loses air pressure, secure your own air supply *before* attempting to assist another passenger—even your spouse or child. The principle applies even more so to your spiritual connection to God. We must spend quality time with our Father, and let Him have His way in our minds. Our natural self, the nature of sin, will rebel and want to maintain its dominance and freedom from responsibility. Give him up to God; let God's spirit rule.

Paul had a keen sense of belonging to God. He was not a free agent, nor did he want to be. His old life, directed by self, had long been abandoned (Phil. 3:4–9). He came, went, stayed, spoke, and wrote as God directed him. We need to take his words as the words of our Father to us, which they are—authoritative, directive, encouraging, and full of grace and peace.

Even with his history in Ephesus, it was important to Paul to stress his divine calling (Eph. 1:1). Perhaps because of his history in Ephesus, with his popularity and prominence in the city, it was especially important that Paul deflect attention from himself. Having received his commission, his mandate, from Jesus Christ Himself on the hot and dusty road to Damascus, Paul was certainly not a self-made apostle nor was he about to diminish the grace of God's calling him to service. He wanted his converts always to remember that the gospel he preached, a gospel full of grace, came directly from the Lord. Its roots are in heaven; its authority is divine. God intends it to be received into the lives of the truck driver and the tax accountant, in fact, into the collective life of the congregation—and obeyed. Can a truck driver or a teacher actually obey the gospel? Can a theologian honestly do any better? The idea of obeying the gospel raises an important point that has confounded and confused many sincere folk as they endeavored to obey a law. Let's try to end the confusion now.

Quite possibly, if not always easily or conveniently, we can obey a law or a rule—or not, as we choose—at least in the eyes of not-so-close observers like police officers and hall monitors in dormitories. I also pondered this question for years without achieving any clear insight into how to obey the gospel. Actually, the answer now seems quite obvious: to obey the gospel is to receive the life, death, and resurrection of Jesus Christ, the gospel in its purity, as my own. We must receive *and* experience grace, that superabundant outpouring from God of everything necessary for life and salvation (2 Peter 1:3). Having received the gospel, and continuing to receive it each moment, we are empowered to live in that state which Paul called *the new life* (Rom. 6:4), in which the self (the still-lingering manifestation of the old nature) is put down every time it raises its lubricious head.

Ephesians is all about grace for *the new life* and what it looks like in the individual and in the body of believers. This new life begins small, like a tiny green shoot, actually like a seed. Growing larger each day with adequate nurturing, it eventually produces a delicious harvest

(Mark 4:26–29). In addition to the rest of our garden, Mirja and I grow a few hundred pounds of tomatoes each year. Every summer day finds us in the greenhouse exclaiming over the fruit and measuring the growth since yesterday. We water, feed, prune, weed, and finally sample the red-ripe fruit from the vine. It is an annual metaphor of the work—a daily work of unmerited and undeserved grace—which the divine Farmer performs in us as we remain in the Vine.

As Paul begins his letter to the church that he loved so dearly, he noted that the members are the saints who *live* in Ephesus. These saints are not long dead folk, somehow still alive and strumming harps on a cloud, whose memories and shrines inspire pilgrimages, prayers, and even pillage. These are real, living people with passions, problems, possibilities, and positions like the rest of us. These saints are people who, like us, need to put in effort in remembering that they are loved by Jesus Christ and God, His Father and ours.

Though Paul very well knew that this congregation, like your congregation, was comprised of fallible folk, who struggle daily with the trials and joys of life and sometimes fall prey to temptation, he still called them *faithful* (Eph. 1:1, 2). How can they, or I, or you be called faithful when all of us were and still are fallible and prove it frequently, if not more often? Once again we see that our Father and Jesus Christ, our Brother, have answers to our questions. They see things from the divine perspective. They are truly the faithful Ones in this divine-human relationship; they cannot deny themselves (2 Tim. 2:13). In Christ we also are "the faithful" (Eph. 1:1), and in Him there is no condemnation for anyone (Rom. 8:1). For all the merchants, laborers, or fisher folk in all congregations scattered across this globe, this is great news. This is news about which we can sing as we chain up the log truck at the top of the steep mountain grade, or as we hammer the slag from the pipeline weld in the fields of Nebraska, or about which we can pray as we gently guide a frightened young calf to its worried, inexperienced mother, or at any other time. We can talk about it, too, as we rest with our coworkers on the seismic line in the northern muskeg or when we share a business lunch with a colleague.

The next two sections in this study are actually a single sentence in Greek. Paul began with praise to God, continued with praise to Jesus Christ, and concluded with praise to the Holy Spirit. Watch Paul raise his hands to God in praise for His glorious and gracious work to save us from our sin and unite us in Christ! It's been more than 2,000 years, and we can still hear that spontaneous outpouring of Paul's joyful recognition of God's unmeasured, unmixed, unimpeded, undiluted, unending, unconditional love for us! By grace we are saved!

Have I Got News for You!

Our Father has given us every spiritual blessing in Christ, and we are truly blessed. We owe Him praise; we need to praise Him for His marvelous gifts. Before He created the world, our Father chose us in Christ to be holy and blameless in His sight. Because He loves us, our destiny is to be adopted as sons of God through Jesus Christ. His pleasure and will are satisfied because His glorious grace is freely given to us in Christ. In Christ and because of His shed blood, we have, right now in the present tense, redemption and forgiveness of sins. God is so extravagant when it comes to dealing with us sinners in need of His rich grace! He absolutely lavishes us in grace with wisdom and understanding of our sinful condition. Not only that, God took us into His confidence and revealed the ancient mystery of His will to us—which He has always intended in Christ. The mystery is no longer a mystery; God intends, when the time is right, to unite all things in heaven and on earth under one head: Christ! (Eph. 1:3–10)

Searching for the Heart of Praise—We can sing and pray and talk and think precisely because our Father is so lavishly gracious. He has given us every spiritual blessing in Christ. The apostle Peter agreed totally with Paul, and agreement is a rare thing for scholars and theologians: *The divine power of our Lord, Jesus, has given us everything we need for life and godliness, enabling us to participate in the divine nature—the Holy Spirit of God dwells in us—and we are empowered to escape the corruption of the world caused by lust, by uncontrolled desire* (2 Peter 1:3, 4). Wow! Even we amateur theologians can understand that! Peter and Paul are in full agreement. Though we are comforted to see solidarity among the Bible writers, it shouldn't surprise us since the same Holy Spirit indwelt them both. (What does that say about us who sometimes disagree in less-than-agreeable ways?) But look again at Paul's words: *Our Father has given us every spiritual blessing in Christ* (Eph. 1:3). He has emptied heaven for us. There is nothing more to give. There is nothing more that we need. Now, that is real grace; that is a real cause for real praise!

Oh, speaking of which, I feel the need right here to ask you a question. What is real praise? Paul gets explicit as he moves from theology to practicality later in his letter, but let's notice here that real praise is much more down to earth and grubby than merely singing songs of praise (though praise certainly is expressed in song). The book of Psalms contains many songs of praise, but Psalm 103 excels in its praise of the gracious benefits of our God. It speaks of forgiveness (we all have sinned and, sadly, continue to do so), redemption (we all were trapped in habit, apathy, fear, or in other such snares), love and compassion (even the hardiest of rugged individuals needs love and compassion), satisfaction (with good things), and justice (even for me, the sinner). This is God's grace in our lives—though I did not recognize it for far too many years.

As a small boy in a Saskatchewan farm-country school, the May 24th sports day was the big event of the spring, and it was anticipated for weeks in advance. To be chosen first by the team leaders was every boy's hope, a recognition of which he could boast with pride to his smiling parents. Because of my skill and physical prowess, I was always chosen last and given a position as far as possible from the action—for the greater glory of the team, of course. But get this: in

Gimme the fastest, strongest, meanest. But God chooses everyone.

Christ we have all been chosen first. In fact, the Creator chose us before this world was created, and we were chosen for a grand purpose—to be holy and blameless in God's sight. We are gratified to be judged the strongest, fastest, most skilled, and most aggressive team player in the opinion of the team leader ... but blameless in God's sight? And holy, too? In the sight of Him who knows the details of our secret musings? Scripture does not lie. It must be so!

Before creation we existed only in the mind of the Creator, but in looking to Christ, His Son, our Creator saw us, perfect, holy, blameless as we truly are in Christ. At creation Adam represented the entire human race; in fact, he *was* the entire human race. At His incarnation Jesus Christ became the last Adam: the human race in one holy and undefiled being (1 Cor. 15:45). God chose to put the ruined race into Christ at the incarnation so that He became for us our righteousness, that is, our justification; our holiness, that is our sanctification; and our redemption, that is our glorification (1 Cor. 1:30).

Our Creator knew what He was doing back before earth's creation—when the universe was pristine. He knew we would experiment with cigarettes, sex, stupidity, and stuff, so much stuff. From the time of Creation, He watched us blow our minds and debase our humanity with drugs and alcohol and debauchery. He knew we would vie for first place on the team and bloody the nose of the girl who got it. He knew we would find ourselves trapped in the rat race and react with multiple addictions. He foresaw the deceptions, riots, mutinies, and carnage that only rebellious children could conceive. He saw all this yet, in Christ, He views us as holy and blameless! What an awesome motivation to actually respond to the gracious invitation of our Creator, to come to Him and experience the salvation that we have in Christ, and to let Christ carry out in us the vision of our Creator.

Is this truly more than a fiction? Can I be an overcomer? Really? In the words of our gracious God through Paul, *I can do everything through Him who gives me strength* (Phil. 4:13). But our Father gives us more than strength; He gives us victory through Jesus! And because of this victory, we can stand firm in the face of all assaults from the enemy (1 Cor. 15:57, 58). Faith is the victory that overcomes every inclination to remain alienated from our Creator (1 John 5:4). I am sure you have heard it said, "If only my faith were greater; if only I had more faith." But Romans 12:3 tells us that God gives us enough faith if we desire it! So, we can have it! God has said so! Faith is ours for the taking; believe it and act on it. Spread those eagle wings and soar!

But having said that, don't you ever wonder why we still struggle against temptation? If God gives us the victory, where is God when we need Him? Why do we go down that same sin road again and again when experience has taught us how we'll feel when remorse kicks in at the end of the road? Could it be that, in God's all-knowing wisdom, He sees that we are not yet ready for victory? If we are even a little bit relying on our own resources, God can't give us the victory. Victory must wait until we surrender the last vestige of self and come to absolute trust in God—to the point at which we give up every subtle, self-generated attempt at righteous living. Only then can God give us victory because that is when we know that it is not I but Christ (Gal. 2:20).

All in the Family—Like most children I was born into a family. I have always belonged to a family, so I have no personal experience with adoption. But I have a memory of an experience that I had at about the age of four. We were traveling by train to camp meeting, and I became separated from the rest of my family. (Of course my mom knew exactly where I was.) I still remember the joy of being reunited after fearing that I was alone in the world. In another incident Mirja and I were about to catch a train from Gare de Lyon in Paris. Destination: Torino. Thousands of people pressed and swirled around us in the cavernous terminal. Trains slipped quietly in and

Alone in a milling mob of mortality.

out every minute. The unarticulated roar of the crowd, color dissolving into color, announcements in an unfamiliar language, and the endless this-way-that-way-round-and-round swirl of human beings rattled me. I could find no fixed reference point. Suddenly Mirja was gone—just gone! Not there! Vanished! Lost! She was nowhere to be seen in that milling mob of mortality. I was again, for a nanosecond, alone in the world and panic swept through me! Then I saw her—right there at my side where she had always been. Relief! Family again! I was not alone in a world of jostling strangers!

I think this might be what adoption is like. We go from alone to family. We now have security, stability, and a base to call home. Because our Creator loves us, He made it our destiny to be adopted as sons through Jesus Christ. We are no longer alone in a universe of rugged individualists, each one scrambling to accumulate the most real estate. We are now part of a family, God's family. Family means caring for the special needs of its disadvantaged; it means participating in family planning and in family activities; it means generously contributing to family expenses; it means graciously helping to solve family disputes and problems. I'm so glad I'm a part of the family of God!

But is it only sons that God is adopting? What about the other half, the daughters? Some people would prefer to substitute the word children in place of sons for an inclusive statement, but I believe the intent of Paul's statement is different. Jesus was God's only Son from eternity. He always enjoyed a special relationship with His Father. Now, when we are adopted into the family of God, we share that same special relationship that Jesus has enjoyed forever. So the word "son" is used as a metaphor to define a special relationship that we now have with our Father, a relationship similar to that which Jesus Christ has always had. So many sons will come to glory, and that clearly includes the daughters as well.

The accumulation of family brings praise to God for His glorious grace. What is praise? Is it singing *praise* songs instead of hymns? Is it singing the first and third verses of nineteenth century hymns only from a book? Can we use drums? Harps? Tubas? Maybe a didgeridoo? Should we sing a cappella? No to all. Singing and music is only a part of praise, and singing from an unconverted heart or singing for my own praise is no praise to God. Real praise comes to God when real sinners turn to Him and find real salvation, receive real repentance, and experience changed lives—for real. Then the hymns or choruses we sing will truly praise God, and it will not matter which we use to express our devotion to Him. Changed, converted lives will praise God now and forever for His glorious grace.

Curses in the Wind—I was sharing a shack on a log raft for a summer with Tom, the logger, and another guy. I had left Mirja and our daughter in the city and found my way to this rickety, unstable contraption moored to the tops of giant trees. It was on the steep shore of remote Williston Lake, a reservoir created by the brand new Bennett Dam on the Peace River in northeast British Columbia. The tree-covered mountain slopes rose steeply to snowy peaks above our heads; below us was 300 feet of water.

For me, this was seasonal work to finance my university expenses. For Tom and the other guy, logging was their life work. Each morning, we shouldered our chainsaws, gasoline, chain oil, and other paraphernalia and scrambled ashore over fallen trees. We would make our separate ways to our chosen sites and commence the day's work of cutting down the tall spruce trees, which would then be collected by the logging company when the water had risen high enough to float them. Tom and the other guy hated each other passionately. On shutting off my chainsaw to fuel it or sharpen the chain, I would frequently hear their shouted curses. Back on the raft, they didn't have to shout but the cursing went loudly on.

I met Tom again at a camp meeting twenty years later. The man was changed! Hardly recognizable, he was a new creation; his sins forgiven, and his life changed. His life was now a praise to God instead of a curse to his enemy. He was a leader in his congregation. The redeemed logger had reason enough to praise God through a holy life, the truest form of worship and praise. His

No longer cursing his enemy.

sins were now forgiven through the blood of Jesus. Only through Christ can we be forgiven. We need to get this straight: our sins are not forgiven for any pleading, penance, or penalty on our part. We do not have to wait until the judgment to find out if we will make it into the kingdom. In Christ, because of what He did on the cross, we have now in this present experience, that is today, redemption, forgiveness of sins, and assurance of salvation.

When I understood this grand truth, it began a change in my life that is still in progress. It motivated me to hate the sin I once loved; it empowered me to turn away from the sin that had so easily entrapped me. Does that mean I have quit sinning? How I wish! (However, in my former experience, I always attempted to work out the problem by my own goodness and willpower. It never worked, as you know from your own experience.) But it does mean that I have the assurance that I can come with confidence (I like the King James rendering: boldly) to the throne of grace (Heb. 4:16) and find immediate forgiveness and cleansing in Christ, who speaks with divine eloquence to the Father in my defense (1 John 1:9; 2:1, 2). This is the extravagant grace that takes a cursing logger and transforms him into a gracious leader of the congregation. This is the extravagant grace that takes a spiritually failing college administrator and transforms him into one who trusts Jesus for past, present, and future. This is the marvelous grace of our loving Lord that enables me to put down my self, my corrupt and sinful nature that despises God, and daily install Jesus in its place.

Go back and read the scripture. God is extravagantly lavish when dealing with sinners in need of His rich grace. Think of the thinness (or thickness) of our skins; the hardness of our hearts; the stiffness of our necks. Think of the size of our egos. It takes divine understanding of our sinful condition to reason with the opinionated cowboy on his high horse. It takes divine wisdom to caress the thick skin of a wounded, case-hardened nurse wearily coming off a twelve-hour shift plus two hours overtime dealing with the bloody results of reckless living. It takes divine wisdom to assure the struggling owner-operator whose rates have just been slashed by the company. God's grace treats us as special individuals in need of His special attention. He has the special remedy custom made for each special welder, trucker, saw filer, artisan, day care aide, choker setter, and for all others.

While working my way through college, I set chokers[1] for three or four months behind a D7[2] in the mountains of western British Columbia. I swear that a more brutal, body-and-mind-destroying job has never been conceived since the days of the galley slave. Try dragging 200 pounds of iron through a tangle of treetops in a foot of wet slush, fall to your knees and hug those snowy trees while wrapping the cable around them, and inserting the knob into the bell. Unhook the second batch of chokers when the D7 rumbles back after about fifteen minutes; get those chokers out of the way fast (but be able to find them when the drag of trees leaves). Stumble and drag the twenty-five pound bull hook to the pre-set chokers, and drop the choker loops over it. Now, scramble out of the way before the speedy young driver pulls the clutch lever—or be ground to mush under the trees as they are snaked to the landing.[3] Now find the set of chokers that you stashed behind a stump and do it all over again. Can you imagine doing this for ten or twelve hours and then going home to do housework, play with your children, have some quality time with your spouse, and spend an hour with God? Want to bet there is a lot of energy left for anything? What we won't do to make a living!

Work nowadays may be less brutal in some respects but definitely no less time consuming, stressful, and destructive of the body that our Creator gave us. But our God is extravagant with His grace; He is wise in His understanding of our human condition. That gracious wisdom with which our God deals with us mortals comes overflowing with mercy, patience, goodness, and truth (Exod. 34:6, NKJV). He does not condemn us for our struggles to earn our livings on this sometimes-hostile earth. Those livings are frequently hard to come by. Frequently the jobs we would like, that would give us the income, time, and energy to spend with our families, are just not available, or our skill sets do not match the

---

[1] A choker is a short length of cable with a loop at one end and a knob at the other. Between the loop and the knob is a sliding bell into which the knob is inserted after the cable is wrapped around the end of a log. The loop is then dropped over the bull hook on the D7.

[2] In the 1960s a D7 was a mid-to-large size Caterpillar tractor used in road construction, logging, excavating, and other types of industry.

[3] A landing was the central location for preparing the full-length trees and loading them onto trucks for transport to the mills.

requirements of the job. In my case I had the skills and the equipment for the falling job I was promised, but I was just too good at that mindless choker-setting job. We take what we can get. And sometimes we leave it. One cold December day as a westerly gale drove snow plumes off the peaks around us, I paused on my way out the door and said with conviction, "Enough is plenty; I'm out of here!" With Mirja and our daughter, I returned to the city and found another job to put food on the table until resuming my studies at the university.

I think God wants first place in our lives whatever our jobs might be; He wants our first and most-alert thoughts—usually at the beginning of the day. On some jobs thinking of other things is not difficult; while hugging the snowy tree or pushing the broom, our minds can turn to God. Instead of cursing the driver, warm and dry on the D7, when he actually does knock me down and drag the tree over me (it did happen, and I should be dead; the one-legged bucker,[4] who witnessed the incident, came hopping over with his chainsaw expecting to have to cut a corpse free, but I was actually safe in a hollow—was it the hollow of His hand?), I can keep my mind focused through song, prayer, or Scripture. There is time in a gruelingly busy day to focus on our God—always.

We are important to our Creator God; He respects us and considers us to be family and friends. He proved this by taking us into His confidence and revealing His plans, the ancient mystery, to us. Mysteries, especially the ancient ones, are exciting, aren't they? Friends and family talk things over, share secrets, and have intimate knowledge of one another that is not shared with others. Jesus assured His disciples that they were His friends and were privileged to share in His plans (John 15:15). What about this ancient mystery that God has always intended to reveal in Christ? Well, God has revealed the mystery to His friends and family. The familiar order of life on this sod will change, perhaps one life at a time, but change it will. Everything on earth and in heaven is to be united in Christ when the time is right.

As we soar through Paul's Ephesians, we will see what this unity looks like and how it happens in the present, in our own lives, and in the life of the congregation. It truly will affect the life of the poor grunt setting chokers. It will affect the life of the harried school teacher, the welder with burned fingers, the nurse who sees too much of the results of living on this earth, and the carpenter with a blackened thumb nail and splinters in his fingers. For this change, the time *is* right. We do not have to wait to some future, cataclysmic event for this change to occur. Change happens when we turn our lives over to the Master Builder, the Carpenter from Nazareth, who for us was suspended from a splinter of His spoiled creation with nails through His hands. Little by little He takes the raw material we offer Him and transforms us. Unity in heaven and on earth? That sounds like paradise! Paradise it is! And it starts on earth. The time is right! You can simply and sincerely pray, "Our Father, You have my permission to work in my life, in my congregation. Transform me. Unite us all in Jesus Christ." And, lest we forget: the work of re-creation and transformation belongs to God as does the praise for the new creation.

---

[4] A bucker, in those days, would cut the full-length trees to log length on the landing.

God Works Out His Purpose; Don't Stand in His Way!

God is working His purpose out, make no mistake about that, and we Jews, who were the first to hope in Christ, are included in His purpose. We have been chosen and predestined in Christ to praise His glory. For you Gentiles, the gospel of salvation is your passkey to inclusion in Christ. The gospel is the word of truth, which you believed and, having believed, you were sealed with the Holy Spirit of God. The Holy Spirit living in you is a deposit in your life; He is your own personal guarantee of salvation, written in your hearts by God. Let's cherish this deposit together until we are all safely out of this world and in God's eternal kingdom, our glorious shared inheritance, redeemed to praise God eternally—for His exclusive glory! (Eph. 1:11–14)

What if There Is No God?—I used to find myself wondering, "What if there is no God? What if these stories are not even nice stories because they promise us a hope that can never be realized? What if they are just myths created by lonely, desperate people seeking a way out? What if they are nothing more than vain musings of unstable minds? What if we are all cave dwellers dressed up, savage, grunting, belching, eating, or being eaten, and in the end, worm eaten? Then what? Nothing?" The alternative to God is not a pretty picture, even if our lawns are manicured, our houses are spacious, our tables are groaning, our cars are polished, and our behavior is impeccable. (By the way, this is not the rule of life for the majority of earth's hungry, struggling, sweating, freezing, despairing inhabitants.) Although we try to deny it, forget it, avoid it, postpone it, and duck it, in the end, be it small or smaller, we kick the pesky bucket. All of us! Done. Finished. Forgotten.

Recently I attended the memorial service of a friend who died too soon. He didn't get to enjoy his impending retirement. A resolute, determined unbeliever, he would not allow me to speak of God in his presence. As an avid reader of histories and biographies of great people, he loved to talk about his books and share them with me. But he would not touch a book of mine for fear that it would contain some hint of the divine that might destabilize his equilibrium—that I would use it as a wedge to breach his defenses. He was compassionate, fair with his staff, and always quick to interpret the rules in favor of an employee. Graying men choked up as they told of their love for him. Will we miss him? Absolutely! Ultimately, for everyone, this world becomes an ugly place because death is ugly no matter how we dress it up or joke about it, and death comes to each of us sooner or later, but it always comes too soon however late.

My friend, like so many others, would not acknowledge the presence of God in the world. He would not admit that he was the handiwork of the divine Creator, but his denial cannot change the purposes of God. God is working out His purpose in this world in spite of denial by puny, arrogant humanity. Our denial does not change the big picture in the slightest. In the days of the apostle Paul, philosophers speculated about origins and endings. They loved to talk and debate multitudinous theories, but they laughed at Paul when he told them of a God with power to restore their decaying bodies (Acts 17:32). Odd, isn't it? But quite usual. Why wouldn't they jump at a chance for restoration? Why don't we moderns jump at the chance?

Marcus Aurelius, a competent Roman emperor and a respected Stoic philosopher of the second century, was a determined, principled persecutor of Christians. He would not step over that line of belief into life (John 5:24). For a thousand years during the period that we call the Dark Ages, the image of God was distorted by teachers of religion, but God remained untouched by human slings and arrows aimed to dislodge Him and change His times and laws (Dan. 7:25). Enlightenment philosophers tried to reason God right out of the picture in the eighteenth century, yet He remained in view in spite of their reasoned philosophizing.

Nineteenth century science, philosophy, and even religion (are we surprised?) made heroic efforts to obscure the evidence of God in the world, but He was still there. The twentieth century bloodied our hands and preoccupied our minds with survival of the quickest, the smartest, and the most righteous. But God did not die. He is still here in the twenty-first century in spite of continuing attempts by the likes of Christopher Hitchens (*God is Not Great*), Bishop John Shelby Spong (*The Sins of Scripture*), and Richard Dawkins (*The God Delusion*), three tireless proselytizers for atheism, to remove Him from the picture. Dawkins has been called the most prominent Darwinian of our age. Practically our entire popular culture is based on the assumption that we generated spontaneously from a soup of inanimate elements in a hostile swamp (well, didn't we evolve?), and when our tour of performance, pain, and pleasure is complete, we return to the same inanimate elements forever. Done! Terminated! Expired! The bitter end! Gone forever! So long, dear friends, it was good to know you. Exciting, isn't it?

In Praise of Praise—Paul championed the presence of God in the world in his time, and he recorded for all future generations the message of a living, caring God. Because we also believe, we are included in Christ with the believing Jews. We also have a role in the purpose of God, which is only made available to us by His grace. Our destiny and present privilege are to live lives that reflect and demonstrate the character of our God and that praise God's glory. We cannot help resembling the God we worship. Because we have freely chosen to worship the Creator God, which is the only God that exists (all others being mere pretenders, agents of Satan, determined to destroy the handiwork of the Creator), we will gradually grow to be like Him in the way we live and in the way we respond to the challenges and pleasures that this world provides to us. It's a lifetime process of recreation (called sanctification in Scripture).

What does a life that praises God's glory look like? It goes far beyond singing praise songs or mouthing the occasional holy platitude—even far beyond carrying the Bible close to your chest as you walk softly in the sanctuary. So, how should I praise God? Throughout the many phases in my life, I have come to recognize different characteristics that demonstrate a life that praises God's glory. I am convinced that praise is as much connected to the daily grind as it is to rhythm and melody.

Dependability: As a contractor renovating a house, you don't make unrealistic promises to the owner and then leave her hanging with tarps spread over a gaping hole in the roof. You don't leave the domestic water cut off and the doors covered by plywood while you disappear for a week to finish a job for someone else. That's unprofessional, undependable, and unconscionable. Behavior like that will get you an unenviable reputation in heaven as well as on earth. If you commit to being on a job, be there—or don't commit. As the Bible tells us, *If you keep your promise even when you are personally damaged, you will please God* (Ps. 15:4).

Last evening after months of procrastination, I finally turned my attention to a box of papers that had been begging to be torched. Surprise! They were records of my long-forgotten last season as a building contractor. I found names of employees, records of hours worked and wages paid, concrete purchased from long-dead suppliers (even a small-load charge), materials prices that would make us smile today, statements from Workers' Compensation and Canada Revenue Agency, and even a building proposal that went nowhere. Memories were stirred. People and events that had not crossed my mind in decades floated past. I remembered income generated and shifts in fortune that took it all away. And I remembered lessons learned: do the job you've committed to do for the price agreed, keep on task until the job is completed, and most importantly, stick to the contract.

Honesty: I was doing a major renovation on a house while the owner continued to live in it. The family endured in good humor while the roof was removed from the kitchen, the floor extended, and the walls pushed out. The end results were great, but while I was working, I discovered that the owner's concept of honesty didn't extend to recognition of boundaries between that which was his and not his. He also seemed to have ready access at his place of work to the belongings of others. One day he presented me with an expensive set of drill bits lifted from his employer. It was a puzzle to him that I would not accept them.

Self-control: I was the senior administrator on my college campus for more than two decades. With almost the full range of personalities reporting to me, I had opportunities to discipline, commend, direct, give orders, evaluate, mediate, arbitrate, and negotiate. I had to terminate, keep order in staff meetings, change the circumstances of lives, and hear complaints; it was always a pleasure to give maximum latitude for decision making under the rules of our organization.

My office door was always open to students, faculty, and other staff. I always attempted to be rational, firm, compassionate, and add a touch of humor to all my dealings with others. A couple of the faculty, G and B, wonderful instructors devoted to their students, loved to talk with me in relay, hoping to wear me down—usually to get my support to increase the course requirement in their program, a budget implication. One day B was hanging in my office door going on about something. After some minutes I said, "Uh, B, maybe you should close the door." As she moved in to close the door, almost choking on my laughter, I added, "With you on the other side." I got away with it for a while.

The people I worked with were the best. It was the inanimate, truly mindless pieces of machinery that could push my buttons—and still can. Machines are supposed to work for me without questioning my authority. I push their buttons and pull their strings. My chain saw should start cold with a max of two or three pulls on the rope (it doesn't). My computer—well, I don't even have words for what can go wrong with that thing. And then there is the pump in my well. It had needed a new pump for several months (I had been procrastinating), and Monday was the day to install it. I spent four hours climbing into and out of the well changing the pumps and getting the new pump primed. Then it refused to deliver. As darkness approached, I took it out and hooked up the old one. I needed a shower. The same process occurred on Friday with, maddeningly, the same result—but no time to put the old one back. Did I feel a desperate urge to drop the pump into the well? I did. I restrained myself. I smiled grimly and took a sponge bath. Friday is not the best day to change pumps. Sunday is coming.

Now consider another perspective: I don't need to fight against the insults and abuse of my inanimate mechanical devices, devilish as they seem at times. Neither is it inevitable that they exasperate me nor cause my old nature, the self, to flare up and take over. I can trust Jesus when the urge to drop the pump into the well begins to assert itself. I can repudiate the sin. Jesus, I trust you to take my exasperation; I ask you to demolish the self that is rising up in me. Thank you, Lord. You are so patient with this poor sinner!

Words: Our words could be the first indicator of character. The stories we tell (or to which we willingly listen) and the descriptive expressions we mouth all shout volumes about the states of our characters. The guy who can remain calm as he watches his neighbor's horses prance through his garden will create permanent impressions. There also is a passive use of language that communicates very well. As a mayor, I frequently drop in to visit our chief administrative officer (CAO). He has an enormous inventory of jokes all delivered in his almost-understandable Sheffield accent; some of them deal with subjects that are clearly outside the lines—my lines, at least. CAO is a quick learner. He has come to understand the kind of jokes that are inappropriate for my ears. We remain good friends respectful of our differing perspectives, but it demonstrates how important our words are. What I say and what I listen to—the words I allow in my life—help define his opinion of me.

These illustrations only touch on the potential for praising our Father God in the humdrum of our ordinary lives. They also touch on the potential for discrediting our profession of faith. Actions have to correspond with words, or the actions are believed and we are seen as people who talk but do not do.

But talk we must! Scripture commands us to be ready to give an answer to the one who asks about the hope we have (1 Peter 3:15). So as you sing at the snowy pull-out while you hook up the tire chains, be ready for the guy who asks: "Aren't your hands just as frozen as mine? Aren't your chains as heavy as mine? Don't you have deadlines just like I have? Didn't you blow a transmission a couple of weeks ago? Didn't they cut your rates when they cut mine? What's going on? Why are you singing when I am cursing?" We could go on with other examples of how to praise God in the daily grind, but maybe you should come up with a few of your own.

Good News! Read All About It!—Most of us are Gentiles. For us, the key to the kingdom is the gospel. But what is the gospel? Basically put, the gospel is simply the story of Jesus, His birth, His death, and His resurrection. Everything else in the wonderful account is commentary about what the gospel has done, is doing, and will do for us. When we believe the gospel, we go immediately into the kingdom of grace in which God gives us the pleasure and privilege of demonstrating the gospel. We are enabled to praise God in the present details of life while we wait for the eyeball-searing-brilliant and waking-the-dead-noisy appearing of Glory, the hope of the gospel (John 5:24).

The gospel comes in many shapes and colors. Because we live in a world of diversity, we have to be prepared to share the gospel with our friends in the format in which they can understand it. Notice, we share it with our friends. My friend would not talk of God, but he loved to talk of history and the battles and inventions that changed our lives. In his final hours as his vitality seeped away and his mind began to lose its focus, did he remember the great battle that forever changed history, present, and future? Did his mind turn to God? Our compassionate Father wants everyone to come to salvation; He knows my friend's heart and mind better than anyone. I wish I knew. Then again, I think I am better off just to leave him in the hands of the One who saved us.

The gospel is the word of truth that we believed, and having believed, we were sealed with God's Holy Spirit (Eph. 1:13). Did we read that correctly? Jesus tells us that in believing we cross over from death into life (John 5:24). Does the Holy Spirit seal us in life when we cross over? When I was a boy the annual *pop, pop, snap, pop* of the lids on the cans as they cooled on the kitchen table told us that the food we had put in them was sealed and safe. I am probably going way beyond the comprehension of most people. Let me back up and explain. Because we had no electricity, we preserved most of our off-season food—garden produce, wild berries, fruit, and wild meat—in cans, and canning was a major annual production. Beginning with the strawberries in July and carrying on to raspberries, peas, beans, pickles, wild blueberries and cranberries toward the end of August, and ending with the moose in September, the *pop, snap, pop*

Sealed and safe.

of sealing lids was almost a daily promise of safe food in the frozen months ahead. Any can that didn't pop was tested again and usually found with a spongy top that indicated a lid not sealed. It was removed from the line, the lid was cut off, and the can was prepared for resealing.

Is the sealing of the cans in my mom's kitchen a metaphor of the work of the Holy Spirit in our lives that seals us in our Father's care? Can we place full confidence in the word of God that, having believed, we are sealed in life? Are we safe like the produce under the lids that went *pop*, with our salvation assured? By continuing in this state of belief, do we have continuing assurance of salvation? We do! *God is faithful. He calls us into fellowship with His Son, Jesus Christ, and He confirms us to the end; having God's Holy Spirit, we are lacking in no spiritual gift* (1 Cor. 1:7–9). The apostle Peter affirms Paul's teaching: *The divine power of Jesus has provided everything we need for life and godly living, enabling us to participate in the divine nature and spurn the evil desires that cause corruption* (2 Peter 1:3, 4).

What about the bad things that I continue to do? Sadly, my life does not consistently demonstrate the divine nature. Too frequently I allow the old self to rise up and dishonor the One who called me out of darkness into His marvelous light (1 Peter 1:9). What shall I do? I could shrug and retreat into an apathetic acceptance of my weak humanity and shuffle on through a spiritless, failing life to face in the end—a bucket. I could then summon my last bit of energy and kick it. But I have just described the ultimate rebellion against our compassionate Redeemer! That is not the destiny to which we have been called in Christ. There is an option, and it is one filled with light and promise! The apostle John describes it so well: *Hey, guys, I have written to you so that you will not sin* (1 John 2:1). Did we read that right? Sin is not a compelling force in our lives? The devil can't jerk us around like his personal puppets on strings? That's the way it's written. That's the way I read it. *But if you [get lazy, careless, self-confident, proud, distracted, over tired, bored and] do fall into sin, there is One who will [powerfully, eloquently, and convincingly] speak to His Father in your defense [and, by the way, His Father is equally eager to acquit you]* (1 John 2:1). *[Just] confess your sin, He will forgive and totally cleanse us* (1 John 1:9). You see, it's all there. We have the amazing and beautiful answer to the bad things we do as believers.

We don't fall from grace every time we sin. The fall from grace would occur if we deliberately, rebelliously, and ultimately refuse to confess and receive repentance from our gracious Father in heaven. Receive repentance? As a gift? I thought I had to *repent* and then God would forgive. It seems that most of us thought so at one time. We are such do-it-yourself people! But our salvation is all God's doing—including the gift of repentance. The Holy Scriptures are quite clear on this: *God's kindness draws us to repentance* (Rom. 2:4); *God exalted Jesus to give repentance to Israel* (Acts 5:31); *Gently instruct those who oppose you in the hope that God will grant them repentance* (2 Tim. 2:25); and one more, *God is not slow in keeping His promises to us; He is patient, not wanting anyone to perish but that everyone will come to repentance [which He is eager to give]* (2 Peter 3:9).

If God gives me repentance, then it must be rank rebellion, stupidity, apathy, and or willing ignorance on my part to remain in my sin. There is no justification for remaining in ignorance. There is no reason to act stupidly. There is no compulsion to rebel. Apathy, well, it's a condition that underlies many symptoms. The Scripture is available and readable in more than 600 languages—in multiple translations. Time can be found, even if you are a sleepy log truck driver (sorry for picking so much on the log truck drivers, but I've been there; I know they are particularly hard pressed as they yawn their way up the narrow logging roads at 2:00 a.m. squeezed between the bulk-fuel prices and the company rates—always needing that extra trip to pay the bills).

All of us are harried. All of us have to set priorities, make decisions, and change plans. Just this morning I was preparing to do some harvesting of the garden and pick a few wild blueberries before the bear gets them all, but then I got a telephone call … so now I am going to feed the bear, postpone the harvest, and help lay out the fire alarm system in the church. Life is sometimes like this. All of us will have to give up something if we are to make room for God's word to us. Jesus wasn't fooling when He told us to *seek His kingdom first* (Matt. 6:33)—not that I equate installing an updated fire alarm system in the church with seeking God's kingdom first; the two aren't related. The alternative to seeking God's kingdom first is not to experience His kingdom at all

Our role in this life is to cherish the Deposit, our personal guarantee of salvation, as Paul writes to the Ephesians. Cherish God's Holy Spirit, hold Him close, walk in His light; experience His kingdom now, even while in this harried life. I've been given a few guarantees in my short life. Far as I can remember, I've never benefited much from any of them other than to have a few minor flaws corrected on my new pickup truck. My usual experience is to have the major break occur just after the warranty expires, but my experience with our Father God is totally different. He assures me that His Holy Spirit in my life can be trusted to the end. There is no expiry date; He doesn't leave after seventy years. I can never outlive God! His guarantee is as enduring as God Himself! He will see me through this life and through the gates of glory when the time is right.

Paul Prays; Things Happen

I've been hearing things about you—good things. The rumormongers tell of your faith in the Lord Jesus and your love for all the saints. I am thrilled to hear these rumors, and that's why I never stop giving thanks for you in my prayers. Specifically, I want our glorious Father, the God of our Lord, Jesus Christ, to give you the Spirit of wisdom and revelation that is, in fact, God's Holy Spirit. Thus, you will know God even better than you do now. I also ask that your mind and feelings may be enlightened in order that you may know in your present experience the hope to which our Father has called you. This marvelous hope is the unimaginable richness and glory of God's inheritance in the saints. And much more: I pray that because you believe in Him, you will experience the ultimate power of God in your lives. How much power is ultimate power? More than you imagine! That power is the muscular strength of God that He exercised and gloriously, brilliantly demonstrated by raising Jesus from the dead and seating Him at His right hand in heaven. Do you understand? Jesus is in heaven where He exercises rule over every authority and power your mind can conceive—and more—now and in the age to come. Jesus is superior to all things and head over everything for the church, His body. Now understand this: the church, you believers assembled in worship, is the fullness of Christ. He fills you as He fills everything in every way. This is God's will. (Eph. 1:15–23)

The Rumors I Hear!—The rumors we hear usually are those that appeal to our lower instincts. When people involve themselves in scandalous affairs, it seems to get our attention. It gets our attention even faster if the scandal originates in the church. The TV preacher suavely scamming elderly widows and other vulnerable folk to finance expensive projects, vacations, condos, and private jets gets headline coverage on the national news—as it should, I admit. This ungodly behavior brings enormous dishonor to our Father, to Jesus, and to His body on earth.

At the local scene, we are all too familiar with the hissy fits, family breakdowns, ego trips, frauds, frictions, and general disorders that raise their oily heads in many congregations and distract the saints from the mission of the church. I was going to say these conditions characterize many congregations but perhaps that is too harsh. Even so, it seems we are much like the saints Paul exhorted in Corinth. But while we beat ourselves up, let's not forget that Paul addressed his letters "to the church of God in Corinth, to those sanctified in Christ Jesus and called to be his holy people" (1 Cor. 1:2). That is an awesomely high calling addressed to each believer in each, however troubled, congregation of believers.

The rumors that Paul heard about the church he had raised in Ephesus brought joy to his heart. How could he help rejoicing in the news of the faith and love of the believers? He had nurtured them for twenty-seven months, teaching them daily from house to house and in his rented hall. I want to focus on this idea of nurturing for a moment because here is an incredible example for us welders, day care aids, and other ordinary members of the body. On our own level, we have people we nurture daily whether we are conscious of it or not. I submit, however, that our nurturing should be deliberate and planned. Our nurturing should be continuous and reliable. It should be directed and sustained by the Spirit. The spiritual welfare of our coworkers needs to receive priority attention. The questions are these: how do I give priority attention? How do I break through the prejudice and preoccupation of my friends? How do I get past barricades of mountain-climbing sleds, mud-bogging quads, expensive pickup trucks, and just plain stuff—all of it under the curse of the second law of thermodynamics? How do I speak of eternal things to someone apparently totally focused on the passing things of this life?

I learned an important lesson when I was administrator of my college campus. I'm not a sports person. While I still enjoy indulging in a fast, noisy, aggressive game of Ping-Pong or the quiet swishing of my cross-country skis in the fresh powder, I find myself utterly unresponsive to the fever of viewer sports that sweeps the country. I did go to a hockey game once, but that was more than fifty years ago. I've never watched soccer, football, basketball, tennis, or even Tiger Woods for more than a few minutes. So how can I feel sympathy for the pain or joy of my friends when their teams score or not? What can I contribute to the excited conversation in the hall when the Blue Jays just put one in the net—or is it baseball that they play?

My lesson? I have to be at least minimally conversant with the things that capture the interest of the people with whom I work. I should know who is playing whom today (at least this season)—painful as it might be to learn. Much more importantly, I have to know whose kids are playing where and with what results. The dear hearts and gentle people of my hometown have sent their sons and daughters to the Olympics on several occasions. They have sent them to confront the Taliban and to stand brave in other theaters. Know your friends and take interest in the things that are important to them. Sure, it takes time, but that little bit of genuine interest might be the key to the soul of a proud mom or grandpa.

Paul's sources reported to him that members of the Ephesus church loved one another and were strong in their faith in the Lord. That is a good report! How does a body achieve such a degree of love and faith that the conference president hears only good news because there is only good news to be told? How can we have a body so securely connected to the Head that the right wing and the left wing beat in harmony? To put it in simplest terms: if we had to generate this love and faith out of our own church resources, programs, services, charities, inner personal goodness, well, we could say it would be hard, but we'd be quite wrong. It's not hard; it's totally impossible; don't even waste energy trying. But how long does it take for our God to perform a miracle? How long does it take for Him to change a stony heart into a heart of flesh (Ezek. 11:19)? How long does it take for Him to infuse a dead body with life or to restore a wasted leper to pink-fleshed health? How long does it take for our Father to pour His life, His peace, and His love into a wounded congregation? How long?

I read that our God is more willing than any loving parent to give us the things for which we ask (Matt. 7:10, 11). I also read that when the leper confessed that if Jesus was willing, He could make him clean. Jesus was willing, and the leper was made clean on the spot (Matt. 8:3)! How long does it take to bring life and vitality to a congregation of dusty farmers, greasy mechanics, harried teachers, weary elders, hungry unemployed, restless teens, and scrambling contractors, who get paid every ninety days but must pay their own obligations not later than every thirty days? Well, how long does it take to ask? Not long. I can ask for love even if I don't feel like loving that more-grace-required person; I can ask for faith any time. Ask and receive (Matt. 7:7; John 18:24). Because we ask, God gives (Isa. 37:21).

So maybe the changeover doesn't have to be a long time in coming. We don't have to rely on our own resources to generate love. God, our Father, is ready, willing, able, and eager to pour His own *agape* (divine love) into our hearts and into the body of Christ if only we ask. We don't have to desire it. We just have to ask. I am asking. Now. God, pour Your *agape* into our congregation today. Cleanse us from evil. Transform us into the people who will give a witness that this community cannot ignore. Thank You, God. You are wonderfully gracious!

But what keeps us from asking individually and collectively for God's *agape* to overwhelm us? Is it busyness? Is it busybodyness? Is it our personal histories of failure? Is it apathy? Is it unbelief? Yes—and more! But all of our weakness and sin together in one stewing pot is not sufficient reason to shrug our shoulders and resign ourselves to the status quo and hope that something will change. Now is the only time we have. Our God has promised to answer us and help us in the day of salvation (Isa. 49:8), and that day is now (2 Cor. 6:2). This is not the time to debate over details of differences. (What we see depends on where we stand. Why not stand on the Rock?) God's sun is shining on us, and when the sun shines, it's time to make hay. My farmer neighbors know that instinctively. God's sun is shining on us, and His Son is speaking in our defense. Let's make hay; let's pray. Now is the time to ask. And if we ask, He will be given to us (Luke 11:11–13; Matt. 7:7). Now is the time to shed all our encumbrances under the prompting of God's Holy Spirit. Why should we dally with destruction when love, life, liberty, and true happiness are ours for the asking?

Let's consider some of the encumbrances that still divide and enfeeble this body of Christ. A few examples should be enough. Theological differences, for example, bend us right out of shape. Paul referred to similar disputes in Corinth (1 Cor. 3:4, 5). We are very much like Corinth with the range of theologians and theological perspectives to distract us from the clear word of the Bible. If we stick to the Bible, we will come to see the light as the Holy Spirit sees fit.

Aside from theological disputes, there are few things more powerful to split a congregation and set one faction against another than family infidelity. Probably no congregation has escaped its devastating results, but there is a way of escape! While families may split, and there is no way to keep together that which is determined to part, there is still the Holy Spirit to direct the response of the congregation. Our own congregation has experienced family breakups. Years later we still feel the pain, though we soldier on. Is there a better way? We cannot right the wrong; can we ever fully reintegrate the broken parts? Do these dear souls have to be sort of fringe members until the end? Maybe our human memories need divine adjustments in the present. Perhaps we need to ask our God for the gift of forgetfulness for the hurts we have experienced as a congregation.

And finally, there are underlying causes for every effect, true in the material realm but also in the spiritual, where the visible effects are not always immediate. Cause: we spend time with the enemy of our souls instead of with the Savior of our souls. Those very-popular Hollywood productions steal our time, open our wallets, and close our minds to the call of the Holy Spirit. This is no accident. They are carefully designed as part of a worldwide conspiracy to steal our minds, our money, and our morals (even if the producers are unaware of their part in the conspiracy). The same holds with pop music, with empty reading, with aimless surfing of the Internet, with playing video games, and I am sure I have not exhausted the list. The time spent on these mindless diversions is time lost; time gone forever. This is time we are not spending with the Holy Scriptures, sharing our faith, or contemplating the work of God in our lives. It weakens our defenses, puts our guards to sleep, and actually turns over the keys of our minds to the enemy who always destroys. How can we expect to have a strong, living-faith experience personally or in the congregation if we willingly harbor the enemy in our personal lives? In order to model our congregations after the church in Ephesus and ensure the spreading of good rumors, we should rid ourselves of these distractions.

What Time Is It?—We have considered things that will weaken and divide us as the body of Christ. What will strengthen and unite us? What will increase our faith in the Lord and our love for all the saints? The answer is simple, yet reality is complex. I was clerking in Mirja's store when a woman walked in looking for a quick fix. I had no quick fix for her, and there is no quick fix for anyone. The fix she needed would have entailed some basic changes in her lifestyle that she was not willing to make. The coffee-and-toast breakfast would have to change to something more substantial. That would mean she would have to get up earlier in the morning. That would mean she would have to go to bed earlier in the evening. That would mean she would have to forgo some of her usual evening activities. That would mean … see what I mean?

I experienced similar resistance to change when I was campus principal of my college. "Adult Basic Education" is just what it sounds like. It's simply an opportunity for adults who have missed out as children on the foundations of readin', ritin', and 'rithmatic. The problem was that in order to get to class in the morning, the student had to be able to tell time—time to go to bed, time to get up, time to eat a wholesome breakfast, and time to go to class—but especially time to go to bed. So, we first had to teach many of them that they could not soar with the eagles in the daytime if they insisted on hooting with the owls at night. For many, the absence of basic life skills was the major handicap in their lives.

But what will strengthen and unite us as the body of Christ and increase our faith and our love for all the saints? The process is time sensitive and starts with telling the time: now is the time of salvation; now is the time to turn away from *all* the distractions that use up time and leave us feeling harried and distracted; now is the time to draw close to our Father in Bible study and prayer. I won't enter the debate of night person or morning person. That debate is also a distraction that takes time and yields nothing of value.

Whatever our circadian rhythms, the first thing still has to be spending prime time with the Head of the church. My prime time is in the morning. I can't fully function intellectually after about 8:00 p.m. My mind seems to shut down. Oh, I suppose I do have the ability to install a new pump in the well in the middle of the night and go to bed after a shower at 3:00 a.m. (Been there; done that—more than once; sure don't hope to ever do it again.) Writing seems to keep my mind more or less alert a little later into the night—if I am on a roll. But to read someone else's writing ... sorry. So I need prime time to read the Bible, to listen to the voice of God, and to share with Him my fears and hopes. This, I believe, is the key to love and unity in the church, to building up the body: pray without ceasing; store the promises and warnings of God in our minds; contemplate the greatness of our God and Father; remember His leading in our past; give an answer to the one who asks about the faith that sustains; connect regularly with the other members of the body; exercise faith—and start with prime time experiences.

What does it mean to exercise faith? I think it simply means to obey God. When He says jump, then jump. When He says go, then go. You get the idea. When He says give up your resentment for your perceived or real injury, give it up. There is no load heavier than resentment. It will break you. Have you followed the instruction in the Bible on dealing with your enemy in the body? Do it now; love your enemy, and leave the results with the Head of the church. Go down your road smiling. The disciples once asked Jesus to increase their faith (Luke 17:5). Jesus responded with a story about doing our duty—in other words, about obeying.

A member of the body came to me requesting that I mediate between him and another member whom he alleged had treated him unfairly. He wanted a witness when he attempted to make this *reptile* (his word) apologize. I declined. To cut off the head of a *reptile* is not the answer that brings lasting peace and unity in the body. That is the work of our Father in heaven. For us, reconciliation is the only answer. I would have gone with him had he been willing to give up his resentment and go with the idea of reconciling regardless of the response of the *reptile*.

The Head of the church is quite clear that forgiveness and reconciliation are the only solutions to disputes between members of the body (Matt. 5:24). So, let's do it without delay. Let's obey. Let's experience the results of obedience in the body. Let's feel the ripple of smooth muscle in sync with the Head of the body as we go, jump, stop, shout, or cover our mouths at the command of the Head. Paul's example in Ephesians is to be taken as a command of God: never stop giving thanks for the body of Christ and *all* its members. Resentment cannot stand in the face of thanksgiving.

Paul's explicit request to the glorious Father for the Holy Spirit to be given to the body of Christ should be our daily prayer as well. This Spirit of wisdom and revelation is exactly what we need. Faced as we are with so many unknowns, we need the wisdom of God to navigate us through the maze of daily decisions, obstacles, and those deceptive easy rides. Christ is called the wisdom of God and the power of God in 1 Corinthians 1:24. The congregation I am a part of is facing some rather formidable challenges that require the wisdom, power, and revelation of God to solve. We desperately need a new facility for church and school. What are the providences of God that He has placed in our way? Are there spiritual obstacles that we harbor that need our attention before further providences can be revealed? Are we failing to obey our Father in some of the clear indicators of His will? Obedience to God's clearly expressed will opens the door to understanding His more obscure plans for our good.[5]

God's will is clear about His requirement for us to love one another and live in unity. But if we look in opposite directions on apparently nonnegotiable issues, how can we ever get together? Try standing face-to-face instead of back-to-back. It will be easier to feel the humanity of your enemy when looking him in the eye. It will be easier to read the body language; it will be easier to have sympathy and recognize that this other child of our Father is your brother or sister in the family of God.

Unity is possible in the body even if we are not all on the same line on some matters of theology. It was Jesus, our Head, who told us that it was love (*agape*, not sentiment) that identified us as His disciples (John 13:35). Theological correctness with uniformity might give us warm feelings, but don't take correctness and uniformity as the definitive indicators of discipleship. We also learn through Paul that our Father takes responsibility to bring us to common understandings of those points of doctrine on which we have different perspectives (Phil. 3:15). When all the different theologians from all around the world sit down to eat together in the kingdom, they will have plenty of time to laugh over their different theological perspectives as they savor

Theologians laugh at themselves as they bond at a heavenly feast.

the delicious menu spread before them. I'm sure they will each discover that they all have been a little bit wrong at least some of the time. *Agape* love, not flawless theology, identifies us as disciples (John 13:35)! And I have a feeling that *agape* love in our souls will open the door to clearer theological understanding.

When we receive this love, we will know God even better than we think we know Him now because God *is* love. I long and pray for that Spirit in the congregation that impels us to reach out to every member. The Spirit inspires compassion, forgiveness, understanding, teachableness, humility, and service. He brings us all the qualities that are captured in the little word "love" (*agape*). Our Father in heaven, may Your name be hallowed in this congregation of truck drivers, teachers, contractors, ranchers, want-to-be lawyers, and used-to-be college administrators. This will answer the prayer of Paul. This will answer the prayer of Jesus that we may be one and by our unity prove to the world that Jesus was sent by the Father (John 17:21). To what higher calling could we aspire?

---

[5] Since this writing a new facility, opening huge new opportunities, has been richly provided.

The Long Road to Grace

Walk in the Light—Our Father has turned on the light, now blazing in full-spectrum glory all around us, and Paul urges us to walk in this light! What more can He do than He already has done? So, Lord, grant me grace; open my eyes to the light. There is only one place in which the light of life can be clearly seen—the written Word of God (Ps. 119:105, 130). Some may presume to get their inspiration from other sources, even from nature and, truly, there is much in nature to inspire and instruct us. But there is also much to distract, mislead, and even cause us concern. Here the written Word becomes indispensable. Let's walk in the light while it shines on us.

I recently completed a mind-and-body-testing backpacking journey into the mountains with two of my teenage grandchildren and their father. It was a wonderful, cross-generational, bonding experience. At night we spread our sleeping bags on the spongy moss beneath us. We named stars and traced the silhouettes of trees and mountain cliffs with our fingers in the dark; we felt cool zephyrs brushing our faces. We imagined we saw what we didn't see—and enjoyed the adrenaline rush. When the clouds rolled up and the rain came down as we hiked the trails, we were soaked to the skin and our boots squelched with God's wonderful water. From the tops of ridges we had enchanting views of soaring peaks and plunging valleys, with ice and snow hanging from the pinnacles and waterfalls thundering with great joy into the gorges. We stopped in the bear's diner to pick our fill of blueberries and huckleberries clinging to the brink of sandstone cliffs. Then in the evening we took our weary bodies down to rest in the tree-sheltered campsite by a stream of pure water. Here we quenched our thirst with satisfaction, pleasure, and utter confidence.

But all is not well in that pristine wonderland. We did not entirely let down our guards. While we had observed scat and torn logs all along the trail, on day three we were in ideal bear habitat—a moist, level lowland with scattered clumps of small spruce trees among tall grasses and shrubs. Every few steps we loudly announced our presence, promising not to eat any more of the berries (we lied), only desiring safe passage through the wilderness. In spite of the messages we clearly sent, we still came face-to-face in a close, thirty-five yard relationship with the king of all grizzly bears—a massive, gorgeous, brown-streaked-with-amber-hair-flowing-in-the-breeze solitary male. He truly was a marvelous example of our Father's creative genius. One thousand pounds of muscle and blood, skin and bone, and bear intelligence to match his beauty looked directly at us with his round bear eyes. In two hops to the left he covered five yards. He stopped! And turned to face us again! Our adrenaline surged. He assessed the situation, counted the numbers, and weighed his options (ours were rather limited). I was in front with my granddaughter, Caitlyn. Ryan and Steve were right at our heels. We stared back

Will the king of the wilderness obey the King of kings?

quietly, very quietly, sending mental messages: "We only want safe passage; we won't eat any more of your berries; we'd like to drink a bit of your water—if you don't mind; we won't litter; we'll go quietly if you just let us go." In incredibly long seconds, the king made up his mind. Two jumps took him out of our sight, leaving us to marvel that we have even laid eyes on this greatest of all kings of the wilderness—and with our skins still intact!

If I was limited to only nature, I would most likely come to some erroneous conclusions like Darwin and his disciples. Could I be certain that God is love? I could certainly think of Him as powerful, majestic, awesome, remote, austere, fickle, capricious, and even dangerous like these mountains. But loving, caring, compassionate, and interested in me? At least superficially, the evidence would not be totally or immediately convincing. There is too much hurting, too much decay, and too much destruction in the mountains, cities, and pleasant rural homelands for me to clearly recognize God as love. I need a revelation to come to that knowledge. I need the Written Word to interpret the natural, to explain why I fear the king of the mountain and why he fears me. I need the Written Word to explain and interpret all the otherwise inexplicable conundrums in this world. But can I not depend on the Spirit to interpret wilderness truths?

Yes, we can always depend on the Holy Spirit sent by Jesus to interpret our passage through this hostile world. But there are many other spirits lurking all around us whose only joy is perverse and whose purpose is to amaze, annoy, baffle, befuddle, contradict, confuse, delude, deceive, entertain, enthrall, frustrate, and fleece us to ultimate destruction. The Written Word of God, the lamp in the darkness of this world's uncertainty and the full-spectrum light of our Father, is our only sure guide by which we test all spirits. Let's walk in the light while it shines on us.

It is only through the written Word of God that our minds and feelings can be enlightened—"The entrance of thy words giveth light" (Ps. 119:130, KJV)—so that we can know, in our present experiences the hope to which our Father has called us. The king of the wilderness taught me profound respect. He demonstrated his power through restraint. We didn't panic, but we were fully conscious of our mortality. As we marveled at his massive bulk, we could only wait and hope and pray that he would choose the option that favored our continued existence.

Our Father, the King of the kings of the wilderness, must have whispered in his ear, "Leave these guys alone. See that sweet little girl there by the old guy; she's My precious one. And the old guy, he's about ready for the grave, and his meat is too dry and stringy for your taste. Let them pass. They come in peace. They're not littering your trails. The few berries they eat you won't even notice. Let them pass, I say!"

But there's another hope, and it is more certain than any hope we have for temporary survival on this planet. It is hope given in the Written Word that we have eternity to spend with our Father, with Jesus Christ, with the Holy Spirit, with all the angels, and with every redeemed soul from Creation to the present-day. Hey, that's exciting! So, ultimately, it does not really matter if the king of the mountain roughs us up here and takes us out of circulation. It will give the masses opportunity to talk about us instead of to us. But it *really does matter* that our lives here are "hid with Christ in God" (Col. 3:3, KJV). And I can only know that from revelation. So I read my Bible, I test the spirits, and I compare the evidence of Creation with the full-spectrum light of divine revelation—and I get truth. Let's walk in the light while it shines on us.

No Limit on Hope!—What is the hope to which we are called? Why, the certainty of enjoying eternity (where maybe the king of the wilderness will give me a ride) no matter whether the bear eats me, whether I perish on the road in a mangled car, whether I die peacefully in good health, or whether I live to see His appearing! I have indescribable and unimaginable hope without limit. We are God's inheritance, you and me. Our Father calls us saints, and we are invited by God to live with Him forever. Hard to believe? Hard to accept? Not at all! It's a simple choice. Trust in God; it's a simple choice. He, not I, is the faithful One (1 Cor. 1:9; 2 Tim. 22:13; Heb. 2:17; 1 Peter 4:19; 1 John 1:9).

We experienced the presence and power of God in the mountains. We experienced His gracious care. But we have a greater experience of ultimate power when our Father intervenes to put the brakes on the ultimate devourer. Satan would have free reign to toy with us and destroy us were it not for the great power of God. This power was exercised through Jesus when the Father raised Him from the dead! To infuse a dead body with life and turn gray skin again to the tints of life takes real divine muscle. This is the power that is available to take our wasted lives, long dead in sin, and infuse them with spiritual health and vitality now, in our present experience. There is no spiritual enemy meeting us on our paths through the mountains and plains of life that will not immediately fall before the power stroke of the Almighty if we ask for His intervention.

But strange infatuation! Strange, twisted thinking! While we gladly accept timely protection from the fang and claw of the great bear of the mountain, we are slower than quick in asking for immediate intervention when the devil aims his artillery at our vitals. Don't ask why. There is no answer that makes sense to anything but a perverted mind. The heavenly Father can forgive our sin and restore a right mind within us. Jesus is in heaven, but His grace extends to earth for us (Heb. 4:16). He understands our temptations, having been through them all (Heb. 4:15), and He will exercise His power in our defense (like Father, like Son).

We've been looking at God's power for individual need, but isn't this the same power available for the church, the body of Christ? Absolutely! As a congregation we have full access to all the power of God exercised through Christ, the Head of the church. That is an awesomely comforting thought. To realize that the Head of the church can infuse this moribund body with vibrant life and scintillating vitality should bring courage and joy to each praying saint. I say praying for a reason. Just as to the individual, divine power will not be sent to the congregation that does not ask for divine power. Remember Hezekiah and Sennacherib? Maybe not. But Hezekiah was rescued from Sennacherib's violent clutches *because* he prayed (Isa. 37:21, 22)—because he asked for immediate deliverance. What if he had not asked?

Scripture tells us that Christ is head over everything for the church. This means that His interests are centered in creating a church body that lives, breathes, and moves to the divine command—and does so with alacrity and joy. This means that He intends to create a unity out of the diversity of members that will honor Him in every way. Think of the most well-honed human body imaginable. The fingers can pick up the tiniest object; the arms and legs, in synchronized unity, can propel the body over seemingly impossible hurdles; eye, hand, and toe coordination coupled with enormous strength can carry the body up a shear precipice. When a toe bangs on a rock and needs attention, the rest of the body jumps to immediate help without criticism. All the body parts respond to clear instructions from the head. This is the church, as it moves smoothly to the clear instructions of the Head and acts in synchronized unity. When one member hurts, the body responds immediately to help without criticism. Are we spiritually there yet? No, sadly we are not there, but thankfully, our God is patient, and He does not want us to perish in our sin (2 Peter 3:9).

How do we get there? We simply have to *ask* for this unity and keep asking until we are ready to receive it from the Head. We have to ask as individuals and as a body. Our Father is not reluctant to give but only by our asking can we be made ready to receive. Jesus is in heaven exercising rule over every authority and power imaginable. He also respects our free wills. Submit our wills to Him, and He will make short work of the power of Satan that was wont to control us. Does it seem too simple? No, it's impossible! But what is impossible for us is possible and simple for the King of all kings.

Just *ask*!

Encouraged by a Thought—The church is the fullness of Christ. What does that mean? Simply that everything that is Christ is embodied in the church; we make up His visible presence on earth. Like the facets of the diamond displaying its beauty from every angle, the multifaceted membership of the church is exactly what He wants to display His awesome Self in the community. How else could He display His values, His patience, His love, His compassion, His grace, His mercy, His truthfulness, and His goodness than through the synchronized, harmonious association of disparate members in the body of believers? There is no other way for Christ to be revealed in the community than the way He has chosen.

Think of it; one hundred vastly differing personalities that look at the world through colored glasses of a hundred shades and filter their data through sieves of a hundred differing meshes, are working, giving, even sacrificing for each other in unity, peace, and harmony. Harmony in the church is the ultimate miracle. That's why the church was created. It is not a work of humanity, but a work of God. He intends the church to display His power and majesty in the world.

The people on the street won't recognize God in the body unless the body submits to the miracle-working power of divinity and is transformed into a coordinated, articulated unit that responds with harmony and joy to the Head. Ah, Lord, take away our stubbornness and give us a spirit of willingness to submit to Your miracle-working power.

Will we ever, on this earth, see eye-to-eye on all theological questions? Perhaps not. We are all growing in our understanding, and we grow at different rates. We are all standing on different vantage points. When hiking the steep mountain trails, I finally scramble up to the outlook on which you are standing, deeply breathing the pure mountain air and marveling at the wonder of God's creation. You are ready to move on, but I must rest a while and take in the scene. Yet, I won't see exactly what you have just seen, even if you tell me all about it. The expansive view will be the same; the great, unifying truths of sky and earth and the marvelous, unchanging landmarks will be the same—but not the detail. Sun and shadow have subtly shifted; they now reveal and obscure differently.

This illustrates how we advance in understanding of the Holy Bible. We see the grand panoramic sweep of God's truth and marvel at its beauty and integrity, but in some of the finer points we may understand things differently.

Do you see what I see? Do you hear what I hear?

While I pause to ponder the truth from my perspective, you could be moving on to clearer understanding. This should not trouble us. We should be glad for each other, recognizing that in God's good time, He will bring all things to our understanding (Phil. 3:15) and unite us, even in our theology. "Only let us live up to what we have already attained" (Phil. 3:16). Let's not deny that we are on the same mountain just because we haven't noticed every detail that our climbing partners have seen. Let's not say that our climbing partners are lying and deceitful because they report things that we haven't seen. Let's not say that a member of the body is a Jesuit mole, for example, just because he is preaching a truth that we haven't quite grasped.

Yes, I believe God can and will take away our stubbornness. He will rid us of our pride in the ability to see the detail and our reckless determination to be first up the mountain. He will give us a spirit of willingness to submit to His miracle-working power to recognize that the one coming up later might have seen a detail that we missed in our haste. We believers, assembled in worship, are the fullness of Christ. He said so. Paul wrote it down for us. Are. Present tense. Now. What we are in Christ, we can be in experience. We can demonstrate divine unity in our human diversity that will give glory to Christ, to our Father, and to the Holy Spirit. Christ will fill us in every way when we give our wills over to Him as individuals and our collective will to Him as the body. This is God's will. Let it be done in us, and let it happen now!

Chapter 2
The Dead Become One

God Raises the Dead; Makes Us Alive in Christ

You Gentiles used to be dead in your transgressions and sins. You didn't realize your desperate condition as you followed the ways of the world, which are dictated by the ruler of this world, Satan, who had you completely in his power. His spirit is still at work in those who are disobedient.

You had lots of company as you blindly followed the devil. All of us were there with you at one time. The cravings of the sinful nature, the self, were very much alive and active in us, and we gratified them to the full. We were totally comfortable with sinful desires, thoughts, and actions. We were just as rapidly heading for destruction as you were. In fact, we were by nature objects of God's wrath, doomed to destruction as you were.

Ah, but there is a grand solution to our desperate condition! God's love for us is great; His mercy is rich! We, who were dead in sin, He made alive with Christ—so great is His grace. He saved us from His wrath, but there's much more! God raised us up with Christ; He set us down with Christ in heaven, where Christ is now. And why did He do it? He did it simply because He wanted to show to the universe His incomparable grace that He so kindly provided to us in Christ Jesus.

You see, we have been saved by the grace that was freely given to us by God in Christ. You received this gift by faith as we did (faith itself is a gift of God). You didn't work for grace. Don't ever think so. God's gift leaves you no room to boast. We are totally God's workmanship (imagine, being the handiwork of God!). You might say we are His work of art, both in our original creation and in our present restoration, our new creation. God intends that we glorify Him by good behavior, which He has prepared and described for us in advance. So, in a single sentence, we are saved from God's wrath by His grace to honor Him by good works, which He has already prepared for us to do. (Eph. 2:1–10)

Wanted Alive—Not Dead—As a living, breathing Gentile, Paul's words as he introduces the idea of being alive in Christ have a powerful meaning for me. Before I submitted to the grace of God, I was thoroughly dead in transgressions and sins. I see now that Paul wasn't exaggerating because I didn't even recognize my condition of deadness! In fact, being dead in sin, it was as impossible for me to recognize my condition as it was for me to leap into life. I needed the new birth that only God can give (John 3:7). As one who grew up in a Christian home and still clung to the illusion of being Christian, I had the obvious, visible forms of godliness but, dead as I was, I lacked its power (2 Tim. 3:5). These forms of godliness have a powerfully deceptive effect on us. Focused as we are on behavior, we are blinded to our desperate condition. I was following the ways of the world, not in overtly wicked living (though God could see my wickedness), but in attempting to achieve my own salvation through my own sweaty effort. My *self*, my nature of sin, was alive and actively dominating my life. Did my efforts work? Did yours?

Since experiencing the miracle of new birth, some of my overt behaviors have not changed a whole lot. I attend church. I support the gospel. I don't beat my wife. The big change is in my relation to our Father. Through the work of the Holy Spirit I am becoming progressively more conscious of the attempts of the *self* to reassert its place of dominance in my life. The Holy Spirit leads me to recognize things, circumstances, and thoughts that, in my new experience, I want to avoid, to have purged, and to escape entirely. Having restored my soul, *he leads me in the paths of righteousness for His name's sake* (Ps. 23:3). I am no longer threshing through swamps and brambles of despair vainly seeking for a destination that is always out of reach. I no longer see our Father as coolly waiting for me to struggle up through many failures to a level of performance predetermined by my inherent strength and ability to resist temptation (which I must develop by sweaty effort and painful self denial), at which point He reaches down and pulls me up the rest of the way. This seemed to be the thinking norm for the group to which I belonged as a young person, though there had to have been many at that time who lived in a saving relationship with God.

As teenagers in boarding school, we had an old barbell. It was just two round iron balls on the ends of an iron bar that weighed about 100 pounds. We kept it outside behind the dormitory, and we boys who aspired to be tough would gather there to test our strength against one another. I forget all the terminology we used to describe the various acts of bodily abuse in which we engaged. In one particular maneuver, we would attempt to swing the weight over our heads in one clean movement. In another we would bring the barbell to our chests then sort of extend the arms over the head while dropping under the weight. The mighty ones would do that with one arm. I was never able to manage the one arm stunt, though I could get the thing to my shoulder. Then, of course, there were the presses, the bench presses, the curls, and the squats. All of it was intended to impress an audience—preferably from the other dormitory. So on we labored; we pushed our limits, and we tore our ligaments. Every time we achieved a new level of performance, we would raise the bar on our expectations. Nothing was ever good enough. (Without realizing it we set ourselves up for a lot of pain later in life.)

This is a metaphor of my even more foolish attempts to achieve righteousness through performance—or by avoiding performance. I struggled; I worked; I mortified my soul if not my body. I paraded my virtues and attempts through singing bands, ingathering, literature distribution, book selling, and other good deeds. Still, nothing was ever good enough. If I did succeed in resisting a temptation, the sense of personal satisfaction as I raised the bar to test my resistance at a new level might have warned me that the *self* was alive and well and tantalizing me. In fact, the way some of these otherwise good activities were promoted, recorded, and rewarded fostered the already-well-embedded belief in salvation by doing.

Following the ways invented by the ruler of this world, I subscribed to a pernicious concept that never worked. Satan had me in his power. But God is persistent; His patience is great, and more than sufficient for all my sin is His mercy and grace, which He lavished on me in wisdom. I know that now, and I rejoice in the knowledge and experience. This would-be-tough boy doesn't have to prove his strength to overcome. He only has to receive overcoming grace from our God. Am I always an overcomer? No. But I have an Advocate who speaks with power, grace, and eloquence in my defense. He is the atoning sacrifice for my sin (1 John 2:1, 2), and I want to honor Him in everything every single moment of the day.

Cat in the Rain Barrel—Sadly, the spirit of Satan is still at work in those who are disobedient—even ignorantly disobedient. So many people, even within the congregation, are just too comfortable with sinful desires, thoughts, and actions. They think that they are doing good when, in fact, the sinful nature, the *self*, is promoting the behavior. In ignorance or otherwise, they have not submitted to the Spirit of Jesus. Within the congregation these folk would be horrified to realize that the good things they do, plan to do, talk about doing, and neglect to do are regarded as sin by God (Matt. 7:21–23; Matt. 25:45). When is a "good" deed actually a sin? I'd suggest that it's when it is not done by God's grace, in His power, by His prompting, for His exclusive glory; it's when it is done for the glory of the self.

Whenever we hope for a little piece of the glory, for recognition, for praise, for applause, for our picture in the *Review*, we are usurping God's place and just as surely sinning against Him as if we brazenly committed a heinous sin. (I hear the Holy Spirit calling to me, "Hey, you there, staring into the depth of the computer monitor: why are you putting these marks on paper? Do you crave recognition of some kind?" *Oh, Lord, deliver me from myself! If there is anything of value in these words, let God alone be praised for pulling me from the swamp and setting my feet on the Rock!*)

In stating that all of us were there with the Gentiles at one time, Paul makes it clear that the Gentiles had lots of Jewish company as they blindly followed the devil. In fact, Paul would be truthful today in saying that all Christians were at one time with the unbelievers in gratifying the cravings of our sinful natures to the full (and some stay there for a long time, even after they think they are Christians). But this idea needs some unpacking. Each generation is born with the same handicap as the previous generation, whether or not born into a Christian home. We are born sinners in need of a Savior, in need of the rebirth that Jesus gives. We can't take any comfort in being third- or fifth-generation Seventh-day Adventist, Baptist, Methodist, Muslim, or anything else. We need to make this absolutely clear when we teach our toddlers. Being good, kind, and sweet does not win for us the favor of God. Little boys and girls are not made acceptable to God by sharing toys or not pulling hair. Little boys and girls, like the big ones, are acceptable only through God's "glorious grace, which he has freely given us in the One he loves" (Eph. 1:6). This acceptance by God is all the motivation and power we need to please Him in our daily contacts in the congregation and in the community.

As a child and teenager growing up in my parents' home, I always wanted to please my parents—especially if I was doing something I liked to do. They operated a bush sawmill, and there were many things in that operation that I liked to do. Skidding logs was one of them. After I was ten years old, I could handle the horses as well as an adult could, so I got to skid a few logs. Well, actually, it was the horses that dragged the logs; I merely hooked and unhooked the chain and instructed the horses. As I grew older and stronger, the mill became more interesting, and I would vie with my brother for different positions. We both wanted to prove our strength and maturity. Even piling lumber became a test of skill, strength, and endurance. It seemed that in everything that adults normally did, we boys endeavored to excel.

The ranch branch of the enterprise at the north end of the lake was in the very early stages of development while I was growing up. Barbed wire fences were starting to appear and it was not uncommon for us boys to get our clothes or our skin snagged on the barbs as we tried to crawl through a fence. We could do it successfully only with careful attention to the barbs. Try crawling through some of God's hoops.

Why do I tell you these tales from sixty years ago? Well, that is where the tendencies with which I was born were developing and finding expression as attitudes toward life and toward God. It became a simple, natural, and unconscious process to transfer my desire for parental approval through excelling at manual work (usually doing those things that were considered *man's* work) to a belief that God can be reached in the same way. I could say, and essentially that is what I did say, "Look, God, see all these good things I am doing? I am getting up an hour early to read a devotional book; I am going out on a snowy evening to collect money for the poor; I pay tithe on everything I earn; I am not doing those bad things. What is my reward? If I become good enough at the good work and avoid the bad will I make it to heaven some day? What more do I have to do?" There was always something more. I didn't have assurance of salvation because there was always another level to achieve. God was always just out of reach, and I was continually attempting to reach that illusive level of performance that I felt God could accept.

Where were my parents while I was entrenching these unhealthy and destructive, even satanic, attitudes in my thinking? It was during that period that my dad sustained a massive head injury in the mill and was incapacitated for about a year. He then developed a brain tumor, which tormented him for fifteen years before it ended his life. As dad lost his ability to function, more and more of the operation of the home and mill fell to my mother. Those were tough times and with five children, an invalid husband, and food to put on the table, my mom had little opportunity or energy to pay attention to the needs of developing boys. We sort of did what we had to do to survive. By then, we older ones were in our mid-teens and pretty much established in our attitudes. It was time to leave home for boarding school and take our ideas with us. Sadly, boarding school did little to change them.

I graduated and spent the next eleven years getting my first degree. During this period I religiously followed the forms of godliness, but it was all empty and lacking in power. It seems like the devil was quite content to have me zealously practicing the forms. My sinful nature craved the satisfaction of reaching those goals myself, and I gratified it to the full. While recognizing that my performance could always be improved, I was totally occupied with keeping the lid on my sinful desires and thoughts, preventing them from spilling over into actions. I was usurping the role of God in my life. The apostle John, through the gift of the Spirit, warns us to be on guard against the antichrist (1 John 2:18, 22; 4:3). Typically, we look outside for the enemy, but this sounds a lot like the antichrist. The antichrist in the church? Don't put it past him! All these years I was *by nature* an object of God's wrath, doomed to destruction—and I couldn't see it! This was not because of some inherent inability to see, but because of my own obtuse blindness to which I clung like a cat to a stick in a rain barrel.

That is a tragedy of enormous proportions in the making, but God is great; He is persistent; His mercy endures forever; His grace is sufficient for all my needs. I just needed to receive it and follow Him with joy! Now I thank God. What I could never do, He did—with grace, with finesse, with power, and, I believe, with great joy! I was well into mid-life before I recognized the love and grace of God and admitted the glorious, full-spectrum light of the gospel to my darkened mind. The day is dying in the west now, and I know I can lie down to rest in peace, assurance, and confidence in the eternal morning.

Can you imagine being dead in sin and not knowing it, not recognizing your desperate condition? Well, how could you know anything spiritual? You're dead. Just as the physically dead know nothing and can respond to nothing (as we learn from Scripture and experience), so the spiritually dead are blissfully or otherwise unaware of their condition. They go on from day to day in their terminal trajectory performing their rituals, perhaps enjoying the *good life*, perhaps not, maybe even thinking of ending an existence that brings no joy and has no obvious purpose. Then God breaks into their minds with the good news of the new birth—they are made alive in Christ.

There is no other solution for our terminal condition. Buddha tried to find an answer and countless people are still following his futile teachings. We've all tried his solution and found it wanting in power to change us. Zoroaster, in ancient Persia, tried it, recording his efforts in the *Zend-Avesta*. Although he was wrong, dead wrong, and most of us are hearing of him for the first time right now, few of us have escaped at least dabbling, if not immersing ourselves, in his doctrine of salvation by doing good works. This seems to be the way of humanity. It seems to be the way of too many people in the Christian church. We want to do it ourselves, yet none of us has ever achieved the illusive perfection by striving to be good. The new birth, not just taught by Jesus, but motivated, activated, and empowered by Him, is the only solution for Buddhists, Christians, Islamists, atheists, and all others. Christianity is unique only because Christ is unique.[1] He is for everyone!

When leading out in Bible study groups, I occasionally challenge the serenity of the members by posing the question: do you have to obey in order to be saved? Usually I present the question in the context of a particular doctrine dear to the hearts of the believers such as: do you have to keep the Sabbath in order to be saved? The answer is usually open mouths and profound silence. The answer, of course, is unequivocal: no. If I obey in order to be saved, I am still in sin, rebellion, and darkness, never achieving the elusive goal of goodness sufficient to appease an angry, meticulous, even malicious God. In fact, the illusion of obedience outside of Christ is just that—an illusion. I obey (obedience is only possible in Christ) because Christ has already saved me, given me the new birth, removed me from death, and placed me in eternal life (John 5:24). As one now truly in life, I respond to my salvation by attempting to obey in everything I understand. Ah! I see! God's love for me is great; He is rich in mercy; great is His grace! Is that all? Is there nothing more? There is.

Paul assures us that there is so much more.

---

[1] "The main problem is not Christ's uniqueness, but how we articulate that claim. Don't be tempted to give trite answers [to people who question you on the relative merits of Buddha, Muhammad, or Christ] … and don't try to defend Christianity as a religious system. Keep the focus on who Jesus is and what God has done for us all in him because this is what the world needs. This is who the world needs" (John D. Wilson, *Faith Today*, September-October, 2009, p. 36).

Having raised us up in Christ, God now sets us down with Him in heaven. Beg your pardon, Paul. How is that? Are we not still on this moldering earth or do we now experience a new illusion? Let's take this a bit easy—or hard, as necessary. When I was a kid, the truckers hauling lumber from Dad's mill didn't have it easy on the road. Summer roads were frequently muddy, not just slippery-muddy, but deep-rutted-filled-with-muck-and-water muddy. The intrepid drivers would plow into these mud holes with their trucks rocking from side to side as they lunged and bucked forward. Sometimes they made it through and sometimes not. On the not occasions, they would often unload their trucks by hand, rock the trucks forward and back until they were once again on solid ground, reload board by heavy board, and do it all over again in the next mud hole. These guys just didn't give up. It was a way of life. (Dad did eventually get his twenty miles of road worked into a passable condition.) But that's the point when we come to Scripture that is hard to understand. We don't give up on prayer and study. It's the way of the new life. So, let's keep on trucking, and don't forget that when the way is tough, we have a tough driver at the wheel who is taking us through.

Foolishly Simple Salvation!—Paul informs us that *God set us down with Christ in heaven where Christ is now* (Eph. 2:6). To help us approach an understanding of this concept, let's go back to 1 Corinthians 1:30 and 15:45. We learn from these verses that God put us into Christ who is the last Adam, the last representative of the entire human race. Just as the first Adam *was* the entire human race (you know that Eve is also called Adam), so Christ, in His incarnation, *was made* the entire human race, and in becoming us He rewrote the histories of each person. That being so, when Christ died, we died to sin in Him (Rom. 6:2, 6). When Christ was raised, we were raised to a new life in Him (Rom. 6:4). Now we also live with Him where He is (Rom. 6:8; Eph. 2:6). Yet you rightly insist, "But we are still here." Yes, we are still here, but as far as God is concerned (and that's what counts), we are in heaven with Christ. By faith we receive our new history and see ourselves in heaven with Christ where God sees us now. We are motivated, empowered, energized to realize that God sees things not as we see them (1 Sam. 16:7). In God's good time, we shall experience the reality of what we can now only see by faith in One who cannot lie (Titus 1:2).

We might wonder why God would lavish such a blessing on us that in His view we are already in heaven with Christ. Simply because of who He is—the God whose love cannot be measured or described by human methods. He knows that if we accept His gift of salvation with our assurance rooted in His integrity we are safe from the roaring lion. When the time is right, we will in real time with real, unflawed bodies walk with Him into the real kingdom. The entire universe will see and wonder at the incredible riches of God's grace that He so kindly expressed to us in Christ Jesus.

Our salvation is all by grace, freely given to us by God in Christ, no matter how many barbed wire hoops we've crawled through that have marred our flesh and torn our dirty clothes (Isa. 64:6). It doesn't matter how many exhausting tons of iron we've pumped in our own futile efforts to get God's attention, if not His admiration. We already had His attention. He was right there all the time leaving voice mails in the thunder, tapping text messages in the Holy Scripture, sending His own reps in the persons of our friends, parents, pastors, teachers, and maybe even our enemies, trying to get *our* attention amid the plethora of other voices, beeps, buzzes, and flickering lights clamoring to keep us preoccupied with being good, if not completely righteous.

Our salvation is really quite basic, almost foolishly simple (1 Cor. 1:27)—designed for a foolish people. He says, *Come, I will give you rest from all your crawling and pumping. Just come to Me. I'm right here beside you* (Matt. 11:28–30). Salvation is that simple, that basic, that absolutely available and free!

Saved by grace freely given! Take a good look at the tense of the verb and remember what you see. The saving is an act of God already done—and yet somehow not complete. We need to drill a little deeper into this one. You see, there is a power in sin that is greater than our power to resist. There is a penalty or a consequence attached to sin that cannot be evaded or postponed. There is also the presence of sin that is in our faces everywhere and every day. And still we are saved? Yes, we are! At the cross Jesus saved us from the penalty of sin by taking it on Himself. This is an accomplished fact. A penalty, once paid, does not need to be paid again. Let's not insist on paying any or all of it. Jesus, who knew no sin, was made to be sin for us in order for us to be made the righteousness of God in Him (2 Cor. 5:21). What a novel idea! Only Divinity could think of a solution like that; only Divinity could carry it out!

Having assumed our penalty, Jesus also neutered sin, He took away its power to enslave and compel. But the presence is still around us, saturating our environment, and within us in the person of the old nature, the ubiquitous *self*, which will continue to harass us until this mortal puts on immortality (1 Cor. 15:53, 54). Though we are in the world until the glorious appearing, we are freed through faith from sin's hideous presence as we sit with Christ in heavenly places (Eph. 1:20). And, also in Christ, we have victory over the most alluring and powerful temptations (Phil. 4:13).

A Really Funny Story (... Not)—I once knew a young man when I was just a little younger than he was. In those days many of the workers in the woods did not own their own vehicles. They would catch rides with a lumber truck or with someone who owned a car. The cars were frequently out of commission for various reasons usually related to the rough and muddy roads combined with inadequate maintenance. Occasionally there was no other option than to use our feet. One cold winter's day, this young man discovered that his tobacco can was empty. That was really about as bad as it could get, and there was only one solution. There was no car to borrow, beg, or steal; he would have to use what he had—his feet.

Twenty miles in a gale from the north at minus twenty degrees Fahrenheit! What a bitter chill that was! Then return. Funny, isn't it? What you gotta do, you gotta do. There are some things in life that just can't be ignored and a strong tobacco addiction squeezing every nerve in the body is one of them. I wish there was a happy ending to this story. The ending is not happy. Twenty-five years later this young man, having lost his family and everything but the clothes he wore, died alone in a bare, cold room with his boots on. He was forty-five and a victim of the devil's deadly weapons.

Tragically, he had allowed the faith he had had as a child to atrophy; little by little he made choices that propelled him ever farther down the slippery road to the yawning, but fully awake, abyss. I met him on the street of a northern city a year or two before he died. He was begging. This man was my cousin. I had six other cousins whose stories more or less paralleled the story of this young man. Come to think of it, it's not a funny story at all. These tragedies need not have happened. God's grace received would have changed everything.

This life-changing grace is abundantly and freely given. Wow! We receive this grace by faith in Christ, the giver. Our faith is also a gift of God. God has given the measure of faith to everyone (Rom. 12:3). How big is that measure? I don't know. Frankly, I don't care. That's a debate over nonsense like asking how many angels can dance on the head of a pin. I do know that the measure is quite big enough to connect me solidly to the abundant grace of God. That's all we need. But be warned! Satan hurls all kinds of trials and temptations at us; he insinuates into our lives the most subtle of circumstances designed to divert our attentions to anything, maybe even something intrinsically good, that could come between us and our Father in heaven. He throws pain at us, surprises us with disease, wounds us with betrayal, and alienates us from those we love. He even flatters us through prosperity and popularity.

These varied circumstances require us to face up to the choices we are making. Faith comes through the Word of God, a word that we have to hear if we are to receive its benefit (Rom. 10:17). If we let work, sports, TV, Internet, friends, fishing, last week's newspaper, or any other diversion come between us and God, we put that measure of faith at risk. Choices! God has given us control over the choices we make. Evolution is desperately trying to prove that free will is a myth—that our minds are planning to act before we are conscious of the idea. It just isn't so. God gives us the ability to choose. We can seek His kingdom and righteousness first (Matt. 6:33) or we can play with Satan's flimsy stuff. We can't do both at the same time. I've seen the results in my own life.

Twenty years ago I started to get acquainted with a God of grace. I had known *about* Him since childhood, but when I actually got to know Him, my life began to change. Mine is somewhat like Paul's experience: I haven't already come to know the full power of Christ in my experience, but I "press on to take hold of that for which Christ has taken hold of me" (Phil. 3:8–12). Only faith connects us to God, and faith takes prime time to maintain. That all sufficient, big enough, strong enough measure that God gives to everyone needs maintenance through reading Scripture, meditating on Scripture, sharing Scripture, and ultimately through obedience of Scripture. All of this takes prime time; I can't emphasize it too often or too much. It takes time that cannot be used to amuse ourselves with anything intrinsically good or overtly evil. The simple words of Jesus apply here: *Seek first the kingdom of God and His righteousness, and all things you need will be given to you* (Matt. 6:33). These things include our livelihoods, our social support networks, and our intellectual development; in fact, they include everything that is good and relevant to our circumstances.

God, the Artisan!—Paul goes on to assure us that we are the workmanship of God. We are His personal work of art both in our original creation and in our new creation. That is pretty awesome! I have this little mental picture of God's workshop where He has every tool you could dream of and infinitely more; all are arranged in perfect and efficient order. It's a working workshop; some tools are on the bench and some are in the racks. Each tool has a function. Though they are beautiful tools, none are there solely for decoration, and the great Artisan is a master in the use of each. The workbenches are clean and organized; the lighting illuminates every detail of the project; the supplies are arranged on the shelves within easy reach. And to render the shop totally effective, He made it portable; He takes it wherever He goes.

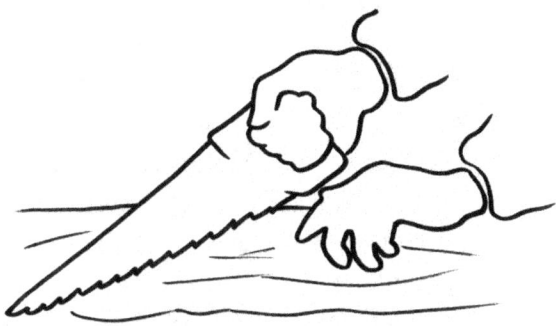

There's a work of art concealed in this splinter of nondescript wood.

I have a shop in which I work with wood, glue, nails, screws, and fewer tools than I think I need. I love wood; I am pained to throw out a piece. Who knows? It might have a use someday. And if I use the piece of wood on a sunny day, it won't be there to use if I need it on a rainy day. Do you feel my dilemma? So I have wood in the rack that has been around for decades—maple, birch, alder, walnut, tigerwood, zebrawood, spruce, pine, aspen. Each has color, density, aroma, compression strength, and other characteristics that make it useful in ways that another variety cannot be used. Each has beauties that appeal to eye, touch, and smell that are not found in another variety. Concealed in a scaly birch burl bursting from the side of an aging tree like a giant wart are goblets, bowls, pens, and lidded boxes that simply beg to be released, admired, caressed, displayed. The skilled artisan will find in a piece of nondescript wood, apparently fit only for the fire, a work of art that elicits exclamations of wonder and admiration in the appreciative viewer. The handiwork of the Creator is not always readily apparent to the casual passerby. Do we see a lesson here?

This illustration speaks to the great Artisan's work of reclaiming lost humanity and saving us from the fire. He finds me, steeped in sin, twisted, and bent out of shape. I am morally and spiritually scaly, knobby, and checked; I'm really just not nice to look at. Any lesser being would throw me into the trash bin or the fire, but God takes me into His workshop and transforms this unlikely lump of protoplasm and twisted thinking into a work of art that will bring glory and admiration to the Artisan when the time is right (2 Thess. 1:10).

As the artisan rescues the lump of wood from the fire, so God saves us from the final fire, although we might have to experience some very intense heat here. I was about 15 at the time and was working in Dad's sawmill. Regulations on burning sawmill refuse were less advanced in those pristine days, and the progressive operators had developed a system of fast belts running in troughs through the mills to carry slabs and other debris to the open burn pits. When a slab dropped into the trough, it took a few seconds for it to catch up with the belt. By the time it reached the end of the belt trough, the slab had momentum to shoot forty feet or so out into the inferno.

Stepping over the trough one day, I found myself in the bottom with the belt burning past under my belly. I was accelerating feet first to destruction with no exit in sight. The memory still singes my grey hair. No one saw me. No one would know to what fate I had disappeared. How long would it take for someone to realize that there was no other place to look and begin

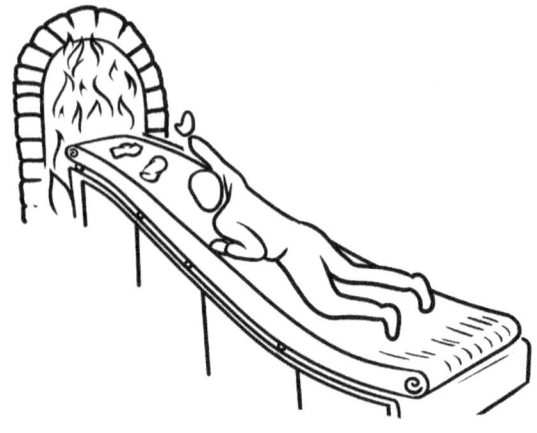

Not my time to burn!

sifting the ashes for a belt buckle or a knife blade? But none of these thoughts crossed my mind as I grasped frantically for some hold. Suddenly, I was out of the trough. I was on my feet and walking, a bit shaky and a little bruised and abraded, but walking. I can only explain my rescue by saying that our God is merciful. He saw that it was not the time for me to burn. The great Artisan had some adjustments He still wanted to do on my character. I know He is not finished with me yet. I want to display His character as He gives me grace and life here, and I trust confidently that He will take me through any fires in my future to the heavenly display in His own good time—His restoration finished.

There is more work for Him to do. Even I can see that. Personally, I would not choose some of the procedures He takes as he shapes my character because I would like to go smoothly into the kingdom. But the way is not smooth. (There is an old song my mother used to sing that tells of the rough road we must follow to heaven with our sore and bleeding feet. The chorus echoed the sentiment, Is it far?[2]) There is much pain involved, sometimes almost more than I can bear. It hurts to see trouble in churches, trouble in schools, and trouble in families. Does it have to be this way? Not necessarily.

Yet God is using these troubles, so many of them of our own making, as His tools. The divine Artisan is working with some very flawed pieces. He will trim and cut and polish as required to bring out the hidden works of art. As with the artisan carefully touching the blade to the wood, so the divine Artisan is right there with sure hands on precision tools as we endure the pain. He knows exactly how much stress, tension, and pain we can bear before we fly apart, like a faulty block on a lathe, and He will not put us to tests we cannot endure. With every test the way of escape is provided (1 Cor. 10:13).

I was turning a piece of ant-holy tamarack one day when my gouge caught in a weak point. Oh, oh! (But, of course, I didn't have time to think, *Oh, oh!*) The piece came apart at 600 rpm and smacked me right in the face shield. The full-face shield was my favorite tool right about then. Our Father, the divine Artisan, never lets a tool catch. His infinite skill ensures that we will never fly apart under His careful crafting. Just as the artisan is praised for releasing a work of art from its prison in a piece of unlikely fire wood, so our Father is praised for converting the unlikeliest chip off the old block—and the old block, too—into something beautiful.

On earth, this beauty is revealed in our behavior that God has prepared and described for us in advance. We learn to demonstrate love, patience, fortitude, honesty, integrity, endurance, peace, kindness, goodness, and faithfulness. We learn how to treat with compassion the sister or

---

[2] George F. Root, "O the Way Is Long and Weary," The Cyber Hymnal, http://www.curate.us/s/2Jxu (accessed June 12, 2014).

brother who has injured us, and we do it with the joy of the Lord, our strength (Neh. 8:10). Just so we don't start thinking that those little growths are our doing, we are told they are called the fruit of the Spirit (Gal. 5:22). For many of us, this learning takes a lifetime; in fact, for all of us, this learning takes a lifetime. Colleges promote lifelong learning in efforts to draw adults into their programs to generate revenues. Our Father promoted this concept from the beginning of time to salvage our lost souls.

So, to put it in a single sentence: we are saved from God's wrath by His grace to honor Him by good works, which He has already prepared for us to do. It is all God's doing; we cannot boast in anything that we are or do. Perhaps we need to take stock of our behavior from time to time—daily, in fact—to ensure that we are placing ourselves in God's care, receiving His grace, reveling in His mercy, and doing what He would want us to do.

God Makes Us One in Christ

Because God has already made you alive in Christ, remember, you who were derisively called uncircumcised by those who prided themselves on being the circumcised (that physical operation which they have performed on themselves), and do not forget that you were then separate from Christ. You were excluded from citizenship in Israel. You were foreigners to the covenants made by the promise of God. You had no hope of salvation and were without God in a hostile world. But now your circumstances have dramatically changed. In Christ Jesus, you, who used to be far away, wandering in a desolate wilderness so to speak, have been brought near through the blood of Christ.

Christ Himself is our peace. He has made us to be one. By his blood He has brought down the barrier of hostility that separated us in the past. Christ abolished in His flesh the laws we had erected as barriers to keep us distinct and separate. His death actually put to death our mutual hostility. Unity and peace among us was His purpose—one body and not two. But this did not complete His work. Having created one body, He intended to reconcile us to God by His death on the cross. Jesus Christ, in His death, preached peace to you Gentiles who were far away and peace to us Jews who were near. Only through Christ can we, together with you, have access to the Father through the one Holy Spirit.

Because of this marvelous act of God, you are no longer wanderers in a desolate wilderness, no longer foreigners and aliens, no longer unwanted refugees. You are citizens with us, members of God's household with us; we are one united, integrated family! We are a beautiful dwelling place, built together on the foundation of the apostles and prophets; Christ Jesus, Himself, is the Chief Cornerstone. In Christ the whole building becomes an integrated unity. In Him the whole building rises to become a holy temple in the Lord. And don't ever forget this: in Christ you are part of this building with us. We are together in Christ, and we will become a dwelling in which God's Holy Spirit will live forever. (Eph. 2:11-22)

Remember! Do Not Forget!—We forget because we don't remember. We usually use our remembering to reconstruct past experiences: Remember when we climbed Old Baldy as kids in the spring to pick the first crocuses? Or remember that boy who ... ? Not being a specialist in the psychology of memory, I won't try to describe the brain functions that result in conscious recall, but I'm pretty sure of this: we need to allocate much more purpose-directed energy to remembering if we intend to improve our recall. That allocation of energy will take time, of course, time that then is not available for any other activity however desirable or noble.

It seems almost self-evident that we allocate energy to remembering those things that are important to us: significant names and the faces attached to them; the contact information of people who owe us; the quickest way to get to a friend's house; the password for my *Amazon* account; where I put my keys. Let's see now, where *are* my keys? Was it today that I was supposed to renew my class one driving license?

These are ordinary memory objectives, but we don't always have deliberate systems in place to ensure memory. Perhaps something as simple as using a date book to help us get to the right meeting on the day it occurs is all that it takes. Well, no, it takes more than a book; we have to *write* in the book and then *read* our writing to make it effective. Perhaps a hook in the cupboard where keys are always placed when not in the ignition, the lock, or the hand would be helpful. You know what I mean.

Take your mind back to Ecclesiastes 12:1. But, wait. Before we go there, let me tell you a story, humorous, maybe a little sad, but true, that I just now remembered. I took a call in my office one day from a man who wished to speak with me the following week. We agreed on the time. The day before he arrived, he called to confirm our meeting. We met, and within seconds of completing the obligatory rituals of greeting, I was aware that this man was in the wrong place. His presentation was rational, but he should have been pitching it to someone else. I pointed out to him that neither my campus nor I was in any way connected with his project. In fact, I knew nothing about it. It took some convincing but as he walked out the door I heard him mutter to himself, "I wonder where I'm supposed to be today." Never heard of him again. Using correctly a few memory techniques would have spared the poor guy a lot of embarrassment and some expense.

Do you remember the words to Ecclesiastes 12:1? Probably not without a prompt: "Remember your Creator in the days of your youth ..." (the principle applies to those who still have brain function whatever the age). If I am going to remember my Creator in any meaningful way, I will have to give Him prime-time energy and focused attention. The energy, the attention, and the time will not then be available for any other of the plethora of buzzes, bleeps, chatters, or flashes that occupy so much of our lives. On the other hand, forgetting is passive; it takes no time or energy to forget; forgetting happens when we attach too little importance to the face, the name, the date, or the event to embed it in the memory, file it properly, and make it available on demand. These are simplified explanations of complex mental processes, of course, and are not intended to explain in any way how the processes of memory work, but this explanation works here for our purposes.

"Well," you might argue, "I operate a faller buncher with a satellite phone. I can talk to my wife and remember my Creator as I buzz off those trees and lay them straight for my friend in the grapple skidder. It's called multitasking in some quarters. I can do it in the cockpit of the buncher as well as in the cab of my truck as I commute to work at three in the morning—except I won't be calling my wife at three in the morning." Could be true. But remember, you have to have some data filed away to recall, and filing that data takes focused time. You can't repeat Scripture from memory without having placed it in the memory; you can't rejoice in the memory of past experiences of God's amazing grace without having gone through the experience. The principle applies as well to the business executive, the chamber maid, and to the teen who's texting and talking in a language that I haven't learned. Not to worry, young people, God knows your language.

Having established that remembering takes time, we acknowledge that giving time to the not-automatic task of remembering takes personal discipline, personal commitment, and personal action. Being alive in Christ doesn't make that discipline, commitment, and action automatic; it just makes it possible (Phil. 4:13). The choice still remains with you and me to take the time to embed the truths of Christ and the experiences with Christ in our minds. For me, that means early in the day, first thing in the morning. It also means that there are some things, however good they may be, in which I simply do not have time to indulge. Typically, if I miss that early morning time with God, I don't get it. I get involved in other things, even emergencies. Yesterday, it was plowing the foot of snow that fell on Friday, then off I went to town for an appointment, and then home I came in the evening too tired to do anything but fall into bed. That three hours of snow plowing *would have* interfered with my first things had I let it. Once I get into my wood shop, I am likely to be there for the day, much to Mirja's annoyance. She thinks I should at least take a break for lunch even if she is not home. (Funny that she should think I could look after myself when she's not home.) First things *must* receive first place or they don't happen.

Together!—Occasionally in Christian circles, unbelievers are derisively called pagans or Philistines. Not nice. In fact, this is arrogant exclusivity in demonstration, and those who indulge in it should repent and amend their ways without delay. I was writing a letter last night in which I referred to Richard Dawkins, an evolutionary microbiologist and activist for evolution at Oxford University. On the Christian end of the spectrum, he could be called a zealous, fundamentalist evangelist, maybe a televangelist. This man has great zeal and great faith in his position (I think he would deny any connection to faith). When commenting on his position, I referred to his faith in an uncomplimentary way. On reflection, I removed the statement. We can afford to make our points in ways that are not calculated to be biting or sarcastic. In fact, we can afford to be Christian in all our dealings and communications. God expects this; He also empowers and motivates us.

All of us were at one time separate from Christ. As Paul told us, *[We] were excluded from citizenship. [We] were foreigners to the covenants made by the promise of God. [We] had no hope of salvation and were without God in a hostile world* (Eph. 2:12). Wow! What a sad and lonely condition! No wonder so many of us filled our lives with diversions, with acquiring stuff, with mind-numbing addictions, with wild music and violent, scatological entertainment. We filled it with sugar on sugar on fat on salt on fat in a double-double burger layered with three kinds of cheese and a side of all-you-can-eat fries smothered in gravy at the local *EatMuchEatMore* franchise (or drive forty miles to get it just to kill time).

And so many top that off with days and nights of frenetic activity. We had to do this to get our minds off the hostility of the world. Not hostile? Then how do you describe the fear of certain death flicking his tail and licking his lips there by the big box at the end of life—from which no one escapes (Heb. 2:15)? Even one as learned and erudite as John Shelby Spong, author of twenty books and the retired Bishop of Newark, New Jersey, acknowledges the need for religion as a narcotic. He acknowledges that the human fear of death impels us to fill our lives with activity and stuff. But he insists that he is quite OK with the prospect of death.[3] Sadly, this popular bishop offers no hope of release from hostility in its most flagrant form: death.

If you are familiar with C. S. Lewis and his book, *The Great Divorce*, you will remember (how could you forget?) the Episcopal Ghost in conversation with the Solid Spirit sent to lead him deep into the reality and pleasures of heaven. Even as he stood on heaven's threshold with its grand, panoramic expanse rising up before him, the Episcopal Ghost refused to acknowledge either hell, from which he had just come, or heaven in which it was his privilege to stay.[4] When I heard Bishop Spong on a CBC podcast, I couldn't help it. I had to exclaim, "This is the voice of the Episcopal Ghost! C. S. Lewis wasn't dreaming!"

Now notice the dramatic change in the tone of Paul's letter. A contrast is about to be introduced: *But*. Something has happened, something radically different from our past experiences. *Our circumstances have dramatically changed. In Christ Jesus we have been transported from the desolation of our lonely wanderings and brought near not only to Christ but also to one another as members of one family through the blood of Christ* (Eph. 2:13). We, who formerly lived our lives, in fact poisoned our lives, through the fear of death, now have new life in Christ. And we are not alone.

We have brothers and sisters who sympathize with us and care for us and we for them. We have Christ, our Brother. Life has taken on meaning, not new or additional meaning, but real, true meaning—original meaning. The blood of Christ, His sacrifice for us, has changed our circumstances. Tragically, Bishop Spong doesn't seem to know that he has a Savior who has *already* paid for his freedom and his life. The bishop doesn't have to hide behind his many books, denying the Creator God and teaching that human life is accidental. He doesn't need to deny the reality of heaven and insist that he is OK with the absence of future rewards or punishments.

More tragically, Bishop Spong is using his considerable platform as bishop and author to discourage others from listening to the invitation to come over the line into life; he confirms them in their infidelity. He alleges that the Christian church does not believe in God anymore. That unbelief, if true, must make him proud. However, not everyone is as sanguine about death as the bishop professes to be. Not everyone is *fine*, as he claims to be. Though Spong is bravely doing his part to ensure that belief in God does not obstruct humanity's mad scramble to avoid the specters of death, maybe some will stop their pell-mell rushing long enough to hear a second opinion, the other Voice. Maybe they will pause, listen, and respond. Maybe even the bishop himself. It has happened before.

We who have been brought near through the blood of Christ are in new relationships with each other. The very nearness in thought, in caring, in emotional bonding is the work of Christ in us. We enjoy a relationship that is not available in

---

[3] John Shelby Spong, *Eternal Life: A New Vision: Beyond Religion, Beyond Theism, Beyond Heaven and Hell* (New York, NY: HarperCollins, Harper One, 2009).

[4] C. S. Lewis, *The Great Divorce* (CS Lewis Pte. Ltd, 1946).

any secular organization. Oh, yes, differences do arise. Friction does occur even in church board meetings, but in Christ we have the motivation and the means to overcome these annoyances and continue to cherish one another as fellow travelers, as family, traveling together on the way to the kingdom of heaven. Bishop Spong, the Episcopal Ghost, and all other skeptics notwithstanding, the kingdom of heaven is real! For the believer, the kingdom is already within (Luke 17:21) because we have crossed over from death into life (John 5:24), and the solid reality is coming. That solid, noisy, brilliant coming is closer now than when we first believed (Rom. 13:11).

Let the Walls Stay Down!—*Christ Himself is our peace because in Him we are one* (Eph. 2:14). We are no longer divided, enraged, or engaged in hostile rivalry for turf on a dwindling earth. The practical, everyday worker commuting bumper-to-bumper, with the eye peeled for the escape ramp, may have trouble with the concept, as may every other human being. The fact that you are meditating on your position in Christ or His position in the world is authentic evidence that the claims of Scripture are reliable, defensible, and powerful.

We accept the evidence of reliable eyewitnesses when they are examined and cross-examined and demonstrated to be trustworthy. We consider these witnesses credible. It does not matter whether the evidence is heard first in a modern courtroom or from documents that have stood the test of time. If, on our early morning visit to the garden, we see little pointy imprints in the soil, we say, "Ah, the deer visited us last night." Then if we raise our eyes into the long light of the rising sun and see the beet tops all nipped off at ground level, we say, "Indeed, the deer was here last night, and he was a hungry, discriminating thief." The evidence is compelling. We don't have to see the deer in the act of eating the beet tops to know with reasonable certainty that he did it.

When walking through the forest, if we encounter a pile of steaming scat on the trail, we glance nervously about and mutter, "Uh … I think … there is … a grizzly bear nearby." (The size of the pile indicates a grizzly rather than the smaller black bear; also griz dung usually contains bells and whistles and smells like pepper—it's a joke!) Then we look up and see him appraising us from the other side of his dinner table and realize that we could be on the menu. Credible evidence appeals to rational minds and elicits appropriate responses.

The testimony of credible external evidence is convincing, but when external evidence corroborates the testimony of internal evidence, the force is overwhelming. How do we recognize internal evidence? We feel it in the work of God in our inner being. By the Holy Spirit, God communicates His love to us—a love that we can feel in our souls. Our spirit responds to the Spirit of God. The fear of death of which Bishop Spong speaks so blandly is changed into peace, not bravado. God's Holy Spirit, standing with our spirits, confirms that we are children of the eternal God (Rom. 8:16). Paul goes on to affirm that if we are children of God, then we are His heirs. In fact, we are one in Him and co-heirs with Christ to share His suffering as well as His glory (Rom. 8:17).

We know that in some jurisdictions people still suffer for Christ. They lose their homes, their families, even their lives. It happens today. But have you ever wondered how you can suffer for Christ in your society? How can you lay down your life for anyone? Not easy, is it?

Opportunities seem scarce, but there actually are countless opportunities, even in the most placid society, to lay down your life for your friends. Your time is your life. Whenever you give your time, you are truly giving your life. But suffer for Christ? Is it possible here in the land of the free? Yes—possible and much too frequent. We members of the family do suffer for Christ. Every member feels the pain when a family breaks up. We all hurt when a member is found in fraud. When a long-time member abandons the faith, we all experience the hurt. It's not embarrassment for ourselves that causes the pain. In our human way, we feel the hurt it does to our Father in heaven.

Early-morning commuter, what more could be said to convince you of the powerfully effective work of Christ in your soul? What more will you require to convince you that the line between death and life is called belief? We belong to the congregation of believers. Do we have Christ's peace? Do we have His oneness? Is the former barrier of hostility lying in rubble at our feet? Let's look at the language of the Bible. Christ *is* our peace. If we believe in Christ, His peace is ours. He has made us to be one. Our oneness is an accomplished fact in Christ. Christ abolished in His flesh the barriers we had created to keep us apart. Downed barriers are an accomplished fact. Let's not re-erect them. Let's not rebuild the hostility.

Your Wrenches in My Gears—In our world things do not stay where we would like them—even in the church. We bumble along comfortably for years until someone new moves into the community. That someone new inevitably brings new ideas and different ways of doing things that act like wrenches in the gears of the status quo. Saints who once wielded significant influence may find their influence waning. The ego hurts. Know what I think? Our Father knows us a lot better than we know ourselves. He is quite aware of the character flaws that lurk in the recesses of apparently committed saints. He knows how to fix them. He brings someone to us who will upset the equilibrium we have established and make us vulnerable to further working of the Holy Spirit. I think He does it with a smile, all the time knowing how He is going to deal with us as we drag our feet, create obstacles, raise barriers, and wish the new people would just go away so we can get back to the good old familiar.

This happened in my church. We experienced a wave of "in-migration," and with the wave came ideas we had not yet explored and practices we had not yet dared to try. Some of our congregants welcomed the newcomers warmly. Others erected barriers of suspicion and hostility. Our Father must have looked down in amusement as we struggled to achieve a new equilibrium. He must think something like, "How simple it would be if they would only yield to the influence of My Spirit (all of them, not just the staid old timers). I guess they all still need a little more time and a lot more polishing." Even the newcomers need to realize that the blending will not be without its tensions and that they must deal gently with the old saints in their comfortably familiar ruts.

Two rivers join not far from where I live. The wide river from the west has been flowing serenely in its deep valley past green pastures for a hundred miles since jostling its way out of white-water canyons in the western mountains into the high plateau country. Its water is pure; its current steady. Suddenly, out of the wild north a brash young river, full of energy and silt, thrusts itself rudely into the wide river's status quo. The young river doesn't have the patience or wisdom to blend gently with the old river. Making a sharp right turn, it empties its turbulent energy directly against the current of the staid old river. The merging of the two rivers is not smooth or immediate. In fact, the two rivers do not merge for many miles. They can be seen as two distinct rivers in one stream bed until, eventually, their waters blend and they become one. The new has contributed to the old and the old to the new. They have created a new equilibrium, a new status quo, a new comfort standard. However, not far ahead, another brash young river is about to dump its turbulent waters into the mix.

There is a lesson here for the church. When new meets old, both need to recognize that each has something to offer to the other (and each will, ultimately, offer something to the other). We need to deal patiently with each other in the certainty that in the good time of God we will come to know and understand each other. We will each contribute to the other, and ultimately, we will be one river. Could this be the headwaters of the river of which John writes in Revelation? The river of life flowing from the throne of God (Rev. 22:1, 2)? It's a thought, but don't make it a doctrine. Actually, I think the saved are going to dance and do cartwheels in the sands of the river of life as they exult in the reality of heaven. Why not join me there?

Bishop Spong, won't you join us? There is plenty of room in the kingdom for you, too. Our Father has made us one in Christ. By His blood He has brought down the barrier of hostility that separated us in the past. There is no law to keep us apart—except the law of sin and death (Rom. 8:2). You see, the death of Christ actually put to death our mutual hostility. But your circumstances are vitally different. We beg you to come over the line. Your unbelief is hardening your heart to the appeals of God's living Holy Spirit. You might boldly deny the existence of God and your need for Him, but your puny words can't put God out of existence. He is still here, and He is still urging you to join Him in the river.

Every dabbling with unbelief, every consorting with Hollywood and her colleagues from hell, every missed opportunity to yield to God, and every refusal to obey the gentle call of His Spirit to move from death into life moves us imperceptibly closer to the pit. Bishop Spong has a lot of company (some of it is in the church), and I dare to say that not everyone on the way to abyss with him is as boldly complacent as he is. The bishop knows not (our Father), knows that he knows not, and apparently is pleased with his position. There are many who don't know that there is a Father; they don't even know that they don't know! What does it take for Him to get their attention before they are eternally confirmed in their unbelief? And what does it take to move those who assume that they know our Father but know not whom they think they know out of their *complacency*? We need to know, know whom we know, and let our lives demonstrate that we know. This is the assurance that evokes confidence in our friends that may lead them to peace with God.

In putting to death our mutual hostility by His death, Christ created one body out of two and brought unity and peace to us. A healthy body does not fight against itself like an autoimmune disease against its own body. Each part working in harmony with all the other parts is a joy to experience. When the hand and the eye respond with grace to the command of the Head, it reveals and expresses the intent and design of the Creator. The evidence of creative power is overwhelming; people cannot come together harmoniously without divine intervention.

Life comes only from life with the divine life of the Creator as the ultimate source. The physical body, itself, is evidence of creative genius beyond human comprehension. The body of believers is further evidence of incontestable creative genius. And, *having created one body, [our] Creator didn't stop there. [Jesus always] intended to reconcile us to God by His death on the cross* (Eph. 2:16). That means that there is peace among us members of the church who, by nature, would viciously, slyly, capriciously, and otherwise compete for positions of perceived prestige, honor, or power, and there is peace between us and our God. No more do we fear and despise Him or even hide from Him, as Adam and Eve did in their first experiment with alienation. We are now reconciled to God, children of the heavenly Father. How then should we live? This is a question that has been asked repeatedly over the centuries and that Paul clearly answers in Ephesians.

The answer seems almost self-evident. Most children that I know who have loving, caring, competent, providing parents want to hang around with them. They love to imitate them. They even want to obey them. This is how we should conduct our lives as children of our Father in heaven: hang around with Him, watch Him in the life of Jesus, imitate Jesus, especially in how we live and work with members of the congregation of believers, and finally, learn what He expects in the details of life and obey Him promptly. This is best done by consistently obeying Him in the things that He has clearly spelled out in Scripture. Do we have a formula here? It seems so simple, doesn't it? Don't become complacent. Nothing is simple in this world. And there is no formula. As C. S. Lewis has told us, all of us are carrying souvenirs of hell that will not be allowed into heaven.[5] Even the most apparently spiritual of us harbors serious flaws that cannot enter the kingdom; only God is really sure what they are. Only God understands how to remove them, and only God is *able* to remove them.

Most of us have crossed international boundaries or booked flights on commercial airlines. We know what not to bring with us as we approach the security agents. We comply with the orders to open bags, empty pockets, and take off shoes and belts. We are free to refuse these orders, but we are also free to stay on the ground. We can't have it both ways. Contrary to what some people want to believe, our compassionate Father in heaven is even pickier than the pickiest security agent. Did you know that? Granted, some security agents could be a little pickier.

Recently, a young Chinese man slipped onto a flight from Hong Kong to Canada disguised as an old Caucasian. He took off his disguise in mid flight and presented himself to Canadian authorities at YVR as the young Chinese man that he was. The only thing we can take into God's kingdom is a character that He has made spotless, pure, and undefiled. Disguises won't work at the narrow gate. Let's not balk at submitting to His processes. Whatever may be brought to us in life, our gracious God will empower us to endure it (1 Cor. 10:13). That is why He allows new people and new circumstances to come into our lives and new members into our congregations. That is why He commands us to meet regularly to encourage and exhort one another as we approach the heavenly security barrier (Heb. 10:25), and we must recognize that heaven does have a security barrier. Jesus called it the narrow gate. Yes, narrow (Matt. 7:13, 14)!

---

[5] C. S. Lewis, *The Great Divorce* (CS Lewis Pte. Ltd, 1946).

Going in Circles—I was part of a team that took groups of young people on a couple of international experiences. There was no end of exhorting as we approached the departure date: passport, money, clothes, passport, that won't be allowed, passport, do this, do that, do it today, do it now, have you done it yet? Oh, and don't forget your passport. Why should it be any different as we approach the gate of heaven? We know and believe that the date of departure from this earth is not far distant. Don't leave the exhorting to the pastor. Every member of the congregation is urged, even commanded, to exhort another and with the exhorting, to encourage "with great patience and careful instruction" (2 Tim. 4:2). The apostle Paul was a great man for encouraging and urging us to encourage. We need a lot of encouragement in this life.

One young lad presented his passport at the first level of screening at the airport and was immediately barred from proceeding further. What a tragic face he presented as he stood there, watching the rest of his friends move past him to adventure; it brought tears to everyone's eyes. His passport was within six months of expiry and no longer valid for a flight to his destination. We did our best to encourage him with the promise that if he could get his document updated, we would find a way to get him on a later flight. (He did. We did. Everything turned out just fine.)

We must know the one condition that gets us into heaven. Paul said, *Believe and you will be saved* (Acts 16:31); Jesus said, *Believe and have life* (John 3:16). Try it! Try it now! Through Jesus Christ, we have access to the Father through the one Holy Spirit. That's the good news of the gospel! As a united family, heaven is ours. We are made one and filled with the love of God; we are reconciled to God by Christ's death. Let's see that not one of us falls out along the way!

This world is full of wandering people. God's creatures are daily uprooted from their homes by war and natural disaster and set adrift with nothing but the meager clothes in which they escaped. I try to imagine the desolation they must feel as they search for a welcoming homeland. Sudan. Sri Lanka. Kenya. Ethiopia. Syria. Just mention of the names evokes pictures of hunger, wretchedness, hopelessness, fear, pain, disease, shattered dreams, and uncertainty. I have slept in barns, in borrowed beds, and in truck-stop restaurants waiting for a ride. I've been hungry and cold. I've even paced and stomped my feet to keep from freezing to death during sleepless nights beside the highway. I have felt lonely, but never in all my years have I even approached the level of desolation a refugee mother must feel as she runs for her life, helplessly dragging her children behind her. Try to imagine the anguish our Father must endure as He looks down on our foolishness, our stupidity, our unbelief, our hatred, our fear, and our rebellion. He pleads with us, "When will you believe and be saved? When will you return from your wilderness wandering?"

We were all desolate wanderers in the wilderness when God found us. We were no better off than the most destitute refugee. And we didn't know it. Yet, by the *marvelous act of God, you and I together are no longer foreigners and aliens. We are citizens, and members of God's household—one united, integrated family* (Eph. 2:19)!

Beautiful Houses—And now Paul changes the metaphor. He tells us that we are a beautiful dwelling place. Sixty years ago when I was a child, my family was following the rough wagon trails through the wilderness, rattling and bumping through the bush behind a team of magnificent Belgian horses; my parents were searching for just the right place to call home. We approached a lake teaming with fish flashing through clear water in the sunlight over a sandy bottom. Mom said, "This is as far as we go. Here we stay." And stay we did. I can still look out from my office window and see the lake lying peaceful in the sun, mirroring the hills rising from the western shore or churning under the buffeting of the south wind.

Every log needs shaping before it's ready for the house. Not so in God's house.

Our first shelter by the lake was a tarp stretched between the trees, and after days in the wagon, it was, indeed, beautiful. We were content for the time. Our first project: build a solid dwelling place to keep out rain, wind, snow, mosquitoes, and bears—a house that didn't flap in the wind. Constructed of aspen logs snaked out of the bush behind Skip and Dick, the gorgeous team of Percheron horses we had brought from Saskatchewan, and carefully fitted together by my dad, it was truly a beautiful dwelling place.

But in Paul's metaphor, *we* are the beautiful building, and our Father is the Master Builder. The apostles and prophets laid the foundation, and Jesus Christ is the Chief Cornerstone. He is the anchor point, the reliable reference, and the solid rock. With our Father as the Master Builder, we can have total confidence in the work He has done and is doing. When my dad skidded the logs out of the bush with all their knobs and bumps, they were not ready to form the finished wall. They required pealing and much shaping before he pronounced them ready to be fitted into their places on the rising wall. Occasionally, a log was found to be unfit for service in the wall and was reassigned to the firewood pile. But even before the wall could be started, he had to prepare the ground and lay down the foundation.

Just so, our Father must apply the tools to our flawed selves to make us suitable parts of the beautiful dwelling, but there is a significant difference in the two dwellings. While my dad had to shape and prepare the logs before they could be raised into position on the wall, our Father calls us a beautiful dwelling while He is still working on our characters, our personalities, and our behavior. None of us, however knobby or deformed we appear, is relegated to the firewood pile. We are all precious components of the dwelling declared beautiful by the Master Builder. He declares us beautiful because He is looking at us in Christ. Even so, let's not become complacent and self-satisfied. Let's not resist the shaping of the divine Artisan.

I was reading Richard Dawkins one evening. He has some scathing criticism of religion, in general, and Christianity in particular. I have to confess with shame that some of his criticism of our behavior hit the mark squarely. Professed Christians have been (and are) hateful, spiteful, ignorant, stupid, and frequently proud of it all. We are everything that sin is. We must all be prepared to be pressed a little harder to the sanding wheel. Don't complain when the Master Craftsman sets the blades a little deeper or chooses sandpaper with coarser grit. There is rot there that has to be removed. Thank You, Father, that You are doing the shaping and not Professor Dawkins. I sense that with him, it would be three strikes (maybe two) and out.

I had been working on a twenty-four-inch-diameter segmented wooden bowl of blue-stained, beetle-killed pine for several months. A huge pile of shavings removed eventually revealed the hidden beauty of the wood. The shape and contours suited my discerning eye. The power sander had done its fine finishing, and I pronounced the work finished. Numerous coatings of oil brought out the color and the grain. A wonderful piece of art had emerged from nondescript chunks of wood, but after having it for several days in the house, I began to be less sure. I could feel tiny ridges between the segments that were too small to be seen. Clearly, there was a problem revealing itself in the structure of the bowl. It was not ready to be displayed. In fact, I had to take it back to the shop, remove the finish, and sand, sand, sand. This time, I am waiting to see if the problem has been fixed before I apply the finish. Several weeks have gone by, and I know that it must go back again to the shop. This is like me (and you) in the hands of our Father in heaven, the divine Artisan. He has taken me back to the wood shop many times. In fact, He also has taken me to the wood shed. You?

A few lines up I wrote that we Christians are everything that sin is. Only in one sense is that true. We also are simultaneously everything that our Father says we are—one in Christ: perfect in Him, alive in Him, united in Him, and brothers and sisters in Him; we are the children of God. In Christ we are born again, and in Christ we live the new life for God's glory. Even so, our old nature of sin continues to live in us, now in tension with the new life, until the end. This old nature, the unruly *self*, will rise up at every opportunity or provocation to knock us down and bring shame to our Father. Our role as Christians is to keep the old nature in a state of total starvation. He begs to be fed, but we can't afford to give him any nourishment.

Even the smell of his favorite foods is enough to revive him, stimulate his domineering instincts, and set him prowling to find something more filling. This is what Richard Dawkins doesn't understand. He calls us hypocrites because we are not yet perfect in all our behavior. The fact is, in contending with the *self*, we do frequently fail to receive the deliverance God freely provides and because we slip into the do-it-myself mode, we sin. But thanks to God, there is forgiveness and restoration for the most egregious affronts to our Redeemer. He brings the sanding wheel against our rough spots again and again until we are polished to His satisfaction.

The church, *the beautiful dwelling place built together on the foundation of the apostles and prophets* (Eph. 2:20), is the forum in which the work is accomplished. The church is God's workshop from which we go to display His skill and discerning eye to the community. The church is also itself the work of art created to display the skill, grace, discernment, and love of God, our Father. The apostles and prophets laid the foundation of truth that God delivered to them. Their tears, blood, sweat, and prayers are mingled in the structure. They are also its foundation, and Jesus, the Cornerstone, is set prominently for all to see. As we submit to being included in the structure, the Cornerstone becomes progressively more noticeable and attractive. We, the people, serve exclusively to highlight the Cornerstone.

I have built a number of houses, so I am somewhat familiar with properly placing a foundation, which is, in my experience, the most difficult part of erecting a house or any other building. A true and level foundation with the strength to hold the structure above it will make the construction of the rest of the building not only possible but also positively pleasurable.

A while back our congregation decided to build a house for one of our members who was living in substandard conditions. Years earlier the owner had built the foundation himself with cement blocks reinforced with concrete and rebar. I had the responsibility of bringing the project to the sub-floor stage, laying out the walls, and preparing the headers, corners, and cripple studs so that the crew would not be handicapped in raising the rest of the structure. To my dismay, I discovered that the foundation, though level and structurally sound, was out of square by several inches with one side bowing in four or five inches. The foundation was unmovable, but I had to make a floor that was square and true for the house that would rest on it. It was possible, of course, but the labor to do it must have been doubled. With about twenty-five workers in the construction crew, with the food ready and delicious at mealtime, with materials on site, with nothing to hinder the work, from sub-floor to finished roof this remarkably bonding effort took only two days.

Workers in harmony make the job light.

The apostles and prophets have laid the solid and true foundation of the church. The Cornerstone is absolutely flawless in beauty and perfection, and He is unmovable. But we building blocks are in desperate need of squaring, truing, chipping, and sanding. Still, if we stand resolutely on this foundation and resist every inducement to leave, if we submit to the divine processing, we will be shaped and polished to reflect the glory of the Cornerstone.

One block does not a temple make. One person does not a congregation make, or a family. Some seem to resist what they choose to call organized religion, not realizing that God is the author of organization—and of religion (though humanity has done much to pervert God's design). And God organized the entire universe to function in harmony.

This harmony is fundamental to the way we live our lives. Just imagine the sun as it wakes up in the morning, yawns, stretches, and then decides to stay in bed. The chaos of such a scenario would be unbelievable. Imagine a one-of-a-kind block (that the Builder shaped for a certain purpose) that decides that it does not like the idea of structure and stays in the quarry. Imagine an ER nurse who decides he doesn't like the way the staff is organized, and just walks away from the work place. Imagine a star football player having a dispute with his coach and stomping off into some cow pasture to play his own game, all by himself. How many fans would be following the action? Events like this don't often happen—happily. Each of us has a place in God's plan, and ultimately, each will be happy to have submitted to being shaped and polished, to being fitted to fill the position the Master Builder intended. It could be that the shaping process does not always make us comfortable or happy, but in the end we will be happy that we submitted to the careful attention of the Master Builder.

Paul writes of unity in the building and holiness of the temple. Unity and holiness are not qualities with which we are born or which we achieve by vote of a board or by a hard-fought decision of a committee. In Christ, where God put us (1 Cor. 1:30), we *grow* into unity and rise into holiness. These are time-taking ends or outcomes, and Jesus is the means by which they are reached. The Means has justified the ends. God is patient. He has the time it takes to transform our rough and uncouth characters into the likeness of the Cornerstone if we only let Him transform us. My prayer is that we parts of the building will be willing to submit to the processes. Even if we are unwilling, still we can confess our reluctance and submit to the processes.

The stones of Machu Picchu are some of the most intricately fitted construction stones known today. How they were cut remains a mystery. How they were transported from quarry to construction site remains a mystery. Why they were assembled there on the mountaintop remains another mystery. Still, the stones of this pre-Columbian site virtually shout to us of the skill, the dedication, and the artistry of the builders. God's work, as He painstakingly shapes us for important positions in this eternal holy temple, is mysterious. But His reasons He has revealed: He is Love personified; He is Patience deified; He is Mercy in human form; He is Grace made visible; He is Truth walking. He wants to walk with us and talk with us forever in paradise; He wants us to be filled with His Holy Spirit forever! He is the Means, and He justifies us, the ends.

Chapter 3
A Mystery That Reveals

The Greatest Mystery Story Ever Told

Because God made us alive in Christ, uniting us in Him, creating you fellow citizens with us in God's kingdom and members of the family of God, I, Paul, the prisoner for the sake of you Gentiles, kneel before God the Father for you. I want you to know that I am not a prisoner of the Jews or the Romans but of Christ Jesus. I am wearing these chains as badges of honor for Christ. Please do not be discouraged because of my sufferings. They are your glory.

You must have heard of the ministry that God gave to me for you. In the past it was a mystery, but the shrouds have been removed and the spotlights turned on. God has revealed to me the glorious news of His grace, [the message of reconciliation, as I described it to the Corinthians five years ago (2 Cor. 5:25), and I had the rich blessing and the high honor to have been God's ambassador to you with the same message of reconciliation]. When you have read my letter, you will be able to understand the mystery revealed to me by Christ. Past generations were not granted this indescribable honor, but God has seen fit to reveal it to His holy apostles and prophets in these times. This is the mystery: through the gospel the Gentiles will inherit with Israel; through the gospel the Gentiles constitute one body with Israel; through the gospel Israel and the Gentiles share together in the promises of Christ Jesus.

By the gift of God's grace, through the working of His mighty power, God called me to serve in this ministry to you. I freely confess that I am an insignificant member, less than the least of all God's people, yet God gave me this grace: to preach to you Gentiles the immeasurable riches of Christ; I am to make plain to everyone, Jews and Gentiles, the mystery only now revealed by God, the Creator, after being hidden in Him for ages past.

God intends that now, through the church, which welcomes people from every tribe and language, His many-faceted wisdom will be made known to all the intelligences of the universe. This is God's eternal purpose, which He accomplished in Christ Jesus, our Lord. Always remember that in Christ we may approach God with freedom and confidence. In view of these mercies, I once again urge you to be calm in your spirit in spite of my chains, which really are your glory. (Eph. 3:1–13)

Living Dead, Living—My brother and I once found ourselves clinging to a driftwood raft being tossed in an eddy at the foot of a waterfall. We had been swept over the fall contrary to our plans. On our hands and knees, we gripped the binding ropes as the waves stood our flimsy craft on end, then on the other end, on edge, then on the other edge—for hours. Clinging to the bits of wood in the middle of the river had our full attention. Only

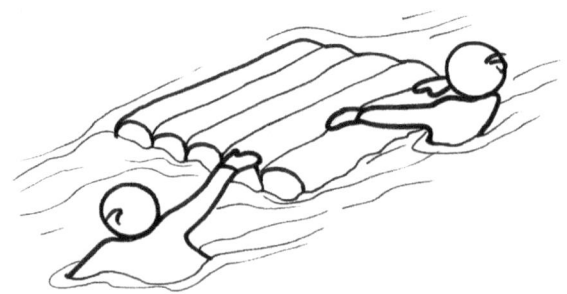

Giving full attention to the task at hand – survival.

the thwacking blades of a helicopter lowering a rescue basket could have diverted our attention from the task at hand—surviving.

We readily admit that once upon a time we (and you) were dead in transgression. The things that pertain to God (gentleness, goodness, humility, faith, mercy, patience, and truth) were not of primary importance to us. The things that pertain to this passing world (pride, acquisitiveness, anger, greed, jealousy, conceit, domination, and lies) gripped our attention with intensity that only the about-to-drown have when clinging to a log in the river.

Just so, things from above, the things of God, do not easily distract the dead in sin from intently pursuing the tasks at hand: getting the job, easing the pain, paying the mortgage, buying the car, escaping on vacation, preparing for retirement, and running after the good life. Getting and spending, the tossing raft on the waves of life, has their full attention. Only external divine intervention can save these walking, running, speeding dead from their mad pursuit of fantasies, mirages, and the rainbow's end. The fact is this: the things of God cannot naturally interest the dead in sin; neither are the dead capable of perceiving them—never mind appreciating their value—until God does a miracle in their lives.

What does this miracle look like? How can the dead be brought to life? The warming up of a body in deep hypothermia will give us a metaphor of the work of God's Holy Spirit in bringing life to the dead in sin. As hypothermia begins to grip the body, the effects can first be detected in the extremities: fingers progressively lose their ability to grip important small things like house keys, matches, or zippers. Without help, the mind quickly follows the fingers and begins to lose its grip on reality. At this point, the body will soon collapse, succumbing to the cold. Only immediate, external intervention with warmth can save this person. And the person dead in sin? Only external intervention by the Holy Spirit warmly wafting over the dead can induce a spark of life; only the Holy Spirit fanning this spark can bring it to flame; only the Holy Spirit continuing to blow over the small, new flame of spiritual life can bring it to blaze. Only the Holy Spirit can keep that blaze dancing. But consider this: does the Holy Spirit respond to the request of believers to rescue the dead?

God uses many circumstances and events in our lives to get our minds off the mad pursuit of the vanishing. Anything, however transitory, that upsets our equilibrium, interferes with our immediate plans, brings pain, suffering, alienation—or even pleasure—can be a tool in God's hands to pry us out of our cozy relationship with the world. Some people move and for a time find themselves vulnerable to the Spirit of God. Some people lose jobs, spouses, friends, and thus are left, for a time, vulnerable to the work of God. Some people lose big in the stock market and thereby open themselves to the arrows of the Almighty. Some people gain a spouse or a friend and thereby become vulnerable to the gracious warm wind of the Spirit.

I didn't lose a job, a spouse, or a stock portfolio. God used another tool to break through my resistance to His grace. He sent me an audio message on a cassette and gave me time to listen to it. I plugged it into my car player and listened repeatedly as I drove hundreds of miles each month between the campuses of my college in the routine duties of my job. The voice of God's Spirit spoke to me through the voice on the audiotape and fanned my dead soul to life. I had never encountered a more appealing and believable account of the gospel.

God raises us up together; He gives us life and unites us in Jesus because, like a football player, we need the team to keep the game going. Like a lone ember, no flame can be sustained in isolation; we need each other to keep the blaze going. These spiritual embers continually require more fuel through which the blaze is perpetuated; they require the draft of the Spirit to unite with the elements of the wood to produce the flame.

My furnace impresses me with this simple lesson once or twice a day during the winter. When my body heat sensors detect a lowering temperature in the house, I head to the furnace room. I find a few embers, too hot to touch, still capable of igniting, but they are very much in need of the new fuel through which their waning energy can be revived. With new logs on the embers to respond to their fading energy, I soon have a merry blaze going again. Is this not something like our experiences in the family of God? If we do not share the warm energy of God regularly and frequently with other members of the family, we begin to grow cold ourselves; we lose our energy. If the family does not reach out to pass its energy on to those who are dead in sin, the whole family will eventually become black, cold, and lifeless.

I guess that is what a family is all about. Sharing. We are a family to share our hurts and our joys, our pain and our pleasure. Over the past two years, several of our church families have experienced one or another form of cancer, a terminal reminder of the fragility of life as we know it. These families have been comforted by the deep caring and generous response of the family of God. People came through for one another in ways we would not have imagined. Warm food appeared at doors. Wonderful prayers were sent up to our Father. Compassionate telephone calls helped the sufferers carry the burden. *Because God made us alive in Christ, we are members of the family of God* (Eph. 2:4, 5). I really am glad I am a part of this family of God; I'm glad to be His adopted son. His creative energy at work in us lifted us from the vortex of sin and united us in a living, caring family. How can we respond even more effectively to meet the needs of our members?

Paul, in his prayers for the Ephesians, gives us an example of how we should continually intercede for one another as we go through the various experiences of life. Paul was in chains, yet he did not let his enforced immobility interfere with his praying for the members of the family of God. This is step one in bringing life to the dead in sin. Though they cannot appreciate the things of God, when believing saints pray for them, we open the door for Him to exercise His miracle-working, life-inducing power on their behalf against the clamors of Satan. At the request of the praying believer, the angry forces of hell are driven back while the gentle wind of the Spirit fans to life the soul now experiencing the miracle of new birth.

Did You Hear Your Father Call You?—This is how God made us alive in Christ and united us in Him. This sense of unity, in spite of the diversity of our backgrounds, warms and cheers us. In our congregation we have people who didn't know this wilderness existed, whose lives circulated in great metropolitan cities—until moving to this small, northern community. They've been accepted. They've found that they do fit in, and we are enriched by a wonderful diversity of cultures. God has united us in Christ and made us family.

Paul thanks God for this unity, this greatest of all possible proofs of divine power and grace. Our unity was so important to Paul that he willingly submitted to cruel imprisonment and galling chains in order to communicate the message of grace to us. From his prison he continued to shepherd the flocks he had raised up to praise God. Never concerned about his own discomfort, Paul encouraged the believers to meet their trials with grace and fortitude. He insisted that prison was his choice and that he was honored to wear the chains for Christ. What a witness to the grace of God!

When I see Paul writing to the believers and preaching to the saints, still chained to his guards, I see a man I want to be like. I see a guy whose life inspires confidence in his message. I see a man I could follow with confidence! Come to think of it, I can follow. From the beginning the path is clearly marked with Paul's blood, sweat, and tears—all shed for the love of God and the salvation of the people he loved. Where should I start? Where am I now? I simply need to follow the path laid out for me. I watch for doors to open or windows of opportunity to close, and I go or not as God's providence indicates. God gave Paul a ministry, and I believe He has given ministries to each believer.

In a congregation of a hundred people, there are at least a hundred ministries, a hundred ways in which saints can bless saints and honor God in the process. Let's keep it simple, like we are. One ministry might be no more than to smile a genuine smile and say hello as you meet someone on the street. Another could be to organize a work bee to repair the rotting-out floor of the kitchen in the house of an aging member—just to make his last years or months on this earth more pleasant. Some people are called to clean the church while others are called to quietly tally the offerings, out of sight of the rest of the congregation. A few, not many, are called to sing and lead the congregation in singing. Everyone is called to reach out to someone with the gospel of grace. Will someone be lost if I don't witness? Maybe.

You've Been Called—We have all heard of self-appointed spiritual gurus who create their little power bases in backwoods communes into which they lure unstable people and their money with hollow promises of safety from worldly temptations, immunity from the terrors of the last days, and one-way tickets to heaven some day. (Jim Jones and David Koresh come to mind.) Sadly, many of these disciples never escape the charismatic hold of the so-called leaders and will cross continents and spend fortunes to sit at their feet. These poor folk are blind to the falseness of the worship they give to self-styled prophets and teachers (2 Tim. 3:6).

Not all prophets are self appointed and false, but Paul takes a hard rap from some people because of their distorted understanding of his calling and message. We have only two options with Paul's writings, as with all Scripture: accept them as the inspired word of God or reject them as the ravings of a sexist egotist on a centuries-long power trip. The apostle Peter, not always on the best of terms with Paul, accepted Paul's writing as inspired. Peter warned us to be on our guard lest we be carried away with the musings of lawless men (2 Peter 3:15–17). For this reason Paul repeatedly emphasizes that he did not appoint himself to his ministry but received it from God. Unlike the work of the gurus, Paul's work produces results for a glorious eternity and a productive life in the present. These results, observable in the day-to-day lives of believers, are the best indicator of authenticity.

Through Paul's Ephesians we see God's grace revealed in all its majesty. Paul helps us see that we are connected to the grace of the Almighty, and this grace is no longer a mystery. This grace changes lives (and *nothing* else will). This glorious grace enlightens the formerly dark recesses of our minds, revealing to us the character of God and motivating us to desire that character more than any other blessing. The news of God's grace for sinners is a message of reconciliation—God's reconciling sinners to Himself! What a contrast to our way of doing things!

Some bury themselves in convents and communes to escape the temptations of the world while attempting to achieve reconciliation with God that was, is, and always will be unachievable by human effort. There are those who simply bury themselves in stuff—stuff of the mind (pride, greed, fear, lust), or in houses, cars, boats, or even the stuff of the body. We, the people, tend to bury ourselves in anything that lets us not notice that God has already reconciled us to Himself.

Paul asserts that, having read his letter, *we also will be able to understand the mystery revealed to [him] by Christ* (Eph. 3:4). So the onus is on us: read and understand. But there are those who read and don't understand. Recently, I sat through a YouTube lecture by Bishop John Shelby Spong about whom I wrote earlier.[1] Bishop Spong apparently is a determined, focused atheist. The author of twenty books, he seems intent on communicating his message of atheism as far and as wide as he can. He professed to have started his career as an evangelical and to be able to quote the Bible as well as Billy Graham, but he does not accept the Bible as the Word of God—a God in whom he does not believe. Bishop Spong perceives the Bible as a human work expressing human ideas too frequently in ways that inspire hatred, conquest, and abuse. During the entire lecture that lasted almost ninety minutes, the bishop did not once let his face slip into a smile. I saw only anger against the idea of God, hatred for the Bible, and even moments of possible despair. Why did the bishop move from evangelical belief to atheism (and retain his position and prestige as the Bishop of Newark)?

I think he dropped a few clues to this change of mind as he inveighed against the Scriptures, and in some of his accusations, he spoke truth. Some believers carry a heavy responsibility for promoting false ideas of God, false ideas of biblical interpretation, and false ideas of human relations. They assert these ideas as correct interpretations of Scripture. False interpretations of Scripture are dangerous and damaging to our Father's work on earth. They have met untold numbers of people at the tipping point and eased them over into unbelief. Examples from Spong, which he attributes to evangelicals, do not bring glory to God.

Believers who promote these false and dangerous ideas cannot have understood the words of the captain of the Lord's host, as he confronted Joshua on the plain of the Jordan: *I am not on your side or on the side of the enemy; I am the Captain of the Lord's army* (Josh. 5:14). While Spong is responsible for his own conclusions, so-called believers who promote false ideas of God and the Scriptures are not innocent.

We find a strong indication in John's letter that we need to be careful of our doctrine (2 John 1:7–11). There is an accounting we yet may have to make to the Judge of all the earth for easing a person on the brink over the edge of the abyss. "But," says I, "Surely it can't be me, Lord, doing the easing. Would I hurry another soul into perdition? Would I betray you again?

---

[1] Episcopal Bishop John Shelby Spong, "The Terrible Texts of the Bible," (Burke Lectures, University of California, November 18, 2004).

Tell me it's not me (maybe the preacher or the deacon—though I stand in the need of prayer)." Paul asserts that when we read his letter, we will be able to understand the mystery revealed by Christ. That being said, if we don't bring to our reading a willingness to believe and obey the message, it will convey no grace of understanding to us (Phil. 3:16).

Clearly, this is where Spong and millions of people miss the point and power of Scripture. They read the Bible as they would read a piece of ancient literature—as a human work describing a god of human invention, deserving of no more respect than any other artifact of tribal musings. Indeed, the bishop's interpretation of the Word of God is decidedly dangerous and damaging because, not only is it false, it appears to be carefully designed to turn vulnerable people against the Inspired Book. His agenda is hostile to Scripture and to the God revealed in Scripture. (Can my agenda be hostile while I think I am right? Do I sin most egregiously when I think I am right? Does the love of God motivate and permeate every encounter?)

Is there then no hope for the bishop? Well, does he still breathe? As we noted earlier, the warm Spirit of God is still wafting over the earth. God still does miracles of raising the dead in sin. Does He need my permission? Is He waiting for me to ask before He moves against the forces of evil guarding the mind of this son of Adam? Well, I'm asking, "Please, Father, if it will work for Your glory, blow a gale on Bishop Spong, if there is anything left in him with the capacity to respond to Your Holy Spirit. Do Your life-giving miracle in him. What a testimony it would be for the bishop to retract publicly, on nation-wide television, the false ideas he has so widely promoted about Your non-existence—with a smile of joy and peace on his face."

Can you imagine Spong (and Dawkins, too) with the same zeal, now sanctified, that he formerly demonstrated in his hostility against God, now as God's ambassador, carrying His message of reconciliation! It has happened before! Wouldn't it be wonderful to see Spong and Dawkins and even Hitchens and Hawking go arm-in-arm-in-arm into the kingdom they have so angrily and confidently opposed, to sit down with Adam and Eve at the grand welcoming reception?

And Called Again!—In view of what we have just said, what should I do personally to smooth or encourage the transition of Spong and Dawkins to the kingdom of grace? What should my congregation do to create a welcoming environment for these prominent thinkers? Of course, we are not likely ever to encounter them in this life, but what about the mill workers and gas-well technicians? What about our neighbors who hold the same aversion to Scripture, the same abhorrence of God, but without the skill or the platform or the need to express it? This is where our accountability becomes palpable.

The message of reconciliation about which Paul is so passionate must become a reality to me and to my congregation. We need to be infused with a passion, a zeal for the gospel like Paul's that is obvious to our neighbors and friends. We need to be ready to provide credible answers when people ask us about our faith. But more than preparing to give theological answers about Sabbath keeping or diet, our lives should stimulate questioning because of our good behavior.

The apostle Peter agrees quite heartily with Paul on the importance of good behavior (1 Peter 3:15, 16) in our ordinary routines: the contractor needs to deliver the job within the terms of the agreement—and with a smile; the employer must treat his workers with dignity and pay fair wages on time; the merchant must receive the returned goods with a smile and a blessing as the customer leaves; the secondary student in the local high school must respect the rules of the school and work hard at his studies.

There are countless opportunities to live the good behavior urged by Peter and Paul as evidence of the light that we have as believers (Eph. 5:8, 9). Only our lives, reflecting the grace of God as we communicate the message of reconciliation, will have any impact on the people like Spong and Dawkins with whom we work and play. Only by the grace of our Father can we hope to deliver a credible witness. So why not ask daily for that grace—the indwelling of God's Holy Spirit?

Mystery of Unity—Paul is fond of using the word mystery, and now he explains the mystery: it is simply the uniting of disparate people through the gospel of salvation. Before the coming of the Sacrifice for our sin, humanity could not have fully comprehended the work of God. Prophets did their best to look into God's mysteries and communicate the message of hope, but their efforts fell far short of the reality in Jesus (1 Peter 1:10–12). Now, through the birth, life, death, and resurrection of Jesus, we have the gospel in its visible, glorious totality. There is nothing to add to the work of Jesus: His miraculous birth introduces divinity to humanity; His perfect life demonstrates the lives He empowers us to live in Him; His death takes away our sin; His resurrection brings us the power of God for the new life—not the good life too many of us wastefully seek (Rom. 6:4).

Because we were crucified with Him, we are now dead to sin and free from its power (Rom. 6:6, 7). United with Christ in His death, we are united with Him in His life also (Rom. 6:5). What a mystery—revealed! Now people who formerly hated, despised, avoided, seduced, defrauded, or murdered one another live in harmony and reconciliation, themselves brothers and sisters in the faith they share. They care for one another, encourage one another, and hold one another to account (2 Tim. 4:2).

Holding to account with the spirit of Jesus is evidence par excellence of caring for one another in the congregation. Our inherent desire to please, to ease ourselves through rough places, to avoid confronting painful issues, is hard to ignore. We tend to put off the pain of confronting for so long that we are embarrassed to bring up the issue, but time is not the great healer. A wound ignored, especially a spiritual or moral wound, only festers beneath the surface and erupts in an ugly sore. The person who committed the wrong is left in uncertainty. No closure is

Christ's perfect life demonstrates the lives He empowers us to live.

achieved. No restoration of harmony is possible. Failure to take this step risks leaving an already-wounded person to imagine that we do not care enough to engage him or her in a restorative process—that we don't really care enough to want him or her back. That failure would be a far more serious sin than the sin for which we rightly confront the person. Our prayer must be not for help and wisdom to do it right but for God to work His will through us.

In allowing our Father to work His will through us for the unity of disparate believers in the gospel of salvation, we are giving evidence of the great power of God. No human agency can unite people like the gospel unites (and probably nothing divides like the gospel misunderstood). True, people can unite to achieve a common objective, and even enemies can unite temporarily against a common foe, as did the Communists and the Nationalists in the face of the Japanese invasion of China in the 1930s. But the gospel produces a different order of unity.

The gospel unites us permanently and, ultimately, in perfect harmony. Believe it or not, even those holding contrary theological perspectives can be united in the agape of God that inundates us. Do we have to be told that this is important in the church? We know that, ultimately, we will see things as they truly are. In the meantime we have to use the sieves and the lenses that we have to filter and examine the data that is flowing all around us. Through God's continuing grace, some of us may change our filters and lenses, but we always view reality through the tools that we have.

Some of my farmer friends are more inclined to move slowly, cautiously, when dealing with new ideas. They understand their theology through the lenses of the seasons, the soil, the seed, the cattle; they filter their ideas through the meshes of fuel bills and equipment repairs, through searching through the dark and snowy cold for the new-born calf hidden in the bush by the silly young mother and through the unseen roots of the grass. They don't need to be told that the crops will mature in due course provided the conditions are favorable. They know their role in nurturing the crop and in harvesting the produce of the soil. Their land base is vitally important to them; they are highly independent, yet interdependent, as they wait and watch, and care.

I, on the other hand, take my cues from other metaphors. In administering a college campus, I learned that a qualified "yes" was usually the best response to a valid idea. Whether it involved adding a new course to an existing program, providing a class set of computers, or building a new facility, the process was the same: engage the people with whom I work. People were my major resource, and my role was to build and maintain the environment in which people could achieve their potential as teachers, clerks, or mid-level administrators while experiencing career satisfaction. In my role independence would have been a major impediment.

When we bring these different perspectives to the church board or business meeting, there is opportunity for misunderstanding, friction, even heat, as we discuss colors, designs, budget shortfalls, or, dare we think it, evangelism, a reason that we exist. There is also opportunity for the Spirit of God to demonstrate His soothing, smoothing, shaping power as we work through our differences.

This is why Jesus didn't identify His disciples by their theological points of view or by any of their various ways of approaching the world. This is why discipleship is based on love (John 13:35) and not on uniform understanding of sometimes-obscure passages within the Bible. This is where Martin Luther in Germany and Ulrich Zwingli, a Swiss reformer, failed to unite against a common deadly foe. The two obstinate reformers had not yet matured in their walk with

God to the point of grasping the essence of religion—oh, I think they might have understood the essence of religion. Not surprisingly, it was the essence of faith and love that still eluded them. This is where too many of us modern religionists still miss the mark (sin): we are intent on maintaining our theological fine points to the detriment of the essence of Christianity: the agape love of God shaping our lives and governing our relationships for His exclusive glory. We are such slow learners—even the fastest of us.

Paul Bites the Dust—Heat! Dust! Dark! Saul gropes about for something by which to orient himself. A hand is laid on his shoulder and the familiar though concerned voice of his guard penetrates his fog. "Saul! You OK? What happened? Come into the shade of this rock and rest a while. You look stunned." Saul, the proud Pharisee and ignorant enemy of God, spits the dust from his mouth and takes his first tentative steps toward Paul, the humble servant of God and never-give-up evangelist of the message of grace and reconciliation.

Paul now reasserts God's graciously calling him to a ministry for the Gentiles. In his own eyes, Paul is insignificant. He sees himself as less than the least of all God's people, yet he is a powerful minister of grace and discipline. Consider this too-prevalent attitude among believers: a false concept of humility or meekness that intrudes itself between our potential for honoring God and what we actually do in His service. False humility is really a subtle form of rebellion. It's simply pride in masquerade. It manifests in a whining sort of refusal to fill the gap when asked to serve in the church. It manifests in remaining quiet in a church business meeting then burning up the telephone lines after the decision is made. It manifests in a feeling of self-pity with its attendant blaming of someone else for my feelings.

This reminds me of a beautiful day, calm and blue, with a barely detectable hint of autumn in the air. I was cutting winter firewood. The chainsaw was sharp, barking a deep-throated assertion of real power as it ripped into the solid pine tree. Chips were flying. Just then, my thought sentinels contacted my consciousness to report on the activity of my mind. You gotta believe this: my mind was indulging in a sort of game with my head. I was mulling over what people were saying about me. And how did I know? I didn't know, of course. It was strictly imaginary. Since I was rapidly falling into a pit of self-pity, I had to rein in my wayward imagination in a hurry before further damage could be done.

Prayer is the only effective restraint for a wayward mind. Paul's humility didn't display itself in these ways. Although less than the least of all God's people, he was foremost among the apostles of Jesus in preaching the message he received from God: the message of grace, forgiveness, and acceptance. His message also included unambiguous, unmistakable reproof for sin in the body of Christ.

Moses is another example of genuine humility. In fact, Moses is known as the meekest of men (Num. 12:3). But, does repeatedly facing the pharaoh with a demand for freeing the slaves look meek? Does ordering the execution of hundreds of rebels at Sinai look meek? Does reasoning with God in an attempt to save the Israelites from

Prayer is the only effective restraint for a wayward mind.

destruction look meek? If not, then what is meek? What is humble?

When we study the lives of Moses and Paul, we see that we cannot equate the common understanding of meekness or humility with the strength of character displayed in their lives. We cannot equate the common understanding of meekness or humility with their firm resolution in the face of open sin. Webster defines meek as "humbly submissive, too mild, lacking spirit."[2] Really! I don't picture either Paul or Moses as too mild or lacking in spirit. Paul declared, "When I am weak, then I am strong" (2 Cor. 12:10). Paul had no issue with weakness or with strength. He recognized that there were times and places to display either, and he recognized the source of his strength (Phil. 4:13).

This leads me to confess that my little brush with self-pity there in the wood lot is not an example of meekness. Self-pity isn't humility. Ordinary, smelly pride precipitated the whole affair. True meekness is, indeed, expressed in humbly submitting, but Webster does not go far enough in his definition. The submitting must be to the ultimate authority figure—to God. Moses did not submit to the pharaoh; Paul did not submit to Nero. Both submitted to God through years of personal hardship to the point of death. Both left us examples of how we ought to submit to God in the daily rituals of personal mind control, work, play, spiritual outreach, and church business. I am convinced that when we do that as individuals, the little church in the vale will prosper as it has never prospered in the past.

Paul was daily sustained by the gift of God's grace and through the working of His mighty power. This is also the source of our daily power. When I try to do it on my own initiative I find myself failing miserably. When I try to do it with the help of God, I fail. When I let God work His will through me and in me, He has complete success. I need to learn and remember that only when I am weak am I strong (2 Cor. 12:10). When I die to my *self* (the ultimate expression of weakness), only then can I live for God. When I am dead to my self, I cannot respond to the arrows aimed at me from within. I can respond only to the working of the mighty power of God, that muscular strength that brought Jesus back from the dead.

Paul was called by God to preach to the Gentiles the immeasurable riches of Christ. What are those riches? As a born-again Gentile, how will I recognize them? I will recognize them when I believe. How will I experience them? I will experience them when I believe. As Paul so confidently asserted, "Believe in the Lord Jesus, and you will be saved" (Acts 16:31). Salvation is the immeasurable riches of Christ. Jesus said, *When you believe in Me, you cross over from death into life* (John 5:24). Living in salvation, living life the Jesus way, is to display His immeasurable riches, the salvation that I now experience.

But the paradox of living life the Jesus way is that we must die daily, crucified with Jesus, moment by moment in Him, so that the lives we live are then His life in us (Gal. 2:20). We no longer see the evidence of our trying hard and failing fast. As we progress through Paul's letter to the Ephesians, the picture of the Jesus way will become more and more distinct, like the sun revealing little by little the golden hill across the lake as it burns off the mists of a foggy October morning. We will come to realize our own inability to live His way. In fact, we will become more

---

[2] *The New Lexicon Webster's Encyclopedic Dictionary of the English Language,* Canadian edition (New York, NY: Lexicon Publications, 1988).

and more conscious that God's way, the Jesus way, is not at all our natural way (Isa. 55:8). We will learn that there is nothing that can be done to fix our natural way; it has to be abandoned, repudiated, disowned (Isa. 55:7) or, as Paul said, crucified (Rom. 6:6). Only then will it be possible to experience the new life in Jesus.

In Paul's mind the sufferings he endured for the sake of the gospel were of no account. He saw it as the greatest blessing of God that he was called to share the gospel with Jew and Gentile—and to share the sufferings of Jesus. Paul's is the attitude I admire: *God gave me this grace,* he writes, *to preach … the immeasurable riches of Christ* (Eph. 3:8). By grace is the only way he can preach; by grace is the only way we can live and preach. We cannot for long drive ourselves to share a message in which we have no joy; we cannot for long pretend a gospel we have not received. Yet, so many of us try to do just that. Now the mystery of God's grace has come home to me. The preaching of Paul has penetrated the mind of this Gentile. God is good! His grace is all I need!

Body, Building, and Church—Paul has written of bodies and buildings. Now he writes of the church that welcomes people from every tribe and language. The Architect and Builder of the church designed it to display His multifaceted wisdom to all intelligent beings in the universe. With the breaking down of barriers between the nations of the world, with the mingling of colors and accents in the congregation, God's glory has a venue visible to all and understandable by all. The church is not a last-day human invention. It has a divine Author (and divine authority) with a history that goes back to Creation. Let's take a trip back to our beginnings as a race and as a church to see if there is something we should learn about our Father's plans for His church today.

Once upon a time, the people were the church; the building we now call a church did not exist; the meeting place was a house or a tent, perhaps under a tree or under the sky or in a cave. People came together to pray, praise, and petition. They may have had little or nothing in the way of teaching aids, but they had much in the way of teachers. Matriarchs, patriarchs, prophets, priests, angels, and the Creator Himself led them in worship and understanding.

In the beginning God established the church and carefully instructed His congregation, the newly rebellious-now-repentant couple, how to worship and why to remember. Remember the Lamb. The serpent will not always prevail, but watch the Lamb or be misled again and fall away from salvation. In different words the same message must be given today: every discourse should uplift Jesus, the Lamb of God, and give us assurance of salvation. The first church on earth was established to help our first parents remember that they were not abandoned to be food for the serpent; the serpent would be destroyed by the Lamb (Gen. 3:15).

Could Adam and Eve take credit for establishing the church and the modes of worship? Not any more than they could take credit for Creation and the weekly cycle. It was because of the church that Adam and Eve maintained their faith through more than 900 bittersweet years. It was because they watched the Lamb that one day, very soon now, they will see again their Creator—the Lamb of God who has taken away their sin, our sin, and the sin of the world (John 1:29).

Time passes and memories grow dim. A new era is being established in the world. New traditions and new ways of thinking are fastening themselves on the minds of human beings as they spread over the recently devastated world. Spirit worship, animism, idolatry in myriad forms is captivating the minds and emotions and taking captive the bodies of people. The Creator God is willingly forgotten (Rom. 1:21, 28; 2 Peter 3:5). *Godless men ... change the grace of our God into a license for immorality and deny Jesus Christ* (Jude 1:4). These conditions of which Jude wrote in the first century AD are already corrupting society in antiquity.

Then God acts again. He reaches down into a populous society bent on forgetting about Him and picks a man and his wife, Abram and Sarai, and invites them to move far away from everything familiar and dear and establish another church (Gen. 12:1–3). In effect, they were to perpetuate the original church in the context of their times. God, not Abram and Sarai, takes the initiative and He provides the doctrine and modes of worship.

Abram and Sarai are not the fastest learners. They have a few tough lessons to experience before they can be written up as people of unfailing faith. Take, for example, the lesson of faith for which we remember them. God had promised them a son and countless descendants. After years of waiting for the promised son, the impatient couple challenge God and offer to make their general superintendent, Eliezer, heir of the promise. God graciously declines the offer and repeats His promise of a son with their DNA (Gen. 15:4). Scripture reports that Abram believes, and his belief is credited to him as righteousness (Gen. 15:6).

Sadly, belief again grows dim with passing years and an aging couple. Once again, Abram and Sarai attempt to help God out with His work. They will do their best, and God can do the rest. What a marvelous idea! Ever hear that sentiment spoken? So, Ishmael is born, and Abram presents him to God as the promised son that he, Abram, has done his best to produce. But God responds, *No, Abram, it doesn't work like that. I will bless Ishmael for your sake, but the promised son is all promise. In your faith relation with Me, there is no such thing as your doing your best and My doing the rest. I do it all. Can you believe that?* (Gen. 17:20; 21:13; Rom. 9:8; Gal. 3:18).

God has not changed. In our salvation relation with Him, there is no such thing as our doing our best and God's doing the rest. To emphasize the promise, God changes the names of Abram and Sarai to Abraham and Sarah and renews the covenant when Abraham is almost 100 years old. Only then is the promise realized and Isaac born (Gen. 17:5, 15; 21:1–3).

It was God's church at the dawn of time. Adam and Eve could take no credit for its creation or its doctrine. It was God's church 4,000 years ago. Abraham and Sarah could take no credit for its creation or its doctrine. God promptly, forcefully, patiently, and unmistakably repudiated their efforts to help Him out. Consequently, we are able to remember Abraham

No credit to Abraham and Sarah.

as the father of the faithful, and I guess that makes Sarah the mother of the faithful.

For the next 2,000 years, the system of worship God gave to Abraham and Sarah changed very little, if at all. Certainly it got more complex with the population explosion of the Hebrews, but the fundamental tenets, the old landmarks, did not change. In fact, the old landmarks were so well entrenched by the time the Lamb of God came to take away the sin of the world that the church had forgotten their significance and worshiped the landmarks instead of the One to whom they pointed. Humankind had succeeded in corrupting the church of God, but it was still God's church, weak and enfeebled though it was—still the object of God's supreme regard.

Now it was time for the Creator to intervene again. For millennia He had attempted to get the attention of His rebellious children through symbols in worship, through fire, water, thunder, disease, and war, through prophets, priests, and rulers. He would succeed for a while and then His children would forget Him again and begin to think that it was they who had created all things, including the church, and they worshiped themselves and the things they had made.

God Becomes One of Us—It was then that our Father, looking down from heaven, knew that the time had come for Him to intervene like He had never intervened before. It was time to bring on the full measure of His glory, as He had planned from the beginning, and intervene in a way that would get the fickle attention of His rebellious children: He would become one of them. He would weep with them, laugh with them, work with them, and play with them. All the symbols He had given to all the past generations, the old landmarks, would come to life and flower and fruit in the Lamb of God, who would take away the sin of the world once and for all. He would establish a new church that would have the power of His Spirit to convince the world of His undying love and compassion. His grace, integrity, and justice would be freely given.

So He came to His own and, would you believe it, His own did not recognize Him (John 1:11). His appearance was just too foreign to their way of thinking. He didn't fit their expectations. A few folk did recognize divinity in that very human baby, and they worshiped Him in the cradle. A few recognized divinity in the carpenter of Nazareth, and they followed Him. A few recognized divinity in the man on the middle cross and believed in spite of the evidence.

That man was the Rock on which the everlasting church was planted, and the gates of hell have not overcome it, though they viciously return to the battle after every defeat (Matt. 16:18). Once again, God had taken the initiative. Once again, God had established a church. Once again, we humans cannot take the credit for the work of God—though we try and try and try.

War Against the Divine—For the following 2,000 years, the gates of hell certainly did try to overcome the church God planted in Jesus. Right at the beginning, Peter attempted to prevent Jesus' going to the cross. Pilate even offered Him His freedom. Let's not forget the three times He was tempted by an assortment of people to come down from the cross. The early church waited for violent persecution before it left Jerusalem to spread the good news abroad, and the spirit of rebellion was already working in the church when the apostles preached the good news to the people of the Mediterranean basin (2 Thess. 2:7). Judaisers tried to return the new church to the worship modes and beliefs, to the old landmarks, that had failed in the old church (Gal. 1:6, 7).

Very soon after the death of the last apostle, serious doctrinal aberrations began to be taught: Origen tried to introduce a deadly twist in the meaning of *agape* in the second century just twenty-five or thirty years after John died. Augustine succeeded in the fourth century where Origen failed in the second. We are still feeling the effects of his work today. The *agape* love of God was perverted and came to be taught as charity—a sort of partnership with God in which we do our best to effect our own salvation and God does the rest. It was very much like what Abram and Sarai tried to do 4,000 years ago. Humanity, in its unregenerate state, has not changed for the better.

We are familiar with some of the other heresies that were brought into the church to obscure the clear vision of Father, Son, and Holy Spirit. God's grace was shrouded by so many futile attempts to *do our best*. We sought to buy His grace through self-flagellation, payments of dues, and exhausting pilgrimages. We solicited the saints' useless intervention by our prayers. We tried to impress the Almighty through carefully done good deeds. Many other distractions and distortions of the truth kept us in darkness while the light was freely to be received.

The purpose of the father of lies (John 8:44) was to make God invisible in the church that claimed to be holy, the body of Christ. He almost succeeded as worship of Mary and the saints became all but universal in Christendom. Virtually every church building, chapel, and convent provided for the adoration of relics and vied with each other to attract the most worshipers with their purses. Intervention of the priests was seen as necessary for salvation. Sunday sacredness, with the consequent obscuring of the knowledge that we are saved by grace alone, became a dominating theme in the Christian church. Compromises made with paganism would render the church popular in the world but ineffective in its witness for our Father. The idea and action of compromise still renders popular today.

There are those who presume to know the workings of God's mind better than others. They coerce, compel, cajole, or otherwise use their power, authority, or position to bring conformity to their thinking in standards of behavior and doctrine. We have examples in Caiaphas, Nero, Cardinal Cajetan, Charles V, popes, presidents, and ayatollahs, as well as deacons, elders, pastors, and parents who believe that they are the interpreters of what you and I should believe and do. In effect, they bend, mutilate, and distort the Word to make it conform to their ways of thinking. Even they do not agree together, and there is rampant confusion in the body of Christ that is supposed to represent Him to the world.

Where is the One who established the church and promised that the gates of hell would not prevail against it (Matt. 16:18)? Was He mistaken? In this confusing world, we need to see evidence that what we believe and teach is not a myth. Thankfully, we have the truth of God, and we can see that He is still working in His people to accomplish the objectives that He has established. What will be the ultimate evidence to prove the truth of what the church teaches? The only evidence is a family that demonstrates God's *agape* love for each other (John 13:35), a family that is united in Him. God always takes the initiative. He works through fallible and defective human beings to accomplish His divine purposes. And we can be thankful that He does because that is what we are—fallible and defective.

Light—Through the hundreds of years that we call the Dark Ages, when more than spiritual light was obscured, if not obliterated, by the foolish traditions of human beings, God had His lights here and there. Individuals and small groups of people maintained some vestiges of truth and faith amid the moral and spiritual darkness of those bleak centuries. The Waldensians in France, Italy, and Bohemia spread points of light all over Europe for hundreds of years, but darkness dominated still.

The Dark Ages blend into the Reformation—slowly, so very slowly from the human perspective. But with God there is no haste and no delay. A day is like a thousand years and a thousand years is like a day (Ps. 90:4; 2 Peter 3:8). Wycliffe, now called the morning star of the Reformation, was God-preserved in the face of deadly threats near the end of the fourteenth century. Wycliffe translated the Scriptures into the English of his time and distributed hand-written copies throughout the English countryside, its villages, monasteries, and castles. Printing had not yet been discovered, and the Word spread slowly; but spread, it did.

Half a century later and half a continent away, in what we now call the Czech Republic, Huss and Jerome read Wycliffe and believed. The teachings of Huss and Jerome spread rapidly through their writings though the writers themselves were torched. Jerome, for fear of the flames and after being kept in a revolting dungeon for a year, recanted and repudiated the teachings of Wycliffe and those of Huss and himself. However, remorse soon moved him to repent of his cowardice, take back his recantation, and go singing to the stake. A century later God took the initiative again and Luther burst on the scene with the power of the Holy Spirit. The gates of hell have not surrendered, but they have been severely damaged. Though unable to compel, they are still seductive.

We might say that the Reformation began with Luther when he nailed his ninety-five theses to the door of the castle church in Wittenberg. That would be a true but incomplete statement. In keeping with our belief that God is the initiator of all good things, we have to acknowledge that Luther was only one tool in the hands of God to precipitate the Reformation when the time was right. Others were raised up in France, Switzerland, and elsewhere in Europe. (Printing had now been developed in Western Europe, and the writings of Luther spread rapidly all over Europe.)

We should say that, as free agents, God does not use us as inanimate tools. He has a divine sensitivity to our needs as rational beings. He reasons with us and works with us in our humanity to bring us to the point of willing service—to the point at which God's desires and our desires are congruent. That is, He draws us to the point at which we want to be and to do that which God wants us to be and to do. This was Luther's experience.

Luther had come to this point in his spiritual development by 1517. He was willing to be used by God in the way God saw best no matter the personal cost to himself. For the next twenty-five or so years, protected and sustained at first by the Elector Frederick, who, himself, was responding to the leading of God's Spirit, Luther's understanding of the divine character and the divine way of working with humanity grew. Luther used his talents, planted securely in God's wisdom and love, to write, preach, and teach that we are saved by grace *alone* and not by grace plus something else. We agree with Luther that there is nothing that we can do to merit God's salvation.

God didn't give Luther all the truth that He had in His storehouse. He gave him only as much as he could communicate to the people of his day. Luther wasn't a Sabbath keeper. He resisted the Sabbath when others tried to teach it. Neither was Luther a teetotaler. He mixed his study of the Bible with real German beer. Luther was a believer in his Savior and a powerful teacher of righteousness. You will want to meet him in the kingdom of heaven. No doubt he will be carrying a pewter mug, but in it something infinitely better than German beer—perhaps a heavenly nectar, or aqua fresh from the river of life.

God called many other reformers into battle in the years following Luther's calling. They didn't all agree with each other. In fact, there were serious disagreements among them. Some of them went faster and farther than others were willing or able to follow. All of them were tools in the hands of God to bring about His will on earth. We can rejoice and be glad that they were willing to come to the front when the time was right, some at the cost of everything they had, including their lives.

The spiritual darkness of the Middle Ages receded, slowly in places, more rapidly in other places. Light took the place of darkness. God is very gentle with His wayward children. He knows that we do not take readily to change, especially to change in the traditions of our ancestors. We don't like to be moved out of our comfort zones. He allows us to grow; first a little green shoot pokes its way out of the soil. A few weeks later it will start to form a head; eventually, we will see the ripe grain—a harvest of goodness (Mark 4:28). The Reformation is not over yet. We might say that the heads of grain are forming. There have been setbacks. As in any growing season, there have been periods of dryness, cold winds, frost, hail, and little growth, but the Reformation still is going on. God still is taking the lead role in moving it forward. He is the great Initiator.

Following the struggles of the sixteenth and early seventeenth centuries, in which bloody wars were fought and people were burned for attempting to translate the Bible into the languages of the people, the seventeenth century brought the Bible in English to the people of England. Luther had provided the German Bible almost eighty years earlier, but prejudice and spiritual struggle were not ended. People frequently forfeited their possessions, their freedom, and their lives to follow the Gospel of Jesus as they understood it. Persecution followed the colonists to North America, and the colonists persecuted each other. Nevertheless, God was patient with His children, stubborn and slow to learn as they always are.

By the eighteenth century, serious spiritual decline, especially in England and America, had set in. People were content with forms and ceremonies as they had been for hundreds of years. But then God took the initiative again. With other intrepid preachers, Charles and John Wesley were called out of spiritual darkness to preach the gospel. The story of their journey from death into life is an eye-opener revelation of God's gentle leading.

At first, they preached a dry, spiritless religion without the grace of God. It did not move their hearers to repentance or to service, and it could not remove the fear of a vengeful God from their own hearts. Through a series of miracles, they came to understand and experience God's grace, and that salvation is by grace *alone.* Then God could use them to effect nationwide revivals in England and America. They prepared the theater for the great Advent revival in the first half of the nineteenth century. Christianity is under the Wesleys' influence still today.

The Reformation was not over with the Wesleys. There was still more light to come, and God had His eye on another man, gently leading him from atheism to incipient belief, from incipient belief to deep faith and, ultimately, to willingness to preach the greatest message ever given of the last days.

His name was William Miller, a farmer and an officer in the U.S. Army during the War of 1812–1814. He became the most prominent Advent preacher of the first half of the nineteenth century. Thousands turned out to hear him and be blessed by his message. God used him, along with others, to bring to the world the startling and disquieting message of the imminent return of Jesus.

This brings us very close to the beginnings of the Seventh-day Adventist Church with its unique role in the on-going Reformation—a role designed by the Great Designer and given to all who will accept a part in it, whether Hindu, Methodist, atheist, or Catholic. God is not through with us yet. He will have a pure church, a pure people who rightly understand and correctly handle the word of truth (2 Tim. 2:15) and who clearly display the *agape* love of God in their homes, schools, work places, and communities. All of it will be God's doing. He will purify for Himself a people (Titus 2:14). His people will be so because they have chosen to answer the call of God, to put Him first in their lives, and to glorify His name in the way they love one another. God commands everyone now to repent (Job 36:10; Acts 17:30). With the command is the power to obey. *God intends that now, through the church which welcomes people from every tribe and language, his many-faceted wisdom will be made known to all the intelligences of the universe. This is God's eternal purpose which He accomplished in Christ Jesus, our Lord* (Eph. 3:10–13).

The church has one foundation, Jesus. He is the Cornerstone. He is the Architect. We traced His work to save His children from their sin from the beginning. While many continue to rebel, God's eternal glory still will be seen in the church, His body. It gives me great comfort to realize that God works in my own life just like He has worked with His wayward children since the beginning of time—with mercy, truth, patience, and abundant grace. I have everything in Him that I need for life and godliness (2 Peter 1:3). What more could I ask? Nothing! He has emptied heaven for me!

Paul urges us to *always remember that in Christ we may approach God with freedom and confidence* (Eph. 3:12). We have considered the concept of remembering. We know that to remember takes time, energy, and focused attention. Let's apply ourselves to remembering. The freedom we enjoy is freedom from the fear of condemnation. The confidence we exercise is not in ourselves but in the One who is faithful (1 Cor. 1:9; 10:13). What more could we ask for? God has emptied heaven for us!

We can see that everything good is of and from God, our Father. He set up the church, and it is through the church that He is recreating a people who will honor Him in this present experience. It is through the church that the people of the world will be introduced to His majesty and brought to experience His grace. It is through the church that He is perfecting a people to live with Him forever. What more can we say? What more needs to be said? If God is for us, can anything do us harm (Rom. 8:31)? In view of these mercies, why should we trouble ourselves over the troubles that come to us as we follow the path of Jesus through this world?

Time; No Time? Your Choice—I have great sympathy for those who still struggle with time. Truck drivers, school teachers, hair dressers, merchants, bus drivers, mechanics, and all others not in retirement or independently wealthy must reconcile the very real and present need to put bread on the table, indeed, even to have a table with a floor under it and a roof above, with the even-more-urgent need to feed eagerly and hungrily on the Bread of Life (John 6:48–51, 53–58).

I don't find it in me to criticize anyone for not measuring up to my standard of use of time. Since I don't have a job, I am free to spend as much time or as little time as I choose in seeking the kingdom of God. I have been a worker, and I know the temptation to put off until tonight what I got up too late to do this morning. But we can be sure of this: the One who set up His church in the beginning, who maintains it in the present, and who calls everyone to fellowship with Him in His church will not willingly let any of us perish. He is calling each of us to repentance, to turn away from the futility of running after the fading-fast things of this world. With the call comes the opportunity, power, and grace to obey. Seize the opportunity! Seize the power! Receive the grace!

Paul Prays Again; Are We Surprised?

Because of the marvelous things that He has done in us, I kneel before our Father in prayer. We call Him Father because that is what He is—the originator, the sustainer, the teacher, the role model, the nurturer, the discipliner, and the caregiver. His whole family in heaven and on earth is called by His name. Our Father is gloriously rich and powerful. My prayer for you: that His power will strengthen you, that His Spirit will fill your inner being, and that Christ will take up residence in your heart by faith. He is standing at the door, seeking admission to your soul.

I also pray that your roots will go deep in the love of God and that you will be unshakably established in His agape. This will give you divine power, as it will empower all the saints. God's power will enable you to comprehend the multidimensional love of Christ that fills everything. The love of Christ is great beyond knowledge, yet you will know His love. And by knowing His love, you will be filled to the measure of the fullness of God, our Father.

Our God is able to do more than we can imagine; the capacity of God to do good to us cannot be humanly measured. Nor do we even come close to asking for the blessings He is eager to give to us. Still, His power is at work within us. I pray that God's glory will shine in the church. I pray that Christ Jesus will be honored in the church till the end of time and in the believers throughout eternity. May this be so! (Eph. 3:14–21)

A Day Late and Twenty Miles Short—In the writing of this letter, Paul makes us progressively more aware of the awesome greatness of our Father—a greatness He displays in power and love. The power is expressed in the re-creation of the dead in sin, bringing them to eternal life in Christ. This is not only to eternal life in the physical sense, but to abundant life in the way the born again relate in love to one another, to God, and to unbelievers.

This love is not the love based on sentiment, reciprocal feeling, or shared experiences (though sentiment, feeling, and experience may be present). God's love is the unearned, unending, overflowing agape which He pours into the life of the believer as the believer passes it on to others. Some of these believers are of the "more grace required" variety. That is, they have a capacity to test the genuineness of our *agape* to the limit again and again. I think that our Father intends for us to pass the test. Thankfully, there are the others whose connection with our Father is unmistakable.

I was a day late and twenty miles short of installing my winter tires on the truck, and I had to go to town. There's a steep grade with a curve that's quite negotiable when one is properly equipped, but it can be nasty to the unprepared. A loaded log truck coming down the hill rumbles past me, its Jake brake[3] barking. I am just entering the curve. Suddenly the laws of physics take control of my vehicle, and the truck does a gently sweeping 180 to the left, followed with a more robust 180 to the right, and then ends the show with a stunning and irresistible side-slip into the ditch.

Even without tea leaves or a crystal ball, I see a big tow bill in my future. As I contemplate my few acceptable options, a green four-wheel drive, with rugged winter grips already in place, stops and backs up in front of me. Out jumps a smiling man who pulls a chain from his box and proceeds to attach it to the front of my vehicle and the rear of his. I see his point immediately, and the image of the tow bill begins to fade. Putting his truck in gear and taking up the slack, the smiling man in the well-tired vehicle grinds his way up the hill, with my truck meekly following behind. At a wide spot in the road, he stops and disconnects the vehicles and, with a smile and a wave, he drives off.

So, what's my point? Clear enough, I should think. Our Father does not chide us for failing

God finds us where we are; He doesn't leave us there.

to prepare for emergencies. (How come you're so stupid that you drive on a road like this without winter tires?) He finds us where we are and retrieves us. We are utterly helpless to help ourselves. His love does not criticize or condemn or say we have to pay (I'll just leave you here to pay the tow truck, if you can get one today—and learn your lesson well); it just meets our desperate need and supplies it.

The man in the green four-wheel drive found me stuck on the hill, quite embarrassed, quite exposed to the taunts of those who had prepared for the coming winter. But he didn't criticize me for my tardy behavior or leave me there. So it is with God; He accepts us as we are, but He doesn't leave us there happy (or miserable) in our sin. He changes us from dead in sin to alive in Him.

This is the Father who calls us to be family. We understand that in the language in which Paul wrote, the words "father" and "family" are similar. We can infer that this "family" derives its being and its legitimacy from the Father. The potential peace and joy in association with other members of the family is sourced in God, our Father. The problems and frictions we encounter are our own, the product and the evidence of the uncrucified *self* to which we stubbornly or otherwise cling. Speaking elsewhere of dying daily through the crucifixion of the self, Paul teaches that we need to put *self* down daily, continuously, if we are to have a family life that brings praise to our Father and joy to ourselves (1 Cor. 15:31).

---

[3] A Jake brake is a mechanism that relies on the compression of an engine to slow the vehicle.

If family, then we share a name. What's in a name? What's in the name we share? In our culture names tend to be made, that is, people will begin to associate the characteristics I habitually display with my name, and my name will become either good or bad. I will be seen as dependable or not, honest or not, thrifty or not, stingy or not. My word will be as good as a signed contract or not. Of course, I can inherit a name that is respected, or not, in the community; I may have a hard battle to rise above a bad inheritance, or I may ride into life on an already good name—and tarnish it. Such is life in this world.

The Christian has inherited a good name, and it means something in the thinking of society. Christians are assumed to be good people—or hypocrites. Too frequently the person doing the assuming is left puzzled at the variance between name and performance in the ordinary duties of life. This discrepancy gives ammunition to detractors such as Dawkins and his disciples to discredit the Name.

What's in a name? Specifically, what is in the name *Christian*? Much. As Paul would say, "Much in every way!" (Rom. 3:2). When we take the name of Christ, we take His grace, His mercy, His patience, His truthfulness, His goodness, and top it off with His power, the infinitely muscular power that raised Jesus from the dead, to live the life that honors our Father. That's what's in this Name and this Name is available to anyone who will receive it. It matters not what name we inherited, cherished, or in which we took pride. Each one of us can be born again with a new name that will be written down in glory.

Father, Family—Our Father is gloriously rich and powerful. As the old song rings, "My Father is rich in houses and lands; He holdeth the wealth of the world in His hands!" That's rich, indeed, and so true, but a different sort of riches than I think of now: the riches of grace that took a broken, failing man and set him in the way to the kingdom. Now, that is rich, indeed! The power exercised in my life is the awesome power that brought Jesus to life. I don't know how to relate to power like that—except with belief, with humility, and with great thankfulness.

Six rumbling diesels pull trains loaded with the commerce of the nation over the rocks to the west several times a day. That's real grunt power, but six hundred sixty-six of those engines on full torque could not bring life to one good-looking corpse. The call of our Father, delivered by two angels, was all the divine energy required to bring Jesus out of the grave. This is the power that is available to you and to me. It can put to death the old nature of sin and bring us to newness of life in Christ. Awesome power! Awesome grace! Ask for it!

I heard it said in a sermon: *Jesus needs company on the cross*. I've heard it said before but not so colorfully. Company on the cross? If Jesus dies alone, He dies in vain. A cross is for dying. My cross is not some pain, trouble, or annoyance I have to bear, perhaps without complaining. No, a cross is for death, my death to self, to sin. It has to happen daily; it has to happen continuously. That takes God's muscle power!

Paul, the praying man, asks for God's power to strengthen us. Does he know for what he asks? God's power is life-giving power. This is no toy stuff. How will we use the strength? To polish up the *self* in an effort to make ourselves look good? To keep the self hunkered down out of sight? To smile when the going is difficult? No, no, and no! Use the strength to take up the cross and crucify self. It takes divine strength to do the act.

Paul, the praying man, asks for the Spirit of our Father to fill our inner being. The Spirit cannot inhabit the same inner being (mind) as the uncrucified self. If we would have God's Spirit fill our inner being, we must crucify the self to make room for Him. I have never witnessed a physical crucifixion, but I sense that it creates pain, embarrassment, and despair as deep as one could imagine. There must be a profound sense of powerlessness against the nails and ropes fastening the body to the beam. How utterly awful! I sense that the crucifixion of self will have its own kind of pain as the desires of the old nature are repudiated and exchanged for the new nature. I sense that the old nature is going to resist as long as possible, using every device available to dissuade us from taking the final, fatal action. I sense that when Jesus pointed out that His followers would have to take up the cross daily to follow Him, He understood the pain and emotions that attend a crucifixion.

God's Letter to Us: Laodicea—While we are on the topic of exchanging the old for the new, we should look at the words of Jesus, the faithful and true witness to Laodicea (Rev. 3:14-21). Jesus finds Laodicea quite comfortably ensconced in its assumed wealth—wealth not provided by God. Laodicea has no idea that its perceived affluence is actually a dead weight that will be ultimately and utterly destructive unless exchanged for real wealth.

The Father's wealth in Revelation 3 is described as gold (agape), white clothes (of pure character), and eye salve (of spiritual discernment). For this transaction there is always enough of the phony wealth to exchange for the true wealth of our Father. All of our old stuff must go. We can keep nothing back. At the risk of repeating myself, I will do just that, again. C. S. Lewis reminds us that there is no souvenir of hell that will get past the security gate of heaven.[4] None of our old familiar quirks, sins, secrets, or savings will make it past the narrow gate. Trade them all in for God's enduring wealth.

Paul, the praying man, asks for Christ to take up residence in our hearts by faith. Jesus stands at the door to Laodicea knocking and pleading to be given entrance. He hears all the noise and merriment going on inside. He overhears the boasting of what we have and do and plan to do, or wish we hadn't done. He is praying that, over the din of the partying, someone will hear the knocking and open the door to let Him in. I guess that Paul is actually praying for a lull in the partying so that the knocking will be heard. This world is a noisy, busy, party place. Maybe Paul's prayer will be answered in ways that we would rather not experience. In retrospect, we will thank Paul for his prayer that brought hearing to the deaf in sin—to each of us (1 John 2:16).

The news about every two years is dominated by the Olympics. The buildup to the 2010 winter games in Vancouver had all but sucked us dry and left us pining for something other than hubris to fill dead-air space. However, John Furlong, head of the Vancouver Olympic Committee, assured us that when that little flame came to town, life as we know it would change. Really? It was an idle boast. That little flame burned itself out, leaving us with only the dry smell of smoke in our noses and the feeling of emptiness in our wallets. These Olympic games will be forgotten like every other Olympic bash before them, but of this we can be sure: that little flame and the monstrous cauldron that it ignited will never hold a torch to the flame of God's Spirit who touched the disciples at Pentecost and has never since been extinguished.

---

[4] C. S. Lewis, *The Great Divorce* (CS Lewis Pte. Ltd, 1946).

God is eager to touch each of His praying children as the affairs of this aging earth wind down. Life as the apostles knew it did change after the flames of Pentecost, and life as we know it changes still—no thanks to the events of 2010. Change will continue as long as we listen to the knocking of Jesus at the door, let Him in, and let His flame rest on us! The changing life is a work in progress. So often I feel that the progress in me is slow, tedious, and without effect, but I remember it said that the closer I come to Jesus, the more unworthy I am going to feel in my own soul.

Warning! I should not take my feelings of unworthiness as an indicator of spiritual growth. I should not take my feelings as anything more than the working of my emotions that are affected by many things, including bed times, the food I eat, and the progress on the new sour-gas well down the road.

And so I ask, Lord, help me to trust You and take You at Your word no matter what my feelings may suggest to me. Your word says that You stand at the door knocking to be admitted into my life. Lord, come in. Eat with me. Talk with me. Teach me how to respond to the clamors of this world that would steal my attention from You. Empower me to give up the imagined wealth I suppose I have in exchange for the reality of the true wealth only You can give (Rev. 3:18). And thank You for the divine assurance You delivered and packaged with infinite grace for me personally and for every member of this wonderful body.

Roots as Faith—As a gardener I know a few things about roots: we work with delicate roots when transplanting squash and cucumber plants; they respond poorly to careless handling. Strawberry roots seem almost indestructible. The young strawberry plants come dried out and apparently dead, but once we stick them in the fertile soil, and give them a shot of water and a burst of sunlight, they will thrive. Bury the roots of a young tomato plant deep in the soil and the plant will generate new roots from the stock.

Toss a pigweed on the soil of a tilled bed and, given the least hint of encouragement, it will take root and survive, if not thrive. Clover has a powerful root system that's almost impossible to extricate. Chickweed roots mirror the chickweed plant; they grow indiscriminately, break easily, and die with difficulty. Quackgrass sends its rhizomes every direction beneath the soil—out of sight, it thrusts up new grass stalks as it progresses across the field. These new stocks, in turn, send out new rhizomes until the entire field is choked with quack grass. My mother gardened until she was 90. She conquered the quackgrass each year by digging a trench around the parts of her half-acre garden that were threatened by the persistent weed. Since the rhizomes seem to thrust out at a maximum depth, she was able to keep the quack grass out of her garden by trenching below that depth and ruthlessly eradicating the grass within.

The root system of the spruce tree is generally shallow. In light soil, as in a swamp, a spruce tree left standing alone can be easily uprooted. The same tree, if it has grown up unprotected, will have developed a deeper hardier root system that can better withstand the gales. Pine trees seem to do the same in their habitat. As I look from my office window, I make out the silhouette of a tall spruce tree through the surrounding aspens. It could be the tallest tree on my sixty acres, certainly the tallest in its neighborhood, and it has weathered enormous gales for 100 years. Clearly it has sent down roots adequate for the task.

Aspen trees tend to have sturdy root systems, yet newly exposed aspens will also be blown over in strong winds. Recently in a gale one of our aspen trees broke off at ground level and damaged a fence in falling. On examining the break, I discovered that a type of rot had totally infested the tree at ground level and had, in effect, separated the tree from its roots, from its source of nourishment and support.

Jesus spoke of roots in the context of the seed that fell into shallow soil (Matt. 13:5). The roots of these seedlings were not in touch with the water of life. The plants that sprouted quickly in the shallow soil were unable long to withstand the beating of the sun. Paul urges his Ephesian readers to send their roots deep in the love of God. From the metaphor of the roots above, we can infer something of the importance Paul attaches to roots. Roots provide support. They keep the plant upright as it reaches to the sun, they draw in the nutrients and water from the soil, and they act importantly to propagate the plant. Another crucial function: roots provide storage for plant nutrients. And, in most cases, roots are largely out of sight to the casual observer.

By sending our roots deep into the love of God, we will be unshakably established in His *agape*. That is the true source of every spiritual victory, of unity in the church, and of effectiveness in witness. We have been warned that the devil, in his death throes, will rage like a roaring lion after more victims (Rev. 12:12; 1 Peter 5:8). With roots deep in God's *agape*, we will have continuous spiritual nourishment; we will stand tall against the winds of temptation or oppression as we reach to the Son. The promises and the blessings of our Father and the memories of His past leading will be stored for ready access. These are all the defenses we need against the devil. We will be unshakably established in the love of God. Sealed by the Spirit of God, our inheritance is guaranteed; we wait in confidence for the redemption of our bodies (Eph. 1:13, 14).

How, we must ask, do we send roots deep into God's *agape*? The answer is really quite simple. Our entire experience with our Father is based on faith. So faith may be said to be the root of which Paul writes to the Ephesians. If faith is the root, then it makes sense that the root, the measure of faith with which every person is endowed, is augmented and strengthened by feeding on the Word of God (Rom. 10:17). Our major role in the salvation experience is to pay close attention to the Word of God—pay frequent attention to the Word of God and be careful to obey the Holy Scriptures (Ezek. 36:27).

You might remember that when the disciples asked Jesus to increase their faith (Luke 17:5), He immediately spoke to them of obedience—of only doing our duty. Faith has three facets: knowledge, belief, and obedience. Knowledge comes from the Scriptures; belief comes from the heart; obedience is an act of the will to receive the gift and honor our Father in heaven. There is more than factual knowledge of creation, maintenance, and redemption in the Scriptures. There is power.

Paul described the gospel as the *power of God unto salvation* (Rom. 1:16), and in a letter to the Corinthians, he calls the message of his letter the power of God (1 Cor. 1:18). If the gospel and the message embody divine power, it follows that if we spend quality and quantity time in the Word, the power will shape our lives. It was not an idle statement that faith comes by hearing the Word. There is power in the Word. By sending our roots deep, we are anchoring our souls in Jesus Himself. But we have to hear it—if we still have ears. And the presence or absence of ears is a vital question with which we must wrestle and deal.

Ears, No Ears; Listen Up!—Don't we all have ears? It would appear at first glance that most people have ears—there must be some support for the hardware dangling there. But some have sharper hearing than others. Some hear the high notes, some hear the low notes, and some cannot hear any notes. But everyone *has* ears. If you have ears, then listen to the words of the prophet. Seven times in chapters two and three of Revelation, the prophet ends his letter to a church leader with the admonition: *Listen.* Clearly, the metaphor speaks of more than superficial sound recognition. It calls for closer scrutiny of the message than the sound of a passing gust of wind or the tuneless screeching of dueling cats in the night (unless it's my kitty that is getting beaten up). This message requires analysis, evaluation, reflection, and action—that's real, deep listening.

Analysis, evaluation, reflection, action – that's real listening.

Listening at more than the superficial level of sound recognition and reflexive response is not a natural skill; it is certainly not a skill supported by much that occupies the post-Christian way of life as we dash along in this mad human race. We have conditioned ourselves to hear without analyzing, without evaluating, without reflecting, but we have especially conditioned ourselves to neglect a response. In submitting to the noise of the rush and the rushing of the noise, we have seriously impaired our capacity to hear. Even the most benign of TV entertainment may compromise our capacity to hear at that deep level. Thus, we will be less prepared to respond effectively to practical situations in life.

We became incapacitated without our knowledge. First, we taught ourselves to love the entertainment that demanded no response, in fact, to which meaningful response was not possible. We soon transferred this learning to other areas of life. When responding effectively to life's experiences was inconvenient, painful, or costly, we applied our new skills by ignoring the experiences or pretending they really didn't happen. Eventually, we became truly comfortable with not responding. We enjoyed the comfort; then we required it.

Without our notice we descended further. Level by level we fell to the state of resenting anything tending to move us from that comfortable state of dead center. To be centered on our own comforts, oblivious to the calls of the Spirit to step over the line, is to be like the flywheel of my dad's monster steam engine that hissed and sputtered and belched hot steam in my childhood. If the flywheel stopped in the dead center position with the piston at its fullest extension, the wheel would not restart without a push from outside. Poet Alexander Pope describes the process in rhyming verse: "Vice is a monster of such frightful mien / As to be hated needs but to be seen. / Yet seen too oft, familiar with her face, / We first endure, then pity, then embrace."[5]

If you have ears—if you can still hear, if you have not destroyed your ability to analyze,

---

[5] Alexander Pope, "An Essay on Man," epistle II (1732–1734).

evaluate, reflect, and act on this message—then listen to what the Spirit says to the churches. Listen to what the Spirit says to you. The message has eternal significance. *Listen.*

Listening to the Spirit is not natural. Naturally, we prefer the pleasing sounds of music and laughter. We prefer the diversion of drama and suspense. We prefer sport and work. We prefer chemically induced oblivion or drifting into dreamland with a light story. We prefer the titillation of other people's sins. We prefer to shut out the uncomfortable call to repentance, to service, to reconciliation, to unity. In fact, we prefer almost anything to the knowledge that requires a response.

But we are not locked irremediably into our deafness. There is a way to get our hearing back. We can have our ears uncorked. This utterly crucial process may be uncomfortable, painful, inconvenient, and even embarrassing—such a small price to pay for the ability to hear the voice of God! While the Physician can diagnose the condition, prescribe the cure, and apply the remedy, He cannot consent on our behalf to the procedure. That is our part to do. *If you hear His voice today,* obey Him (Heb. 3:15).

*The Holy Spirit calls;
if you have ears then listen for real.*

The sound in our ears *today* is not tinnitus; it's the call of our Father. If you have ears, then listen. Now is the time of salvation (2 Cor. 6:2). Now is the time to look up with rejoicing because our redemption is closer than we ever thought possible (Luke 21:28). Now, when the call to repentance, reconciliation, obedience, and unity among the members is still going out, we need unimpaired capacity to hear and respond to it. We cannot keep our deafening pleasures, diversions, and titillations and have our hearing too. There are choices to be made. There is a point of no return when the voice of the Spirit cannot be discerned in the cacophony of voices competing for our attentions and for our souls (Isa. 55:6). Now is the time to listen—if you have ears. The root Paul urges us to send deep into our Father's *agape* is faith. Faith comes by hearing. Victory over sin, unity among believers, and effectiveness in witness will follow.

Comprehending the Power—I watched the closing ceremony of the 2010 Winter Olympics on the television and was treated to a program of praise for human greatness and power. Nothing in that vast celebrating assembly of 60,000 souls, the elite and powerful of the nations, hinted at our Father's greatness. The first song, artfully performed in French and English, taught us to believe in the power of humankind, in fact, it was a hymn to humanism—shades of the failed French revolutionary attempt to set up humanity in the place of God. There was much talk of the power of sport to bring us together, but behind the lights, glamour, and rhetoric was bare-knuckle competition to be the greatest. Young athletes had pushed themselves to the frontiers of physical and mental endurance almost from babyhood just to wear the gold of Olympia under the bright lights of the stadium and to stand on the podium receiving the praises of the nations that gave them birth. It was most impressive, designed and executed to prevent our seeing past the glitter of Olympic gold to the gold of Revelation.

The Russians had come to 2010 with a sizzling display to lure us to the 2014 Winter Olympics in Sochi on the Black Sea. Sochi is now history, and you can be sure that no expense was spared to make the spectacle even more brilliant than 2010—the most expensive Olympic display ever. "At an estimated $50 billion, the Sochi games are the most expensive ever, exceeding Beijing ($43 billion) handily and quintupling the most ever spent on a Winter Games—Vancouver, at $9.2 billion."[6] With its national hubris on the table, and that's no small display either, Russia tapped every resource at its command to prove to the world that that ancient nation is not too stiff and bent with age to outglitter the best of the West. Even if it had crippled the nation, and I am certain the pain of Sochi will be felt for years, the price of Olympic glory would have been paid. How vast the power of human pride to drive us to self-destruction (Prov. 11:2)!

In contrast to the glitz of human power, divine power comes up quietly through the roots we have sent into God's *agape*. This is the power that makes the big head small enough to pass through the security gate of heaven (Matt. 7:13, 14), and the great ego humble enough to serve the weak (Matt. 20:26–28). God's power does not attempt to dazzle our senses. Rather it seeks through wisdom to bring sense to our world-bedazzled brains. In dealing with us mortals, God wraps His power in the garb of humility as He did in Jesus, who put off His divinity before He entered the world as a human baby—a very poor human baby.

As a human being, Jesus endured every pain and insult depraved humanity could heap on Him. He took His humility to the extent of giving up eternal life for us on a Roman cross (Phil. 2:6–8). *Your attitude should be the same as that of Christ Jesus* (Phil. 2:5). This, more than anything else, demonstrates the contrast between human values as expressed in glittering Olympic extravaganzas and the values our Father holds.

Our natural inclination is to put ourselves forward at the expense of everyone else. That's only human, and that attitude is displayed in full color and sound at Olympic celebrations. By infinite contrast, coming silently up through the root of faith, God's power will change all that in us. The saints will receive the divine power necessary to be like Jesus in attitude. The prayer of Paul will be realized in each praying saint and God, not ourselves, will be on the podium to receive the glory and distribute the gold. Amen.

Three-Dimensional Love—We understand something about dimension—about three of them, anyway (other dimensions are more speculative)—and that gives us enough data to measure and plan and build. The first dimension is length, like a straight line between two points, having no breadth or depth. The second dimension adds breadth as in the surface of a desk, or any flat surface, but there is still no depth. The third dimension adds the depth, and we have an object that can occupy space or be held in the hand—like a ball, a box, a balloon, a piece of paper or string, or even a horse. All of these objects occupy space and their volume or capacity can be calculated. This is what we consider to be three-dimensional.

---

[6] David Goodsall, "Chasing the Cash in the Most Expensive Olympics Ever," *BC Business*, January 6, 2014.

Paul describes the love of Christ as three-dimensional. We should, therefore, apply our understanding of the principles of measurement to the love of Christ. According to Paul's definition, His love occupies space; it has length, breadth, and depth (Eph. 3:18). Perhaps Paul was simply trying to express the idea that Christ's love fills everything in every way that we can comprehend. When we look to a star, we describe a straight line of sight (we think), the first dimension; shift the eye to a second star in the same plane (if that is possible), and we describe the second dimension; now swing to another star in a different plane, perhaps on the opposite side of the universe, and we are into three dimensions. That's big, and that's Christ's love. We could introduce time and the speed of light, but Christ is beyond time and the speed of light. We start to get a bit wobbly here. I'm not sure that we should try to take this concept further. To know that the love of Christ is capable of taking us in and filling us—all of us—is quite enough.

The love of Christ is great beyond knowledge, yet we will know His love (Eph. 3:19). This paradox puzzles us: Christ's love is beyond knowledge, but we will know His love. Does Paul mean that Christ's love cannot be described adequately in words yet somehow, perhaps by experience, we will know it? I cannot comprehend the vastness of the universe and the interrelations of time and space. What is beyond time? What is outside space? I don't understand how light bends and colors of the spectrum sometimes get lost between source and eye. How does time speed up—or slow down? Does the speed of light change? What is dark energy? Does it exist? Is space, itself, energized?

The simple answers, the only answers we can give, are limited. We speculate based on our observations and theories. We don't really know, and at this point in our journey to eternity, we can't know. Only the Creator knows. But we can luxuriate in the warm rays of the sun, romance in the soft glow of the moon, marvel at the precision of the stars, and scatter the light into its spectrum colors. Just so, we cannot measure, define, explain, or calibrate the love of Christ, but we can experience and enjoy His love and the results of His love every day. We can know the joy of obeying the gospel.

Paul is totally confident that we will know Christ's love. His is the confidence of a continuum of experience. From his first encounter with Christ on the road to Damascus, Paul never looked back. Always looking to Christ, he lived daily in His presence. This teaches me that if we want to experience His love, there is no other way than to put ourselves daily in Christ's presence. By doing so, there can be no other outcome than to experience His unknowable, immeasurable love in our lives.

This experience will be demonstrated in the way we relate to other children of God. In a very explicit letter to the Galatians, Paul gave perhaps one of the clearest statements in the Bible, which defines how obedience to Christ is demonstrated: "Carry each other's burdens, and in this way you will fulfill the law of Christ" (Gal. 6:2). This is love in action (really, the only kind there is). This is the most available way for most of us to give our lives for our friends.

What are these burdens? They come in all shapes, sizes, and weights. They dig into our backs and weary our minds. They are the burdens of repeated failure, the burdens of pain in chronic sickness, the burdens of fear and loneliness when terminal illness strikes, the burdens of discouragement when the pink slip is handed out, the burdens of the crushing weight of unremitting debt, and the burdens of the shock of betrayed confidence.

Fulfilling the law of Christ.

Perhaps one of the greatest burdens anyone carries is the knowledge of repeated personal failure to honor our Father in the daily duties and encounters of life. These lapses don't have to involve the so-called "great" sins. The ongoing burden of repeated failure to give God the honor due to Him for our daily successes or to praise Him for His never-failing mercies can be a huge burden. We must give this over to Him without delay and receive the victory and the power as overcomers.

How can we carry burdens for one another? There are as many ways as there are circumstances. There is the unconditional forgiveness I can extend to the person who wittingly or otherwise sins against me. There is the nonjudgmental shoulder to cry on. There is the load of split firewood delivered to the guy who just injured his shoulder and can't pull the start rope on his chainsaw. There is the encouragement shared with the gal who hit the moose in the dark, on the curve of the road, and demolished her car (perhaps accompanied by a loaner until her wheels are turning again). There is the giving of time to take a lonely, hurting boy to the ski slopes for a day just because you care. And always take the opportunity to give a reason for the hope you have, but do it with gentleness and respect for the sensibilities of the one who asked (1 Peter 3:15).

Because our moral consciousness is flawed, we are not always aware of our sin. In the Psalms David seeks forgiveness for hidden sins and prays for deliverance from willful sin (Ps. 19:12, 13). We need to send up the same petitions to our Father. We need to recognize that the members of our congregations are also flawed; they need the same consideration that we ask for ourselves. This is how we will know the three-dimensional love of Christ. This is how we will share it.

Paul tells us that *by knowing His love, you will be filled to the measure of the fullness of God, our Father.* Wow! *Filled to the measure of the fullness of God, our Father* (Eph. 3:19)! Be like God? What is the measure that defines our Father? Let's go to the kitchen where we keep our measuring cups. Hmm: quarter cup, third cup, half cup, cup, two cup, and of course, there's the pinch. They measure out with relative accuracy the ingredients we put in our food concoctions. But the measure of the fullness of God? How much is that? Surely He doesn't use cups to dole out His grace.

We have several indicators of the size of God's measure: the writer of Psalm 71 spoke of God's righteousness and salvation all day long though he had no idea of its measure (Ps. 71:15); the measure of faith God has given to each person is always enough (Rom. 12:3). In perusing the thirty-five instances of the use of "measure" in the NIV, I get a sense that God measures sin precisely but His blessings and His forgiveness lavishly. I also get the sense that the blessings of God are always enough; as Paul was assured:

"My grace is sufficient for you, for my power is made perfect in weakness" (2 Cor. 12:9). It seems that Paul's weakness, and yours and mine as well, is the ideal opportunity for God to display His immeasurable grace. So, let's be happy in our weakness as we throw all our cares on Him; He cares for us, you know (1 Peter 5:7).

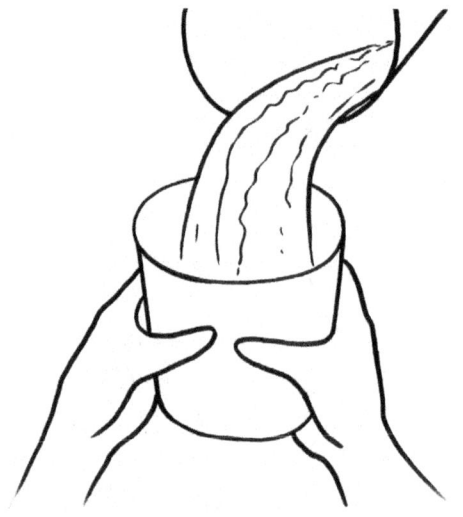

God's measure is big, real big!

So, how big is the measure of the fullness of God, our Father? Big enough to fill the biggest holes in our hearts. Big enough to squelch the strongest temptations we will ever face. Big enough to power up the weakest of the weak. Big enough to raise to life the dead in sin. By knowing God's love, we will be filled to this measure.

What God Can Do (It's No Secret)!—When my grandchildren were small and visiting us, they would play for hours with the simplest toys. Their fertile imaginations carried them into faraway lands filled with bold adventures. With nothing more than a stick of wood and a paper box, they ventured to exotic shores and dined with strange and wonderful peoples. The rare and gifted person retains the gift of imagination into adult years and produces great literature or theological insights, invents the telephone, the personal computer, or some other device that grabs our interest and cleans out our bank accounts.

When I was about five, I was introduced to the ballpoint pen and potato chips—both new inventions. We have so many new inventions today to add to our comfort, to the convenience of travel and communication, and to occupy our dwindling time. Most of them have been developed or refined within the last quarter century. There is such fertility in the unfettered human mind when it is freed to travel with a stick of wood and a discarded box instead of the pre-built toys we find today! Yet we have no concept of what God can do for us other than what He has revealed—or that we have experienced. Our imaginations hit the wall when it comes to God.

We simply cannot measure or even imagine the capacity of God to do good for us. That being so, we are rather well-positioned to leave everything in God's hands and just let Him do His work in us. I cry out in the darkness of the night, "God, I feel a great emptiness in my soul. I don't know how to reach You. I can't see you. I can't feel You. I can't grasp the depth of my desperation. I'm out of my depth, helpless, rudderless, no shore in sight. I don't even know how to articulate my need. But you know. You know everything about me, my history, my present. I leave all that and my future in Your hands. And so, my Father, I place myself into your generous, imaginative hands and trust You to lead me in the path of righteousness for Your good name's sake" (see Ps. 23).

I know that the path of righteousness leads through grace to glory. I am in grace now; are you there, too? Glory is just ahead! The path sometimes will lead us in exhausting ways, over mountain, through swamp, and across the waterless waste; at other times it will meander softly through green and flowered pastures bisected by pebbly, clear-water brooks where silver fish glance in the sunshine. With our limited vision, we'd probably choose a different path, I think, most of the time. But somewhere I've read that we would not choose a different path if we could, like Jesus, see the end from the beginning. We can't. But Jesus assured us that He is with us to the end of the age (Matt. 28:20). "Jesus, as long as we have Your assurance of Your being with us, the path is OK. Paul has assured us that we cannot measure Your capacity to do us good. So, You do the measuring. We'll simply trust Your measuring cups, Your balance, Your line, and Your pinch."

I think we should ask our Father for grace to make His cause our first priority. Remember Paul's assertion that he received grace to preach to the Gentiles. He considered it a blessing and a privilege to preach. There was no other priority in his life. His tent making was only a means to pay for the cost of preaching, and I suspect that he preached while sewing his canvas. His ocean cruises were only so that he could preach again in different places to different people; he even ate his food to give him strength to preach. "Lord, I want this attitude to be mine. Show me the obstacles to receiving it; give me the will to turn them over to you."

But, do I really desire Paul's attitude to become the driving force in my remaining moments? What would happen if I actually prayed with a serious intent to follow the blessing and be vulnerable to the Spirit of our Father? What would change if God took me seriously and actually granted my prayer? What would my day look like? Would I spend any time in the shop? Would I spend my time with people sharing the news of the kingdom with them? Would I actually recognize opportunities when they stand in front of me—opportunities to help a struggling soul fix the roof on his house or wire a renovation—even to fix a faulty sewer?

These are the moments, when we get our coveralls dirty and maybe get a little wood under the skin or draw a bit of blood helping people, when they could be vulnerable to the soft wind of the Holy Spirit. How many lost opportunities are in my history? How many moments that could have been used to share a hope for the world to come where there will be no more broken sewers or leaky roofs?

Our God is able to do more than we can imagine, and we don't *even come close to asking for the blessings He is eager to give to us* (Eph. 3:20). Why not admit to Him that our flaky, dried-up imaginations don't function well, that we are jaded with acquiring stuff, bored with trying to play with it *if* we can get it out of the package intact, and tired of the work it takes to pay for the junk? Let's go back to being children whose imaginations have not yet been seared with prepared cereal, ice cream in a hundred flavors, plastic toys that can't keep our interest, and animated chatter about computer games and awards for best actress or director.

The CBC is about the only radio that motivates me to punch the switch and not very much that it offers gets my time. The hosts are usually filling the air with so much chatter that I cannot bear to hear. Do I really care about the pop music awards, the best movies, and the bouquet subtly detected in the wine glass? I don't need the clutter in my mind, yet sports, music, movies, and wine seem to be the prime topics of their prattle. I guess that the broadcast industry is catering to popular demand—at least to its conception of the popular demand. Sadly, we see that our society has descended to the level of fluff, violence, and empty noise. No wonder that our imaginations are atrophied and our ears are dull.

I overheard a conversation in a bus station. At about 1:30 in the morning two young adults (otherwise apparently intelligent) were analyzing in great earnestness the merits of various computer games and actors as if they were discussing the details of a bank merger or a potential truce between warring nations. I sense that even professed believers in our Father are not immune to the attractions of the popular culture and this, I believe, is a major factor in our lack of imagination as we come before our God for blessings. True, Paul's audience did not have the same trifles that occupy our minds and steal our time and virtue, but they had the pop culture of their own society; it worked the same way.

In spite of the pop culture at work against us, Paul assures us that God's power is at work within us, and that assurance should give us enormous comfort—but not complacency. That being so, we have a power that is strong enough to overthrow all the forces, all the influences, and all the enticements that this world can bring against us. That also being so, the only obstacle to victory over the forces of evil is our own perverse reluctance to turn over the battle to the Lord, whose it really is (1 Sam. 17:47). God is amazing! His patience with me cannot be measured! I join Paul in praying for Jesus Christ to be honored in my life, in my family, and in the church. I pray that we just will give Him the freedom to let His glory blaze. I pray that we will stand back and let Him have the glory that is His—or that we will go forward when He commands and let Him have the glory that is His. Now and forever! May this be so! Amen.

Chapter 4
United We Grow

Unity in the Body

I repeat: I am a prisoner of the Lord, not of Caesar. Christ compels me, not Caesar. As His prisoner I am in a moral position to urge you to conduct your lives in a way that is worthy of the calling you have received and the profession you have made. For starters, believers are characterized in notable ways: complete humility and gentleness. Believers are patient; they bear with one another in love. Indeed, given our ongoing humanity, each of us needs the love of all; all need the love of each.

The unity of the Spirit in a bond of peace is an essential element of the body. Through the death of Jesus, God produced in the church this unity, but to keep it requires total commitment and unrelenting effort on the part of the members of the body. There is only one body, and there is only one Spirit. And you were all called to one hope: in one Lord, with one faith, through one baptism. And there is only one God who is Father of us all, who is over all, through all, and in all by His Holy Spirit. In Him is our unity.

Christ has given grace to each one of us. There is no lack for anyone. This is why it says in the Psalms: "When He ascended on high, He led captives in His train and gave gifts to men." (How can we understand ascended except that He also descended to the earth prior to His ascension? The One whom the apostles watched in awe as He was received by angels of heaven is the One who came to earth as a human baby. He ascended higher than all the heavens with a definite purpose in mind: to fill the whole universe.)

And what gifts did He give? He gave many gifts of grace. To some He gave the gift of apostleship; others received the gift of prophecy; some were designated as evangelists; others were made pastors and teachers. Each received grace to carry out the assignments of the Lord. God's gifts are practical; they are not for decoration of the receiver. They are to be used vigorously to prepare God's people to serve according to His plan and until we reach unity in the faith and understanding of the Son of God. The gracious gifts of God will lead us to maturity in the faith; they will lead us to an experience of the full measure of the totality of Christ.

When we reach God's goal for us of spiritual maturity, the waves and winds of popular, false teaching can no longer toss us about. Cunning and crafty deceivers with their scheming will not break our solid connection with Christ, the Head. On the contrary we will speak only the truth, and we will speak in Christ's love. Though mature in Christ, we will continue to grow in Him. This whole body, of which we are members held together by the supporting ligaments of love and truth, will continue to grow, being built up in love, as each part faithfully performs the work assigned by Christ. (Eph. 4:1–16)

A Unified Body—Can It Be—At Last?—Paul has devoted the first half of his monumental letter to the Ephesians to what we might think of as a theoretical though powerfully moving discussion of grace and justification. In chapter four Paul smoothly shifts his gears and begins a candid hands-on application of the theory: this is what a life of grace looks like in the Kenworth cab when the rubber meets an icy road; this is grace when you are guiding your mount around the barrels under the bright lights of the riding arena, and the crowd is cheering you on; this is grace when you suddenly learn that macular degeneration has robbed you of the ability to read with one eye—and the other is going as well (how could I not have seen this coming?). This is how we recognize the born-again believer in the congregation of believers. This is the product of the justified life. This is the sanctified life in action. This is *applied* grace.

Of course there is no clean division between the two sections of Paul's letter; they blend seamlessly so that readers move easily from the discussion of grace and justification to a compelling look at themselves as products of God's grace. Readers are forced to see themselves in the light of grace, and evaluation of the personal sanctified life has to happen (or the letter must be put out of sight).

Paul once again stresses that the message he is communicating to the Ephesians is a message he is compelled by his own grace relationship with God to share. From the day Jesus redirected his life at the gate of Damascus to his present confinement in chains, Paul's message of grace and obedience has not been concealed. He has boldly proclaimed God's call to repentance to everyone who would listen. More than once Paul's preaching put him under the lash, set him adrift in the sea, made him the target of furious mobs intent on stoning the life out of him, and landed him in jail—and finally in Rome it brought him to the man with the axe.

Because of his divine calling and the events in Paul's life, he is in a moral position of strength to urge us to conform our justified lives to the will of God just as he did. He is on moral high ground from which he has a right and an obligation to urge us to live lives worthy of our calling and our profession. (With clear relevance to the cowboys in our congregations, Hebrews 10:24 in the NIV uses the verb *spur* to activate us—and from my personal riding experience, I know that a spur is not an instrument of gentle persuasion.) Paul is on moral high ground, clearly visible to believers in every age, from which he cheerfully spurs us on to take the high road of life, truth, faith, obedience, and love within the body of believers. Where should we start?

Start Here—For starters, Paul says that we should practice complete humility and gentleness in our relations with fellow believers. So the starting point of my life with you is complete humility and gentleness on my side of the relationship. Is that possible? Really? How can a proud cowboy be humble at all, mounted there on his high horse with gemstones in the tack and spiked spurs dangerously decorating his heals, never mind live in *complete humility* (let's be realistic, Paul)?

How can the coal mine geologist examining the silent evidence of the rocks be completely gentle, having been weaned and nurtured on the law of tooth and claw? How can the business owner reviewing her monthly financial reports be either humble or gentle as she weights all her options? Well, it's not easy. In fact, it's not hard, either; it is simply impossible. On the other hand, it's entirely possible because the humanly impossible is totally possible with God (Luke 18:27).

Pray without ceasing and receive without measure.

Indeed, as Paul assures us, *we can do all things through Him who gives us strength* (Phil. 4:13).

There we have it: complete humility and gentleness in our relations with sometimes obstinate, frequently exasperating, or habitually uncooperative members of the body are ours in Christ. There is a price: our proud and aggressive attitudes (we can't have it both ways). Just give them over to the Lord of your life, and He will throw them into the ocean where the water is the deepest—and that's a long way gone (Mic. 7:19). This has to be the daily routine with each of us believers: commit our lives to God in the morning (or whenever we wake up) and allow Him complete control during every waking moment. No other course will generate humility or support gentleness.

Paul goes on to assure us that believers are patient; they bear with one another in love. Is he telling us something that we should have noticed before? That in this new life of belief in Jesus, patience and love are natural outcomes (and that they are essential elements)? Is he telling us that bearing one another's burdens, fulfilling the law of Christ (Gal. 6:2), is the way of the new life? I believe he is. This is not to say that the former way of pride and hostility is not going to raise its lubricious head ever again. It will, given the slightest inducement or provocation, but in Christ the old nature can be crucified with its passions and lusts each time it tries to assert itself (Gal. 5:24).

Fellow believers who irritate us, strain our patience, and prompt the rising of the old nature, the *self*, just might be carrying burdens of which we know nothing. They could be reacting to hidden pain and not to anything we have done, said, or thought. Our role as members of this wonderful body is to look to our own relationship with the Head of the body and acknowledge that our responses to perceived provocations must be personally owned. They cannot be laid on the shoulders of any other member—however ornery. Our role as believers and members of the body is to carry the burden of the member who is struggling to bear up under pains we cannot feel. We do this in prayer; we do it in kindly responses to abuse; we do it by showing (and saying) that we care.

When we give time to people overwhelmed by the burdens of life, we are, in fact, giving up portions of our own lives for our sisters and brothers. Jesus said, *There is no greater love* (John 15:13). And let's not be smug. Even the healthiest, most well-balanced and articulated of us will, sooner than later, be in a position to appreciate the time, compassion, and help of the body. Given our ongoing humanity, it's inevitable. But have no fear. Nothing can happen to us without the consent of our Father in heaven. He sees each sparrow fall (Matt. 10:29, 31); He numbers our hairs and values us more highly than the sparrows (Luke 12:7). Thank you, Paul, for communicating our Lord's unmixed assurance to us moderns! As we move on through Paul's Ephesians, we will see again that what God requires of us believers in the way of sanctified living, He also provides.

Peace Bond—There is a type of peace in the body of Christ that is entirely of divine origin. You can compare it to a bond posted, the purpose of which is to ensure ongoing unity of the Spirit in the body. God produced the unity through the reconciling death of Jesus on the cross, and He communicates it to the body by the Holy Spirit. Every believer *has* the peace of Jesus (John 14:27). However, some of us don't know it, and Paul is trying to remedy that deficiency.

But having the peace of Jesus and the unity of the Spirit, essential as they are to body health and vitality, does not automatically make peaceful relationships or unify the body. We believers have a heavy responsibility to see that the unity is not compromised. So, how do we do it? Is there a process that we can follow to promote the unity that we already have in Christ?

In my secular college, we made concerted efforts to maintain an outward semblance of unity; we produced manuals and guidelines for conflict resolution (and followed them) and defined harassment in all its guises. The collective agreement was an important document in guiding management-staff-instructor relationships (say what you will about labor unions, a well-crafted collective agreement goes far in defining the basis for peace in the college or in the factory). At the management table, we had an unwritten code of conduct by which we spoke civilly even when sorely provoked. Business happened; decisions were made; and we went from the table to delegate.

Is it unchristian to observe mutually agreed rules of conduct in the various activities of the body? As an employer the body has an obligation to treat workers with respect, to pay an honest wage, and to clearly define the terms of engagement. A worker for the body has a corresponding obligation to give honest work for the pay received. In the body of Christ, we are at a huge advantage that is too frequently unappreciated. Christ has already removed the barriers between the members and has created unity in the body. We have unity!

The Holy Spirit communicates this unity to the body and to each member, yet to keep it in the bond of peace *requires total commitment and unrelenting effort on the part of the members of the body* (Eph. 4:3–5). Why? Simply because the devil has total commitment to unrelenting effort to disrupt the peace and destroy our unity, and he does this in the most basic of ways: he steals our time—time that we might have used to rekindle our devotion to God in the morning; he injects opportunities to gossip when we should be praying; he ambushes us with the most attractive seductions that leave us unprepared when we are T-boned at the intersections of life.

Our total commitment and unrelenting effort means that the guard is *always* in place; it means that the keys to the citadel of our souls are in *our* possession; it means that the pleas of the best of friends might have to be rejected. And all this means that we will have to choose to spend much quality time with Christ in Bible study, prayer, and sharing. If we don't, the guards will fall asleep, the keys will be lost, and the pleas of friends will be overpowering. The peace bond is posted by Christ for every member of this body. In Christ there is peace. His peace is our peace, and we receive it through the Word, which we must study, live, and share—unrelentingly. Interesting, isn't it, that our eternity is so directly related to how we spend our few moments in this world.

One Body; Only One; Love It!—In this life we have only one physical body. From birth to death, this body is ours to nurture, develop, maintain, and cherish as a gift of our Creator. How we care for it with sufficient sleep, appropriate exercise, deep-breathed fresh air, good posture, water in and out, sunlight, and mind control largely determines its health and our happiness during our few moments in this world. Just so, there is but one spiritual body given to us by Jesus Christ. As its Head, He watches for danger signals, prompts our responses to the things life brings on us, and directs us in the details. Thankfully, He has also given us a user's manual containing everything we need to take us safely through the minefields of the world.

These minefields, frequently attractively camouflaged and enticingly promoted, are designed to lure us away from the body of Christ. Appealing to our independent spirits, to our be-in-charge inclinations, to our well-honed tendencies to always be right, to our low-level desire to take it easy, and, let's admit it, to the compulsion to smack you on the nose, metaphorically at least, when your stupid ideas are preferred to my smart ideas, these minefields can explode a church business meeting in a hurry and cripple the body of Christ.

Last June, I drove my aging body through a grueling forty-five kilometer bicycle, foot, and canoe race. For seven hours and forty minutes we biked, slogged through bogs (frequently carrying our bicycles), and dealt with a 700 meter (2,100 foot) change in elevation. The first climb was a six-kilometer (3.6 miles) unrelenting, unforgiving, without-a-break uphill grunt. On top we encountered fearsome gullies and muskegs almost deep enough to swallow us. The downhill was as long, steep, and technical as the uphill section, and even more dangerous. We finished the race with eight kilometers (five miles) in a canoe battling a gusty side wind—with my body still intact, not the case with every racer. How stupid, you say? But did I go into the race straight from the rocking chair? Not a chance! The body needs to be physically ready, the mind mentally ready, for the ordeal—and that takes time and unrelenting hard work well in advance of the event.

From rocking-chair fantasies to the race? You gotta be dreamin'.

Just so, we can't go into the church business meeting (or the work place or the play place) without the necessary spiritual preparation and expect to come out with the body intact. As individual members of the body (the right arm, the toe, the appendix, the larynx), we can't encounter the temptations that surround us at work, at the grocery checkout, or on our personal entertainment devices, without that determined personal training in advance. How foolish and naïve to think we can meet the tempter in our own power! He will come, we can be sure of that, and his arsenal is loaded. But have no fear.

Our God will supply all our needs (Phil. 4:19) as individuals and as the body, but He won't compel us to accept His supply. He has provided the only source of spiritual victory; in fact, He has already won the war, and the victory is His already (1 Chron. 29:11, KJV). The victory is also ours to receive in the only way possible—through Christ, in Christ, the Head of this wonderful body (1 Cor. 15:57). In order to share in Christ's victory, our faith must be grounded in Him (1 John 5:4).

There is only one body just as there is only one Spirit. When Jesus was preparing His disciples (the body) for His return to glory, He gave them the promise of the Spirit (John 16:7). Two thousand years later the promise still holds. The Holy Spirit is still here, still working to shape us into a body that will *be for the praise of Christ's glory* (Eph. 1:12).

For bedtime reading I am currently perusing Cannon's *History of Christianity in the Middle Ages*. It's not a consistently pretty picture—hardly pretty at all. The body that Christ had left on earth to praise Him and bring glory to Him by its unity, peace, and love soon blew itself apart. It fell away and all but destroyed itself in its greed for stuff and power. Consider the political mayhem going around this troubled planet today. The party in power scarcely finishes metaphorically (or otherwise) shooting its leader and the official opposition does the same thing. Politics is imploding at every level; governments are in disarray—but that's politics (happily, as a mayor, I can stay out of politics—so I tell Mirja, but she laughs at the notion. Does she know something I have overlooked?). Should we expect anything else? Not really. But should we expect a different outcome for the body of Christ under the gentle, guiding influence of only one Spirit? Absolutely we should! And the outcome will be different.

Christ will present to Himself "a radiant church, without stain or wrinkle or any other blemish, but [a church] holy and blameless" (Eph. 5:27). That looks like a promise to me, and I know our Father is a promise keeper! The body will survive and, in glory, it will thrive because it *is* the body of Christ, and He is eternal, all-powerful, and fully able. But will you and I still be parts of the body, joined to the Head, in eternity? That is not a given although, never forget it, we do have assurance of eternal connection to the Head. Between John 15:4 and 15:10, Jesus uses the phrase "remain in Me," "if you remain in Me," or "you will remain in [Me]" five times, implicitly indicating that the choice to remain connected is mine—and yours. In fact, Jesus is emphatic that He *will* remain in us if we remain in Him (John 15:4).

It's His promise to every believer, and a God promise is irrevocable. How could we go wrong? How could we lose the way? How could we throw it all away? Jesus even tells us in plain language how to remain in Him: obey His command (John 15:10). And His command is as plain as it can get: "love each other as I have loved you" (John 15:12). Impossible as it is for me to love anyone who is not loveable, He also does the divine act by pouring that love into my soul. I don't even have to want His love. I just have to ask, and it will be given to me (Matt. 7:7, 8).

One Spirit; Only One; Listen to Him!—There are many spirits. Some come in the night; some come in bottles; some are sought in the murky shadows of the necromancer's hideout. But there is only one Spirit. He was given to us by Jesus Christ to be with us along the way. He is the Spirit of God, our guide into all truth as we study the Scriptures (John 16:13). He never speaks in contradiction to the Written Word, so if we neglect the Word, we have no other way to distinguish between the Spirit and the spirits. The Spirit and the Word work in tandem, always in total agreement and cooperation. We find the Spirit in the Word, and the Word is interpreted and applied by the Spirit.

The spirits are persistent demons; they apparently never give up. We infer that they are perpetually hungry (1 Peter 5:8), always prowling, always on the lookout for some indifferent, negligent, or inattentive soul to devour. Personally, I see no good reason to let anything feed on me—not a bear, not a cougar, not a timber wolf (there's nothing else in my world that could do it unless I am already carrion, and I don't much care whether it's worms or ravens at that point); that's why I go prepared. The same principle applies in our spiritual comings and goings. Go prepared!

Our God, through His Spirit, is a total bodyguard—no other is necessary; He will never leave us (Deut. 31:6; Matt. 28:20). The Sword of His Spirit, the Word of God, is ours to swing. We should practice with it often and learn to use it with finesse and skill (2 Tim. 2:15). We should hone it daily and keep it shiny. The Sword must be always available; the only place of ready availability is the mind! One text says it so clearly: "I have hidden your word in my heart that I might not sin against you" (Ps. 119:11). The hiding of the Word in the mind is absolutely crucial to our eternal destiny. Interesting, isn't it, how the time we spend on other things is not available for honing or practicing the Sword of the Spirit.

One Hope; Only One; Cherish It!—We were called to one hope and this is it: there is one Lord, and He is faithful (Isa. 49:7; 1 Cor. 1:9); you and I are not faithful—just check back a few minutes to confirm this fact. There is one faith as old as time. It was received most memorably by Abraham and transmitted to his descendants as Paul says: "The promise comes by faith, so that it may be by grace and may be guaranteed to all Abraham's offspring—not only to those that are of the law but also to those who have the faith of Abraham" (Rom. 4:16).

Paul also teaches us that the faith that saves is a very definite truth that comes from God, our Father, and is not some work, emotion, or feeling generated in our human egos (Rom. 3:21; Gal. 3:23). *The faith* is the gospel of our salvation. It is unmixed with tradition or fable or any other contaminant; there is no other faith or gospel! To receive *the faith* is to receive the promised Holy Spirit, the seal or mark of our salvation (Eph. 1:13). Imagine! Marked for salvation! Sealed for eternity! The only one who can break this seal and erase the mark is the one who has it. Why would I do it? Why would you do it? Why would anyone do it? It just doesn't make sense. It would be like jumping back into the ocean after the lifeboat crew has plucked you out. It would be like throwing yourself back in front of the train after being pulled to safety. Why would you do it? Why would I do it? It makes no sense.

Through the baptism commanded by Jesus (Matt. 28:19), we receive or express or confirm the faith of Jesus. Those who receive this baptism are submitting knowingly and voluntarily to death to sin, to burial, and to resurrection to the new life in Jesus (Rom. 6:4). The new life is a life of total reliance on Jesus for forgiveness of sin and for the ultimate victory over sin. What a marvelous idea! Jesus does it all! I simply submit to what He has done, is doing, and will do!

So we see that this one hope to which we are called is not of the hope-so-maybe-some-day-if-I-make-it variety. Unlike the guarantees with which so many of us have been disappointed, God's guarantee is rock solid, unmovable, sure, eternal, because God is eternal and faithful and won't let us be tempted beyond what we can stand; He will always make for us a way of escape (1 Cor. 10:13). Truly, God is faithful; He "makes both us and you stand firm in Christ" (2 Cor. 1:18, 21). What more can we ask for? What more do we need? The answer, of course, is this: we need nothing more; we could use nothing more. Peter, in full agreement with Paul, tells us, *Our gracious Father has given us everything we need for life and godliness in Christ so that we may participate in the divine nature and escape the corruption in the world caused by evil desires* (2 Peter 1:3, 4).

One God, One Father; Only One; Love Him!—In a congregation that enjoys and revels in the one hope by trusting in the one Lord, receiving the one faith, and expressing this faith through one baptism, the unity of the Spirit through the bond of peace is pervasive. The congregation will work in harmony, and that harmony will be evident in the community. Members, instead of talking about one another, will be talking to each other with the love of God in their souls or, as Paul so musically expresses it, *with psalms, hymns, and spiritual songs* (Eph. 5:19). Jesus will be honored in us. Like the ancient poet writes, *May the words I speak and the thoughts I entertain be pleasing to you, O LORD, my Rock and Redeemer* (Ps. 19:14). Let it happen now!

In the prayer that we know as the Lord's Prayer, Jesus begins with a small but significant word: our. In the English language, this word begins with an O. The O is a circle, and we can see it as a metaphor of the circle that our Father draws around us to take us in. There is only one Father who is *our* Father, and I think we would please Him much better if we also were actively inclusive as He is. Accepting new people (or old people) is not always automatic. It might require a focused effort on the part of the saints to bring the new person (or the old person) into the circle and make him or her feel genuinely welcome. Some people are not quick to intrude. They were not born holding out the right hand in greeting, or the circumstances of life may have left them hesitant and defensive. They need to be deliberately encouraged and encircled.

Wanting in.

When I was teaching school, there was a lad who desperately wanted to be within a circle of young men who were intent on excluding him. They didn't harass or bait him. They just didn't see him; he wasn't their kind; he didn't possess the flair or the funds to finance the flair. He simply was ignored, left to forlornly shuffle about, craning his neck to see over their shoulders, vainly attempting to get noticed. They didn't notice that year or ever; their circle never opened to take him in. It happens too often.

If one God is the Father of us all, it can never be said that we have nothing in common. The most important common ground imaginable belongs to each of us. We are children of the eternal Father, citizens of the eternal kingdom, members of one eternal household, building blocks of one eternal holy temple. Each of us has a special place and special responsibility in the kingdom of God.

With this assurance, does it matter that you are rich, but I have few resources to scatter about? Does it matter that you are a connoisseur of art and music, but I am more at ease with the call of the wild? Does it matter that I have to get out on the road in my truck at 4:00 a.m. come snow, ice fog, or dust, and you get called out to palpitate the heart of a trauma victim? Does it matter that I am old, and you are just beginning your short stint at the game board of life? Does it matter that your skin is smooth, your hair thick and flowing, and I am wrinkled and bald? Not at all! None of these things matters in the great plan of our Father, God. We have in common the only important thing: we know Christ and the power of His resurrection and the fellowship of sharing in His sufferings, and we are becoming like Him in His death (Phil. 3:10).

Nothing else has any value in the great plan

and purpose of God to salvage His creation. Our best thoughts, our most earnest conversations, and our most alert moments have plenty of common ground for sharing good times together—and for supporting one another in the bad times that come to every congregation. There are countless points of interface where we can help each other along the way to the kingdom of glory. One Father, no matter our circumstances, is over all, through all, and in all by His Holy Spirit (Eph. 4:6). Our unity is in Him. Our peace is in Him. Our life is in Him. Our conversation is in Him.

Christmas Every Day—Our human natures love to receive gifts. When I was a child, purchased gifts were few and far between. One particularly memorable incident involved the hoped-for ball. Mom had gone to town for a few days, and we boys knew that she planned to bring us kids a ball. When the wagon rattled up to the house on her return, we galloped into the yard to shouts of "The ball, the ball!" But there was no ball. Our disappointment was keen. I can still feel it. (Either there were no balls in the little Saskatchewan country town or Mom had run out of money before she found them.) The disappointment was somewhat assuaged by the new jack knives she brought—every country boy needed a jack knife.

But in Christ there is no lack for anyone in Him. There is no substitution or disappointment. He has given grace to each one of us, and His grace is more than sufficient; call it abundant, freely given, even lavished on us (Rom. 5:17; Eph. 1:6–8). *This is why it says in the Psalms: When He ascended on high, He led captives in his train and gave gifts to men* (Eph. 4:8). In Ephesians Paul adapts Old Testament poetry (Ps. 68:18) to New Testament circumstances, switching it about so that the Captor gives gifts to the captives—just like Jesus, hey? He also establishes the authority of the One who gives the gifts by stressing the fact that He came to earth as a human baby and, when His work on earth was finished, ascended to heaven—which He did in full view of the believers. This authenticated in one final, culminating, jaw-droppingly awesome act His authority over everything and everyone. Angels of glory received Him out of their sight (Acts 1:9) as He returned to glory to "fill the whole universe" (Eph. 4:9).

This same Jesus will return when the time is right, and if we've followed Him here, we'll follow Him to glory to receive one of those magnificent gift homes He's already prepared for each one of us (John 14:1–3; Acts 1:11)! He just can't stop giving gifts! What a living hope! Heirs of the kingdom, let's spread the word to every power engineer, every rancher, every lumber grader, every high school student, every retired dude hanging out for company at the *EatMuchEatMore*, and to anyone else who will stop rushing about long enough to listen! (I hope we enjoy the reality of a gift-giving Savior so much that people will stop rushing about long enough to demand a reason for our attitudes.)

Let's not lose the significance of Paul's words. The One who fills *the whole universe* has given us gifts. Wow! These gifts are not trinkets or baubles or trifling vanities by which to decorate a decadent body. They are not balls, knives, computer games, or smart telephones to entertain us until we are bored with them or lose them or trash them when the next version comes along.

These are *gifts of grace* for the purpose that Paul introduces in Ephesians 3:8. He tells us that we must use these gifts to share with our neighbors the magnificent, immeasurable riches of Christ. In fact, we have been given enabling gifts that empower every believer for service. They authorize believers to serve, authenticate their service, and, in fact, require believers to serve in the way the gift directs. Jesus Christ, Creator, and Redeemer, who is *over all, through all, and in all by His Holy Spirit* (Eph. 4:6), knows unerringly the gift that each one of us needs. And with the gift He also gives the ability to carry out His assignments.

Gifts of Grace—The first gift Jesus Christ gives is apostleship. Is apostleship first in importance or just first in line? Paul doesn't tell us. But in every lineup, someone or something has to be first. It's the nature of a lineup. Apostleship: the grace of being sent out into the hostile world to give an unpopular message to people who have not invited us into their space. Yes, that would take grace, a bundle of it. Are we ready to accept the lash, the stones, the hunger, the brigands, and finally, the axe for the sake of apostleship? Are we ready to embrace scorn and rejection? No. We are just too ready to shrink from *offending* someone by tentatively offering him or her life.

Paul, Peter, James, and the others put their bodies and lives on the line for the gospel. Of the original apostles, it seems that only John died naturally at a great old age after experiencing along the way some very cruel and unusual punishments for opening his mouth when people, society, and government, didn't want to hear. The lives of all the others were cruelly truncated. Hands up if you are volunteering to be an apostle. Hands up if, like Isaiah, you are saying, *Here I am, Lord, send me* (Isa. 6:8)—and send me now.

Although we haven't called people apostles since the original thirteen were commissioned, I think the gift may still go on. Apostles or not, ordinary people are still being sent on extraordinary missions to people who have not invited anyone into their space. They are not always welcomed. They don't always survive, but God is always glorified when they go, and He is glorified again when people are brought into His kingdom of grace.

On a smaller scale, I suppose that every time you interrupt your busy schedule to point a wanderer in the direction of grace, you are acting the role of the apostle. You are demonstrating the grace of apostleship, and you are, in fact, an apostle because that is what our God is sending us to do. Others are called to be prophets, an entirely different role, though an apostle may also be gifted with prophecy.[1] Paul tells us that prophecy is for believers (1 Cor. 14:22) and that believers should eagerly desire to receive the gift of prophecy (1 Cor. 14:1).

Does this tell me that the server in the local *EatMuchEatMore* could be gifted with prophetic insight and be one of God's called people to speak His message for these times, perhaps a message only for the ears of her clients or her own family or congregation? And what does this imply for the congregation? Should we be open to the expression of the gift of prophecy by our sons and daughters? After all, the prophets have said it would happen in the last days (Acts 2:17; Joel 2:28).

This is going to take some serious adjustment on our part. Not even graduated from high school, this young person could very well be connected to God in a special way! Are we ready to recognize and acknowledge that which God has said would be a feature of the last days? Are we

---

[1] We understand that prophecy is not restricted to foretelling future events, as it is more frequently expressed in communicating God's word to believers on subjects related to our spiritual maturing.

living in the last days or only the last days for me? Yes, to acknowledge the gift in the girl or boy will take some humility, some repentance, and some adjustment on my part. All are gifts of our Father in heaven—hallowed be His name in all the earth and let it start with me; let it start in my congregation; let it flood the earth as the water covers the sea (Isa. 11:9; Hab. 2:14)!

The evangelist has a role unlike that of the prophet, pastor, or teacher. His or her role is more like that of the apostle with the exception that in our time, the evangelist is usually called in, rather than sent out, with the primary role of augmenting the numbers of believers in an established congregation. The term is used only three times in all of the Scriptures. Paul and his companions en route to Jerusalem stayed at the home of Philip the evangelist in Caesarea (Acts 21:8), and Paul urges Timothy, probably in Ephesus, that among his numerous duties and hardships, he is to do the work of an evangelist (2 Tim. 4:5).

We acknowledge that the long-term success of the work of the evangelist depends on pastors and teachers doing their work and exercising their gift of grace. And what is their work? According to Paul in Ephesians, their work, with that of apostles, prophets, and evangelists, is to prepare God's people to serve His plan. Because pastors and teachers cannot help everyone, the long-term nurturing of new believers attracted to the gospel by evangelists and apostles depends on the faithful efforts of every member of the congregation, who are all under the wise spiritual guidance of their pastors and teachers. How can we be sure that the guidance of pastors and teachers is wise or spiritual? You just simply put the spirits to the test according to the Scriptures.

Many false prophets driven by evil spirits are lurking on the coffee table, on the TV screen, on the Internet, on the cell phone, and just about anywhere else you could name. They are committed, equipped, relentlessly vigilant, and determined to destroy you and me (1 John 4:1). We must be on guard, alert, relentlessly vigilant, and uncompromising. In fact, we must test everything by the Holy Bible and hold on only to the good (1 Thess. 5:21). God has given these marvelous gifts to the church: apostles, prophets, evangelists, pastors, and teachers. However, the final responsibility for our doctrine comes back to each of us. The responsibility for our behavior rests with each of us. Blaming the pastor and teacher for personal failure or congregational dysfunction will not fly in the judgment. The only defense that will work is a deep-rooted trust in Jesus for salvation, for renewal, and for present overcoming.

I (and You): Fully and Personally Responsible?— Well, if the responsibility finally rests with me, if I can't blame the pastor or the deacon or the music coordinator, why have all the titles? Why not run a simple, one-person show, deal with God directly and individually, and escape all the tension generated by a congregation of rugged individualists? Yes, there is tension in a congregation of believers, but it is only because we are all still growing as individuals and as a congregation. The more we grow, shift about, explore options, and test the spirits, the more we will need to be patient and understanding with our fellow travelers. We don't grow at the same rate. If your perspective enlarges ahead of mine, it could make me uncomfortable, perhaps even rouse my suspicions; it could aggravate your tendency to impatience. The old nature, the self, could rise up in anger at being disturbed.

Paul warned Timothy to endure hardships and to keep his head in all situations (2 Tim. 2:3; 4:5).

Hardest to bear by far are the hardships generated within the congregation. I don't stay awake at night over a problem in the city council. In city council tax rates are set and bylaws are adopted; problems come and problems go. But a problem or hardship in the congregation has much more potential for causing angst. I hasten to add, however, that a problem or hardship in the congregation also carries infinitely more potential for bringing glory to God than any issue that could rise in city council.

But back to our question: why all the titles? A title should describe a function; it should be a brief job description. The titles simply express the functions and name the gifts God has generously and graciously given to the church. All gifts, received together, work for the building up of the body of Christ. Only a harmoniously functioning, well-coordinated body gives full glory to the One who made the body and is its Head. The little finger might be perfectly formed and beautifully manicured, but in order to function, it must be attached to the hand in the proper place with all ligaments, blood vessels, and nerves connected and with skin covering to protect it from external hazards. Likewise, the hand needs full connection to the wrist, and so on. My friend discovered this basic truth when his little finger made an unplanned contact with a table saw blade. He didn't even feel it go—not even a stump remains. There is only a scar to show where the finger was once connected. Do I really need to explain that it no longer functions as a finger?

A Practical God—Paul tells us that *God's gifts are practical. They are not for decoration of the receiver but are to be used [wisely, joyfully,] vigorously, [even relentlessly] to prepare God's people to serve according to God's plan* (Eph. 4:12). God receives glory and honor when believers work together in harmony. Apostles, prophets, evangelists, pastors, and teachers are commissioned, authorized, and even commanded to teach believers how to live in harmony and to demonstrate this harmony (Rom. 12:18).

God is honored when believers correctly handle the Holy Scriptures. These gifted workers are commissioned, empowered, and commanded to teach, encourage, and require sound doctrine in the congregation (2 Tim. 2:15). In his pastoral letters, Paul expressed profound concern for the teaching of sound doctrine (Titus 1:9; 1 Tim. 4:16). God is honored when believers have a proper relationship with the resources at their disposal. These gifted workers should demonstrate an appropriate relationship to all the resources at the disposal of the members of the body (Matt. 6:33, 34).

In the local congregation, the pastor and teacher (in Paul's Ephesians apparently these gifts are settled on one individual) has the close, day-by-day contact and responsibility for the care, feeding, and leading of the congregation. This gift must carry with it not only the ability to lead, speak, understand, sympathize, discipline, teach, and oversee but also the ability to absorb enormous punishment. The apostle is sent out and moves on; the prophet speaks and the people listen—sometimes; the evangelist is called in to do a job and he or she moves on. But the pastor and teacher is here for the long haul. There is no escaping the daily grind of dealing with people in all their varied circumstances, from pride and bigotry to pain in loss and joy of new beginnings.

Preparing God's people to serve according to God's good plan is not a job for sissies, and it's not a job for the self-reliant. It's a calling that requires total, unrelenting reliance on God. If God is not in the details, the devil certainly will be there.

Wherever two or more come together in God's name, He will meet with them (Matt. 18:20). When God's name is forgotten in haste or weariness or pride or personal ambition, the devil is right ready to take His place and steer the congregation into swamps where we are kept so busy fighting alligators or slapping mosquitoes that we have no time or inclination to remember the reason we came together in the first place.

Pastors and teachers who trust totally in God, who are trained in leadership, who take time daily to connect solidly with our Father—these are the people we need to train us in works of service. They are the equivalent of the disciplined physical trainer. They refuse to coddle us; they lay out the exercise regimen and the diet, and they insist that we follow it. They tell us when we are slacking, when we are walking on mush, and when we are on solid footing.

Discipline—Our annual adventure race draws out dozens of young people every spring. They can be seen peddling their mountain bikes up and down steep trails, as they push themselves to the limit of physical, mental, and mechanical endurance. They are intent on building up the physical body so that it will carry them over the mountain on the great day of the race. As an old man, I don't go at it with the same abandon. I am content to complete the race before dark. Still, I have to build up my body. I have to be disciplined. I have to listen to the advice of the experienced. It takes a lot of grunt work, a lot of sweating, and a lot of pain.

Unity in the faith, God's goal for His church, the body of Christ, is not achieved by a snap of His fingers. It takes much grunt work, a lot of sweating, and a lot of pain. A few lines from a poem by Henry Wadsworth Longfellow come to mind: "The heights by great men reached and kept / Were not attained by sudden flight, / But they, while their companions slept, / Were toiling upward in the night."[2] That's why Paul advised Timothy to endure hardship "like a good soldier" (2 Tim. 2:3). Paul knew that work, sweat, and pain come before the race is over.

Unity and Maturity Only in Christ—Unity in the faith is not a cozy feeling engendered by singing in harmony around a sparkling campfire on a warm summer evening as the last rays of the setting sun illumine the smiles of happy campers. Unity in the faith is a common understanding of the truth that was demonstrated in Jesus. This kind of unity is the result of careful study of the Bible, countless prayers for the guiding of the Holy Spirit, and honest application of the truths we have learned. This is why pastors and teachers are so necessary. They have been down this road ahead of us. They have received an understanding of the faith. They are not willing to let us get away with a slipshod approach to Bible study. Like a bicycle coach who tells the truth about the results of lazy training and demonstrates (again) the proper techniques, the honest pastor and teacher will tell the truth about the results of lazy Bible study (and live the truth).

A related goal of our Father in heaven is unity in our understanding of the Son of God. Who is the Son of God? How does He work in our lives? We could write a formal statement in answer to these questions easier than we could live the experience. On the other hand, a living experience in the reality of the truth in Jesus is ours freely to receive. We don't need a graduate

---

[2] Henry Wadsworth Longfellow, "The Ladder of St. Augustine," *Birds of Passage. Flight the First* (1858).

degree in theology to experience Jesus Christ. We simply have to yield our ornery selves to His gracious will and experience the difference. Of course, interpretation of the experience must be subject to the Word of truth, the Holy Scriptures, and here the gifts of apostleship, prophecy, evangelism, and pastors and teachers come into play. Those who have these church-building-and-bonding gifts need to exercise them vigorously in order to bring the members to full unity in their understanding of the Son of God.

Who, then, is the Son of God? In human terms, He is God, the Lord, the Almighty, the One to whom we owe our existence, our redemption, and our eternal hope. As God, He is the Creator, the Originator, the Sustainer. As Lord, we owe Him total obedience. As the Almighty, He is able to do "immeasurably more than all we ask or imagine" (Eph. 3:20). When it comes to uniting and perfecting the body, His power will bring life to the dead in sin (Eph. 1:19, 20). Now that's a miracle, indeed!

As Paul wrote to Timothy, "Christ Jesus [is] our hope" (1 Tim. 1:1), and He is our hope in the most real and practical of the meanings of the word—Christ Jesus will take us through to the kingdom, and He will do it in style! Just follow Him in the details, and the big hurdles will scarcely be noticed. A congregation united in this experience and understanding of the Son of God will be a congregation with the power of the Spirit. It will be a congregation that affects the community for the glory of God.

Our Father will lead us to maturity in the faith and to an experience of the full measure of the totality of Christ—just follow Him without yielding to the distractions buzzing around us like black flies in an alpine meadow. In the final accounting, these distractions will have less meaning than the squalling of cats dueling in the night. How does a mature believer respond to the pains and pleasures of life? Simply put, they do not disturb his or her equilibrium. Praise or flattery does not incite to pride; personal abuse or pain does not lead to despair or uncontrolled anger. The mature-in-faith traveler, solidly rooted in Jesus Christ, will spurn the temptations of the world. Are you there yet? Well, probably not, and neither am I.

The fight of faith has to be our daily battle, remembering that our Father, by His Spirit, is taking us through this world to His kingdom! He is our guide, our coach, our supplier, our comforter, and our trainer! *He will keep you strong to the end, so that you will be blameless on the day of our Lord Jesus Christ. God, who has called you into fellowship with Jesus Christ, is faithful* (1 Cor. 1:8, 9).

Again to the Corinthians Paul communicates the assurance of our Father: "No temptation has overtaken you except what is common to mankind. And God is faithful; he will not let you be tempted beyond what you can bear. But when you are tempted, he will also provide a way out so that you can endure it" (1 Cor. 10:12, 13). How will a mature-in-the-faith Christian respond to temptation? He or she will get out of its territory fast and not look back (2 Tim. 2:22; 1 Cor. 6:18, 10:14).

Lot's wife became an example of tragically immature behavior. Jesus told us to remember her (Luke 17:32). I think she reluctantly and only partly believed the angels. I think in a sort of indistinct way she wanted to be saved from the threatened firestorm—if she could have Sodom, too. She certainly didn't want to burn, but she just couldn't shake Sodom from her system. She was not mature in her faith; she had not experienced the *totality* of Christ. Having neglected her salvation, having spent her time indulging the carnal nature to the exclusion of her daily time with God, having absorbed the values of her adopted city, she was in no position to obey with alacrity or sincerity. The bottom line with Mrs. Lot was that of unbelief and disobedience—as a habit, a way of life. Her unbelief and disobedience did not start on that salty, fiery morning halfway to salvation! But halfway there wasn't good enough for Mrs. Lot, and halfway won't work for us as the final firestorm approaches.

But let's not go on about Lot's wife and her salty, tragic ending. *The gracious gifts of God will lead us to maturity in the faith [and to] the full measure of the totality of Christ* (Eph. 4:13). As maturing believers we will, step by sometimes-painful step, come to appreciate the values of our Father in heaven. As we come to appreciate His values, we will more and more demonstrate those values in our lives. When temptation pokes us in the eye or slaps us on the ear (as it will), we will get out of its space fast; we won't stop to debate. I think that's what Paul meant when he told us to "flee the evil desires of youth" (2 Tim. 2:22)— and, incidentally, evil desires do not automatically die out in old age.

Not only must we flee from temptation, we must also pursue righteousness as well. One summer during the building-contractor phase of my life, I had a couple of houses and several other projects on the way. I also had a crew and did not really want another worker, but there was a young man, an apprentice, who came around to the sites several times every day to ask for a job. I put him off several times every day until I was worn out with his dogged persistence. He became my best worker and a meticulous craftsman. The mature believer will pursue righteousness just as avidly. But how is this done?

Reject, repudiate, flee every evil desire of youth – and old age! Now!

Let's look at a sampling of ways in which we can pursue righteousness or, as Jesus said in the Sermon on the Mount, seek God's kingdom first. How about spending that daily time with the Holy Bible? How about talking with God even before you get out of bed? How about beginning (and maintaining) a Scripture memorizing program? And be realistic: start with one verse. How about testing everything by the Scriptures— and holding on to what is good (1 Thess. 5:21; 1 John 4:1)? How about making the Scriptures your most-read book? How about sharing as you learn? But most of all, spend that quality and quantity time with our Lord! I have discovered that, as I internalize more and more of the Holy Scriptures, I find it surfacing quietly during the day (and even running through my mind when I wake in the night). Thus, I am given frequent opportunities to refresh my memory and meditate on the grace of our Father.

Most of our resource roads, winding through the mountains and crisscrossing the plateaus here in the great north, are radio controlled. Truckers have to monitor the locations of other vehicles in order to stop in the pullouts to allow them to pass safely. Even here there is opportunity to have

Scripture running softly in the background—provided we already have Scripture embedded in the mind. I dare to say that my dental hygienist could do the same while digging around between my teeth, which would prevent him from asking those entertaining questions I am in no mood to answer. Yes, and the same goes for the taxi driver, lumber grader, house cleaner, clerk, or caddy. I submit that most of us could make much better use of our available moments to connect with God, our Father, and reaffirm our special relationship with Him.

Pursuit of righteousness will lead us through fields of labor and forests of uncertainty. I remember that Jesus spoke of sheep and goats in a scene depicting the final separation of the righteous and the unrighteous (Matt. 25:31–46). The rewards of the sheep and the goats depended on their responses to everyday situations of normal life. The righteous used their time and resources to serve the needs of the hungry, the sick, the prisoners, the unemployed, the foreigners, and the outcasts from God. The goats did not do this, though they shared the same pews, were exposed to the same sermons, saw the same needs, and received the same blessings. They went home to skip in their pastures and smile in God's sunshine—or maybe to doze away the afternoon—without acting on the reasons God called them to service. And, interestingly, neither the sheep nor the goats were aware of the good they did or failed to do for the least of God's children (Matt. 25:40, 45).

And the uncertainty? It seems that there are always multiple options (or no apparent option) for the plethora of challenges a congregation faces daily—and at the meetings of the board. But maybe there is. One answer does fit all. Seek first God's kingdom and His righteousness, and He will graciously supply the answers. Our role is to go forward in the light that we have. When I come out of a meeting into the dark of the night and turn on my truck lights, I sometimes amuse myself with this thought, "These lights illuminate only about 100 meters. At thirty kilometers from home on the dark and winding road, I'll have to sit here until daylight." But then I overrule the temptation, ease my truck into gear, and move out following the light. Funnily enough, the light always moves on ahead of me—a silly illustration of how our Father leads us.

The full measure of the totality of Christ? Thankfully, God does not measure like we do. He richly measures out the totality of everything we need for this life and eternity, and He has given everything to us. Clearly, God's measures are infinite; the totality of Christ is infinite. When He fills us, we are full. There is nothing more that we need.

We might not recognize that we are mature-in-the-faith believers. We might be unaware of the kinks in our characters that need the heat of God's forge and the straightening blows on His anvil. That's OK. Our Father will make us aware; He'll apply the heat and pressure in the right way, at the right time, and comfort us in our pain. Even His blows are part of the totality of Christ! So be assured, the *totality* of Christ includes the pain as well as the pleasure that are ours in serving Him and learning to be like Him. It includes victories gained and failures acknowledged and forgiven. Actually, it means total trust in Him through all the experiences of this life and a joyful anticipation of glory.

The mature-in-the-faith believer will not question God when the way is rough. He or she will not gloat when the way is easy. In joy or in sorrow, he or she will give thanks; in prosperity or in poverty thankfulness to God will overflow. Paul said it this way: "Give thanks in all circumstances; for this is God's will for you" (1 Thess. 5:18). The in-everything-for-everything distinction for giving thanks is crucial. We are to thank God through the pain, the bankruptcy, the alienation, the abandonment, as well as the happy times. He deserves our gratitude when things start and when they draw down to the final breath. God is sovereign; He is love, patience, mercy, grace, goodness, and truth. The mature-in-the-faith believers have learned this lesson and are able to rejoice in that assurance, and it is their desire (and mine and hopefully yours) that we all reach this level of maturity in Christ.

Blowing in the Wind!—There is a lot of stuff going on out there that can lead the unwary down the slippery incline to the abyss. How can I recognize it? Some seem to think that they have to read every blog on the Internet, listen to all the quacks, and subscribe to the much-too-numerous online newsletters just to be aware of all the dangers lurking in the shadowy recesses of this world. I submit that we do not need to know every quirky idea of holiness or the precise hour when the mark of the beast will be affixed. I also think that searching out all the confused ideas purporting to give us the latest insights is a profitless, time-eating activity that leaves us not any wiser and a lot more confused at the end of the day. If we want to be able to recognize error, we have only to be immersed in truth.

If we know the truth, anything that differs from truth must be error, heresy, or worse. Leave it alone! Didn't Jesus promise that the truth would set us free (John 8:31–33)? He did, and He cannot lie. I know that God's freedom includes freedom from all the strange and wordy misinterpretations of the Scriptures promoted by the countless self-appointed gurus, advisors, back-woods teachers, and others more interested in my bank account than in my soul's salvation. The mature-in-faith believer is happy and contented to know the real truth and walk in His light. Let's treasure the gifts of grace that will lead us to this maturity.

Spiritual maturity is more an act of the will than a passage of time. Time's passing is of no value unless we fill it with solid choices based on truth. My decision to put my trust in God and rely on the gifts He has given will connect me to the only solid anchor available against the waves and winds of false teachings or any other distractions. While time is important for spiritual growing, maturity also hinges on the daily choice to walk with Jesus Christ in His light. After all, light is for walking (1 John 1:7). Consequently, reaching God's goal for us is a daily matter of choosing Him rather than acquiring a body of knowledge. Remember this: whatever our level of maturity, God will not allow us to face temptations that He will not also equip us to escape (1 Cor. 10:13).

Our children have a MacGregor sailboat moored on the Peace Arm of Williston Lake. The Peace Arm cuts directly through the Northern Rockies and is subject to frequent expressions of natural energy. We occasionally ship out with them for a few days of sailing where we might encounter no other boats for 100 miles. We are alone to enjoy the ragged peaks, glacier-fed streams, and rare anchorages with crystal clear water. The hundreds of miles of shoreline are steep with few places suitable for a mooring. On one of our excursions we sailed north on a fiord that cut narrowly into the mountain cliffs on the south side of the lake. The wind was light in the fiord. The sun was shining, and the sailing was lovely.

However, as we approached the main channel, we could see a distinctly different weather pattern at work on the water. A gale was blowing from the west, and the waves were running high. We had been sailing without ballast, and our ship was too light to master the waves soon tossing us about. Without further delay we opened the valves and filled our ballast tanks. The change was comforting. The immediate threat of being laid over with our mast in the water no longer received first attention as we angled across the churning sea to the safety of the marina. Just so, the truth and Spirit of Jesus Christ, internalized, gives us the ballast of spiritual maturity that we need to keep our masts pointing to the sky as we steer for safe harbor over the churning uncertainty of life.

We have God's promise that cunning and crafty deceivers will not break our solid connection with Christ. Absolutely true. However, the solidity of our connection is ours to maintain. And how? We must experience a daily renewing of the mind in Christ by prayer and study of His word. We must recommit to Him daily and follow through with obedience to His revealed will. Jesus referred to this as remaining in the vine—with its certain assurance that fruit will grow and, in due time, ripen (John 15:1–17). Paul counsels us through the Romans: *Do not conform any longer to the pattern of this world, but be transformed by the renewing of your mind.* Then *you will be able to test and approve that which is God's good and perfect will* (Rom. 12:2).

If we know and live God's will, we will be empowered to speak the truth in Christ's love. This will be a powerfully drawing influence on those who hear us, and it will be a powerfully uniting influence on the body of Christ, the church.

Grow Up (in Christ)—A body that is properly nourished, exercised, cleaned, oxygenated, watered, and sunned *will* grow (presupposing, of course, a body that is loved and cherished). We are familiar with the experience of infants in orphanages where the staff is overwhelmed with work and physically incapable of giving the children the love that is so essential to physical health and survival. In spite of a clean environment and adequate food, many of these infants fail to thrive or even to survive.

As mature-in-Christ members of the body who are connected to the Vine, we will continue to grow in Him. Could it be, though, that continued growth of a mature member is somehow linked to the member's taking responsibility for the nurture of the babes? While the *spiritual infants* need the nurture of spiritual cooing and cuddling for spiritual growth, the mature could also lose out on essential growth opportunities if they fail to give the nurture required by those in need.

Paul notes that believers, the body of Christ, are held together by the supporting ligaments of love and truth. Like infants, we need this love to keep us growing. Love and truth hold us together. I think of members of the congregation with whom I have worked and prayed for forty years. They are very dear to me. This is so in spite of the fact that for at least twenty of those years I was lost in the barrens "without hope and without God" (Eph. 2:12). "But now in Christ Jesus [I] who once [was] far away have been brought near by the blood of Christ" (Eph. 2:13).

Blessed are the human ties that bind, yet the supporting ligaments of love and truth are superhuman. They come down from the Father of light (James 1:17, KJV). He does not change, and we can depend on Him to keep us well supplied with love and truth. One caveat: we cannot receive unless we function as pipes rather than as sinks. That which we receive must be passed on to others; that is the reason for the body.

And this is the work assigned by Christ: love one another (John 13:34). Paul expands on the command of Jesus: *Let no debt remain outstanding, except the continuing debt to love one another, for whoever loves others has fulfilled the law* (Rom. 13:8). John assures us that we can know that we have passed from death to life when we love one another (1 John 3:14). And then he goes on to describe a very practical expression of love: help for those in need. This help requires the sharing of the material goods that have been entrusted to us by the Owner of all things as well as the sharing of the truth as Jesus has revealed it to us.

As we continually submit ourselves to God by carrying out His will in the congregation, *this whole body, of which we are members held together by the supporting ligaments of love and truth will continue to grow, being built up in love, as each part faithfully performs the work assigned by Christ* (Eph. 4:15, 16). Assigned by Christ? Jesus focused only on two commandments that encompass every other commandment: love God supremely and love your neighbor as you love yourself—that is, to the same degree and with the same unconditional care as you give yourself. "All the Laws and the Prophets hang on these two commandments" (Matt. 22:40). Everything else is commentary and application.

Living as Children of Light

Friends, listen to me, and listen well! This is serious. I have written at length about God's love, His grace, His mercy, and about how He has saved us. Now I am going to tell you how you will live when saved by God's grace. And I insist in the Lord that if you are truly committed to God, you will honor Him in your secret thoughts, your decisions, and your actions.

The lives and behavior of the Gentiles are futile, reflecting their hopeless way of thinking. You must not be like them. Their ignorance of God has separated them from Him and the light with which He would have illuminated their darkened understanding. In reality, their ignorance of God has separated them from life that can be had only in God, and their hearts have become hard. Insensitive to the Spirit of God and to common decency, they have sold themselves as votaries to sensuality and devotees of gross indulgence in every species of impurity. They lust for more but are never satisfied; itching, but unable to scratch, they would rather itch than not.[3]

He'd rather itch than not!

When you learned the truth as it is in Jesus Christ, great changes happened in your minds and hearts with the result that your former way of life passed into history. Having been taught the futility of your old way of life, and of your old nature, the self, you also were taught how to put it off so that you would not be corrupted by its deceitful desires. You were taught of the new mind and heart that is created in the believer. This new mind and heart is like God in purity and holy thinking that yields certain results in holy living.

---

[3] C. S. Lewis, *The Great Divorce* (CS Lewis Pte. Ltd, 1946).

Because this is so, there are changes that have to happen in your habits: you must no longer lie but speak the truth in all things to everyone—especially to the members of the body of Christ. You might get angry, but don't let anger be a cause to sin. Be sure your anger is put to bed while the sun is still shining. Never give the devil a foothold from which to launch his sly and vicious attacks on your soul. If you have been a thief, stop your thievery immediately and get a job with which to pay your own expenses and those of others who may be in need.

As for talk, watch your tongue. Don't let any unsavory speech come out of a mouth that was formed by the Creator. Fact is, all your speech must be such that it will build up the body of Christ of which you are a member—as well as benefit all those who hear you. In all your speech and behavior, consider the needs of others. God's Holy Spirit is gentle and loving; nevertheless, He can be grieved by thoughtless or irreverent actions. See that you do not grieve Him because through Him you are sealed for the promised redemption. If you are bitter or have been in the habit of flying into rages with uncontrolled anger, if you have been a brawler or a slanderer, get rid of all of it now. If you have harbored malice against anyone, get rid of it now. In the place where all this evil once ruled, set up kindness and compassion with forgiveness for everyone just as God has forgiven you. (Eph. 4:17–32)

Paul's a Tough Nut!—Paul is in no mood to mince his words as he transitions from theory to application in the Christian life. Based on a law that obviously still exists, Paul places some clear and definite limitations on our behavior. On the other hand, the new life (Rom. 6:4) taught by Paul is actually a result of the emancipation we experienced when we were set free by God's grace from the slavery of sin. As you know, Jesus defeated sin on the cross before any of us knew Him. It sort of comes as a surprise when we learn that God is looking for us, not we for Him; Jesus gave up His life for us even when we didn't know or care (Rom. 5:6–11). Rather than bemoaning our circumstances as restrictive, grinding us under an oppressive law that we cannot keep, we can now rejoice and be happy in our full freedom to obey. We need never encounter the real slave master again.

A brief statement in Exodus 20 reminds the wilderness campers that they are free people. Because it had been utterly impossible for the Israelites to have freed themselves from slavery, it was the LORD (the Lord Jesus Christ of the New Testament) who set them free: "I am the LORD your God, who brought you out of Egypt, out of the land of slavery" (Exod. 20:2). Then the LORD proceeds to tell them in thunder tones how He expects and empowers saved people to live. We know these thunder tones as the Ten Commandments—and they *are* commandments. The Ten Commandments were not abrogated at the cross as some people fondly and vainly believe. To the contrary and by God's grace, they are fully applicable to everyone in the sophisticated twenty-first century. Every believer commits by his or her belief in Jesus to live out the meaning of all ten of the laws in the details of life.

By "meaning," I refer to the commandments as magnified by Christ.[4] He graciously demonstrated that the commandments are to be expressed in the lives of the believers then and

---

[4] Isaiah speaks to us of God's magnifying the law and making it honorable (Isa. 42:21, KJV) or as the text is rendered in NIV: "It pleased the Lord for the sake of his righteousness to make his law great and glorious." Paul also asserts that the law and commandment is holy, righteous, and good (Rom. 7:12).

now. He showed us that God has done what He promised through Jeremiah (Jer. 31:33), and He has written His law on our minds and put it in our hearts (Heb. 10:15, 16). Thus, by God's grace alone (contrary to the popular misunderstanding that God does not expect or require obedience), believers in the twenty-first century are enabled and empowered to understand and obey the magnificently magnified laws and thereby bring glory to the Creator.

Paul's emphasis on creation as a completed event in history as well as on God as the Creator strikes a dagger deep into the heart of popular beliefs found in today's world. As a society we have bought into the myths of evolution from pond scum to people, from microbes to musicians, from flies to fly fishers. Many Christians attempt to reconcile unprovable dogmas, beliefs, and creeds of evolution with a somewhat-uncertain belief in God. We might as well try to wrap warm flesh and new life around the fossils of the dinosaurs. Jesus assured us that not the tiniest mark would be dropped from the Law[5] until everything embedded in His creative purpose was accomplished (Matt. 5:18; Luke 16:17). Embedded in the Law is the affirmation of the creative act of God. The foundational teaching of the Old Testament is Creation by an act of the sovereign God (Gen. 1:1; Exod. 20:11). This creative expression of God's grace in the beginning of time is affirmed by Jesus Christ and the apostles in the New Testament, and we cannot set it aside without jettisoning the foundations of our faith (1 Cor. 8:6; Col. 1:15–17; Rev. 4:11; John 1:1–5).

Honoring God through thoughts, decisions, and actions is rooted in obedience[6] to a God with the power to create and to recreate. This is the God of whom Paul writes—the One with the muscle to raise the dead (Eph. 1:19, 20). He can take me, dead in sin, and recreate me as a believer in Christ with new motives, new values, and new appreciations for my Creator. Just as evolutionary research cannot prove the rise of life from non-life, I cannot prove the Creator's existence, demonstrate in the laboratory the beginnings of this earth, or even comprehend His presence. But I can experience His power, majesty, love, and grace in my day-to-day life. I can *know* that He exists and that He is worthy of my worship and praise. This worship and praise is most clearly expressed in willing, happy obedience to His Law now written on my heart and in my mind.

Paul characterizes the lives and behavior of Gentiles as futile because they reflect their hopeless way of thinking. As travelers on this sod, we must be cautious in applying Paul's description of Gentiles to non-churched people in our society. There are countless self-professed unbelievers out there whose lives demonstrate integrity, compassion, fortitude, vision, and other virtues society professes to honor.

Paul, however, is seeing the bigger picture given to him by revelation. In this picture are those who reject the notion of any kind of god and especially have no regard for the God of creation or appreciation for the recreative act of

---

[5] The Law of which Jesus spoke at this time was the Pentateuch, the first five books of the Bible. He spoke also of the Prophets. Taken together, the Law and the Prophets constituted the entire Old Testament.

[6] In the day-to-day life, a sincere belief honestly held will lead to corresponding behavior. In reality, we can hold conflicting beliefs simultaneously with a resulting confusion in behavior. For this reason it is crucial that we examine our beliefs and discard those that are incompatible with Scripture (2 Cor. 13:5).

Jesus Christ. They profess to answer to no one, but they fail to recognize that by taking their position of independence, they have set themselves up as gods in the place of God. Others just have no time for God as they madly pursue gods of their own creation—money, fun, education, status, power, or chemically induced oblivion. This type includes a lot of people who call themselves Christian and actually believe they have a fighting chance to storm the pearly gates by trying (most of the time) to be good.

But let's take a closer look at Paul's statement: *the lives of the Gentiles reflect their hopeless way of thinking*. Most ancient Gentiles actually believed that they were controlled by fate and fortune and these concepts have come down to us who live in modern times. Society, in general, thinks in terms of fate and fortune and believes that there is only a faint hope, at the very best, for anything beyond this frequently brutal and always too short existence. Hence, there is a hurried and *futile* pursuit of every opportunity to eat well and feel good because the grave is dark and cold and a long time closed. While claiming and hoping to be Christian, if we think we have to sacrifice time with the Creator for job security or better grades, then, without fail, our lives ultimately will reflect the values we have chosen. It might not be obvious at first, but it is inevitable. Once on the downward slide, our danger might not even be noticeable to us.

Not too many years ago a young couple with their daughter attended our church for several months. They were involved and excited about their new experiences. Then something happened on the job, and they made a decision to trade their new faith experiences for job security. I see them from time to time and sense a coldness and indifference to the things they once were beginning to appreciate. Don't be fooled that as old believers we are immune to such pressures. We aren't. Neglect your salvation for a moment and the enemy will introduce you to something or someone to keep your attention longer—and longer, and longer still. We are clearly warned that we cannot escape while neglecting our salvation (Heb. 2:3).

In Paul's view the futility of life without God is not measured by the quality of life one might enjoy when rated by one's ability to stay warm, well-fed, mobile, and recognized. The futility of pursuing a life without God is measured by the certain result: dark oblivion for eternity. In a sense eternal oblivion begins in the present. Absorbed in getting and spending, we circumscribe ourselves by the stuff of the immediate and, burrowing into these mountains of junk, we lose sight of eternal horizons and ultimately lay waste our lives. These mountains express the hopelessness of our thinking. And really, it doesn't matter if we are rich or poor, the effect of choosing stuff as our god is always the same—futility.

Paul writes: *You must not be like [the Gentiles] in their hopeless way of thinking. Their willful ignorance of God has separated them from Him and the light with which He would have illuminated their darkened understanding* (Eph. 4:17, 18). In reality, they have separated themselves from the life that can be had only in God, and their hearts are now hard. The book of Hebrews links hardness of heart, that is, the inability to respond to the overtures of the Holy Spirit, with unbelief and disobedience (Heb. 3:12–4:6). Unbelief and disobedience grieve the Holy Spirit of God (Eph. 4:30), and persistence in unbelief and disobedience will result in inability to hear the call of the Spirit to repentance.

We are warned by Samuel that "rebellion is as the sin of witchcraft, and stubbornness is as iniquity and idolatry. Because you have rejected the word of the LORD, He also has rejected you from being king" (1 Sam. 15:23, NKJV). Saul's early rejection of God's command was not the unpardonable sin, though it cost him his job. Rejected as king, he still could have submitted to God's discipline and served as God's representative for the rest of his rule. But sadly, it was only the first step toward ultimate rejection of the appeals of God; it established his spiritual direction, which he followed ever further until his ultimate rejection of God at Endor (1 Sam. 28:7).

Paul gives us a more graphic description of the downward slide of human society in his letter to the Romans (Rom. 1:18–32). Because of their desire to deny the authority of God in their lives, ancient society refused to acknowledge the evidence of their senses that spoke eloquently of a Creator God. Because they insisted on having independence from God, He allowed them to experience the natural results of their rebellion: claiming *to be wise, they became fools and exchanged the glory of the immortal God for images made to look like mortal man and birds and animals and reptiles* (Rom. 1:22, 23). The result? Sexual perversion, inflamed lusts, depravity of mind, envy, murder, gossip, slander, arrogance, wickedness, evil, and greed—sounds like the evening news.

Our modern society has taken the slide even further toward the abyss. We are at the point now when to acknowledge God or even to question the questionable doctrines of Darwin puts one in jeopardy of losing a career or being denied the graduate degree for which he dreamed and worked. A really up-to-date example of the secular invasion of our lives is the rejection by provincial law societies of potential law school graduates from Trinity Western University in Langley, British Columbia, because the university promotes chastity, and marriage as the union of one man and one woman. Steeped in hubris, modern society is proud of its independence from God and is hell-bent for self-destruction. All this happens, yet we deplore the abuse of drugs, booze, and sex that gets us into so much personal trouble; we fear rampant wars brought on by our competing interests; we cringe at the specter of economic and social collapse resulting from our overweening greed. We don't recognize, or we refuse to acknowledge, the reason we are in trouble.

At a recent convention of municipal elected officials, I had an opportunity in a public forum to ask a very simple question of the government minister in charge of caring for children and youth. The topic was how to take better care of our vulnerable young people. Many woes were lamented and much money was deemed necessary. I suggested that hundreds of millions of dollars could be saved each year if we cared for the most vulnerable of our young people, the unborn, as we should—and as we could. The simple expedient of *not* inflicting countless thousands of unborn children with a life sentence of FASD[7] would save these lives for productivity and save the treasury untold millions of dollars each year. I also pointed out that we need not delay in providing an example of restraint for the young: would we forgo the alcohol to be served at the various receptions to be held that week and save the first $100,000? Did I get a standing ovation? Did I get the bum's rush? Their hearts were hard.

---

[7] Fetal Alcohol Spectrum Disorder: A lifetime disability of mental and physical functions caused by exposure in the womb to alcohol in the mother's blood. Prevented by the simple and obvious expedient of not drinking alcohol during pregnancy.

Heinrich Himmler, a contemporary of Dietrich Bonhoeffer, was born six years earlier than Dietrich to parents of comparable backgrounds to the Bonhoeffers. Speaking the same language, exposed the same books, playing similar games, immersed in the same culture, Heinrich became a criminal while Dietrich became a saint. Denying the Creator God, Heinrich gave his worship to a monster, becoming like him. His last significant act before his suicide ended an ugly career was to hang Dietrich. Today, Bonhoeffer's books are widely read all over the world by thousands of people who recognize the lasting and growing value of his legacy. We only read *about* Himmler, and the lesson we learn from him is the enormous potential for badness in the best of us. We must be aware of the inevitability of ruin for those who turn their backs on God.

C. S. Lewis, the prolific Christian apologist at Oxford in the middle years of the twentieth century, describes the result of persistent sin as the sinners' coming to the time that, though still itching, they cannot scratch. Their itch has become their only link with their past, and they would rather itch than not. What an awful end for those who reject God and grieve away His Holy Spirit, who became slaves to youthful lusts and flirt with compromise rather than fleeing while they still can run (2 Tim. 2:22).

Change Can Happen to the Best of Us—Let's not go down that road any further. We have already learned the truth as it is in Jesus Christ, and we are expecting great changes in our minds and hearts. These changes begin as we first yield to the working of the Spirit, and they continue as long as we keep open the divine connection. Though the old way of life is now history, it easily can rise up again when we least expect it. The old nature is devilish, sly, and watchful. Give it a moment of distraction, and it will be in your face with a current iteration of the old passions, likes, desires, and habits. Time to run (fast) back to safety with your Bodyguard! Some of the major changes that have happened in our hearts and minds are the ability to recognize extreme danger and the will to run for safety.

Putting Off and Putting On—We were taught the futility of our old way of life and of our old nature that we know as the self, and we also were taught how to put it off. So, how do we put off our old nature? There are positive and negative ways of dealing with the old way of life that lingers as long as we are on this earth—until this mortal puts on immortality and this corruption puts on incorruption (1 Cor. 15:52–54). Get used to the idea. Better yet, stay prepared, keep alert, and remain with your Bodyguard. There is no lion, however ravenous (1 Peter 5:8), that can challenge our Bodyguard.

We must fortify our minds with the truths of the Holy Scriptures as Ellen White so forcefully wrote (*Counsels on Sabbath School Work*, p. 19). And we know that fortifications are not erected in a moment of panic as the enemy approaches with guns roaring. In times of peace, we must hide the word of the Lord in our minds and in our hearts so that we do not sin against God (Ps. 119:11); furthermore, we have the sure promise of God that our lives will undergo a cleansing if we heed His word (Ps. 119:9).

Of course, creating a positive defense against "the wiles of the devil" (Eph. 6:11) takes a bit of planning followed by energetic action. Salvation is free, but there is an opportunity cost: the time spent in fortifying the mind and heart is not available for other pursuits however noble, benign, or pleasing they may be. While God has promised to write His law on our hearts and in our minds (Jer. 31:33), it enters through our eyes and ears. We have to spend quality and quantity time reading and hearing the Word if God's Holy Spirit is to impress its truth, value, significance, and power on our hearts and minds. Then by living God's Word and sharing it with others, we validate it in our own eyes and in the sight of our friends and neighbors.

In order to make our hearts capable of bearing the Word of God, we need to undermine the foundations of the old nature by removing all the familiar stimulants. It doesn't take much to get the old guy going, so we have to be ruthless in our search-and-destroy efforts. Reading and watching habits will have to be changed (they won't change themselves). Recently I read an Andrew McChesney article in which he describes his personal victory over a DVD obsession (his description). He said it right: God destroyed the earth because of violence (Gen. 6:13). Eventually McChesney threw out all his DVDs because of the violence, sexual implications, and vanity inherent in virtually all of them. "God is once again looking at this earth and saying, 'I am going to put an end to all people, for the earth is filled with violence because of them.' He calls you and me to come out of this violent world and not think of what we have left behind" ("My Obsession with DVDs," *Adventist Review*, March 17, 2011).

God also is jealous for the sanctity of His name, yet how can we be entertained by DVDs or TV without being party to someone's taking God's name in vain again and again? God will not hold us guiltless if we take His name in vain (Exod. 20:7). Even vicariously? One important step in putting away the violent and otherwise evil things of this world is to make a decision to put it all out of our sight and follow through on that decision with ruthless thoroughness. You easily could suggest other examples of how to remove the sights and sounds that stimulate the old nature. Anything less than a complete break with the old life will ultimately prove our undoing as we are corrupted by its deceitful desires.

The Scriptures tell us of *the new mind and heart that is like God in purity and holy thinking* (Eph. 4:24). This new self is maintained only by constant feeding on the truth as it is revealed in Jesus, as He is revealed in the Holy Scriptures. Embed passages from the Bible in your memory, and they will be there throughout the day. You will wake in the night with scriptures running in your mind; you will wake in the morning with first thoughts of the God who saved you by His grace; you will meet the trials and the pleasures of the day with the Holy Word. Satan will find no place to set his hooks; your own evil nature, not yet dead, will find no way to trip you up. But if you do trip, the Righteous One is there ready to defend you (1 John 2:1). Yes, God has created in us new minds and hearts. It's His doing, but He cannot force feed our new natures.

As far back as Joshua, we have been urged to make the right choices (Josh. 24:15). As far back as Eden, God gave us the option of choosing life or death. So make right choices today, and many times during the day. Every time the enemy brings a deceitful ploy before your eyes, reject it in the power of our God who is always there for us. He will not let us be tempted beyond our power to resist (1 Cor. 10:13). James goes so far as to say that we are blessed when we endure temptation (James 1:12). However, only in the full-spectrum light of Holy Scripture are we able to recognize temptation. The futility of our old

What you tryin' to sell me? This ain't no full-spectrum light.

way of life and the reason that we put it off can only be understood—and remembered—as we fortify our minds with the truths of the Word of God.

God has given us new minds and hearts. They are like His in purity and holy thinking that leads to holy living. That's where Paul goes now in his counsel for the church. Holy living, not haphazard or accidental, is rooted in the mind that is focused on Christ. But some old habits die hard, and some old habits don't seem so wrong to the newly purified mind.

Changes and More Changes—Paul gets more explicit now about the details of our lives, and he tells us quite baldly that there are changes that have to happen in our habits. His first directive points at our truthfulness: we must no longer lie. Lie? He's writing to *saints*, to people he has addressed as *faithful* in Christ. And he has to tell them to stop lying. Well, yes. It seems that Ephesus may have been a society that tolerated and even rewarded lying (like most societies in the twenty-first century). Cultural acceptance does not a virtue make. According to John's Revelation, liars are shut out of heaven along with murderers and fornicators (Rev. 21:8)—that's how important truth is to God. So these little things that seem so unimportant in the broader culture really are crucially important? Apparently—no, definitely! Truth must be told. Even if the culture has taught us to tolerate convenient, colorful, and even creative untruths, God wants us to see untruth as He sees it—a bar to heaven and a door to hell.

Next Paul addresses a habit that is just too familiar to too many of us in the church and out: anger. Who has not felt hot anger rising up, mindlessly urging us to strike, strangle, smash, thump, whack, thrust, punch, burn, destroy, shout, or withdraw? Paul seems to acknowledge that some anger may be appropriate, but clearly, he expects us to deal with our anger in ways that honor God. Anger that is allowed to contort our emotions and distort our words and actions, even if the cause is just, becomes sin. Some cultures in the twenty-first century let anger drive mob behavior that western culture, steeped in the drive to create a stable business climate, deems inappropriate. No doubt the memory of the great riot in Ephesus (Acts 19:28–35) was not too far from Paul's mind when he penned these lines, and maybe the Ephesians were prone to emotional outbursts leading to mob action. Given that the purpose of the church is to bring glory to God through righteous behavior, anger that leads to uncontrolled action or speech certainly dishonors God. Perhaps this is what Paul had in mind when he wrote to the Ephesians, *be sure your anger is put to bed while the sun is still shining* (Eph. 4:26).

From 3,000 years ago comes this potent reminder to control our anger: *In your anger do not sin; when you are on your beds, search your hearts and be silent ... trust in the LORD* (Ps. 4:4, 5, NKJV). When the indwelling Spirit of God controls our emotions, we don't overheat and require intervention of neighbors or police. If you let your anger be controlled by reason, faith, and the Spirit of God, most people will never know you were angry. Be cautious, however, when tempted to "righteous" anger. According to Paul, quoting several Old Testament statements, no one is righteous (Rom. 3:10). However, the Bible also describes many people as righteous. Can the Bible be divided against itself? No. There are many whom God has declared righteous and whom He is making righteous day by glorious day, but certainly none can claim to have inherent righteousness—or even to be righteous (1 John 1:10). So don't trust your anger too far; test it with honestly directed thought guided by the Holy Scriptures.

We all know that there are so many causes for anger even within the family of God, much of it hidden in family secrecy. These causes destroy families and bring pain and dishonor to our Father. Sadly, there is no question about that. Even if the cause is an elder in the church, a mother in Israel, or a rich financier of church projects, the church is obliged to deal with it as soon as it becomes known. Anger, appropriately expressed, at these outrageous denials of faith might be the closest approach to righteous anger that we will ever experience on this earth (and, I dare say, this is the only earth on which we could have cause for anger). Be sure to deal with it before the sun goes down—and know for sure that this earth's setting sun is sinking low.

Paul said, *Never give the devil a foothold from which to launch his vicious attacks on our souls* (Eph. 4:27). Now, Paul, that seems to be a no-brainer. But is it? If that is a no-brainer, then how come we leave so many grappling hooks lying around? How come we leave so many doors unlocked and unguarded? Mirja and I, when visiting the south of France, discovered that the successful attacks on so many of the fortified castles in the area resulted from careless or willful failures in defense rather than brute strength and clever strategy. The secret door was unguarded or the bridge was left open to the enemy. In too many homes we still see unguarded doors and open bridges, which are the things that the unregenerate nature loves. We still listen to the lyrics that suggest thoughts of illicit behavior. We still retain the DVDs that glorify violence, sex, greed, and dishonesty. Are these not opportunities for the devil to get a foothold in our souls? Are these not open invitations to temptation?

But about thievery—Paul, you can't be serious. We were not thieves even in our old lives. Of course, we didn't pay any more taxes than we were compelled to pay, and if we were not asked about a particular bank account, we didn't disclose any information. It was not our job to do the work of Canada Revenue Agency (or the IRS, or any other tax-collecting authority). And if we found a wallet full of money on the street, we turned it in to the proper agency hoping that the owner would get it back—and we probably didn't think of a reward. We were pretty honest about other people's money and stuff. But we must remember that we are being judged by the law as magnified by Jesus Christ.

Declining to mug the old lady in the dark doesn't brand us honest in God's eyes. He looks more at the way we disperse the wealth that He has permitted us to obtain. Some of us have the Midas touch—touch even a mouse dropping, and it turns to gold. God expects from us the anti-Midas distribution of these treasures. Some of us just get along fine. We are not rich, but we are not hungry either, and we take an occasional vacation. According to that which God has permitted us to touch, we are to give to those who need. To do less is to misappropriate funds and, even in this secular, grasping, money-laundering society, misappropriation of funds is not officially approved. Even the world calls it theft. So get a job, earn your keep, and have a bit of reserve to help someone in need—says the law of liberty.

But there's more. More? You bet.

Malachi was privy to some of the thoughts of God about the resources He puts under our management. Malachi 3:8 tells us all about it: *Will you rob God?* Of course not! That's unthinkable! It's not possible. *But you do.* We do? *By withholding your tithes and offerings you are robbing God of what is His.* So get a job, return your tithes and offerings, give generously as God has blessed you, and have a bit of reserve to help someone in need—says the law of liberty. And, in the meantime, be careful that you are not clouted on the head by those blessings tossed out from the windows of heaven (Mal. 3:10).

Now About That Lubricious Member in Your Mouth—Given half a chance, your tongue will run away without your mind, like the horse that has slipped its tether and is kicking up its heels— already creating a stir that will not be easy to fix. The Bible has a lot to say about careless, irreverent, and hurtful use of the tongue as well as of the praise and blessing of which the tongue is equally capable. Incongruous, though, is the use of the same mouth for both blessing and cursing. As the brother of Jesus taught us, this ought not to be (James 3:10). How can it be, and how does God feel about the evil that emits from the mouths of members of His body? The answer to that question is pretty clear from Paul's next statement: *Don't let any unsavory speech come out of a mouth that was formed by the Creator* (Eph. 4:29). Your mouth and mine were created to sing, shout, and whisper praise to its Creator and Redeemer and to bless and honor its fellow beings made in the image of God. So what is unsavory? Like flattery, for instance? Or gossip? Boasting, even?

Flattery is a subtle, or not so subtle, attempt to gain position or profit for one's self by hypocritically stroking the ego of another. Scripture associates flattery with gross evil: covetousness (1 Thess. 2:5), witchcraft (Ezek. 12:24), entrapment (Prov. 29:5), lying (Prov. 26:28; Ps. 78:36), gossip (Prov. 20:19), adultery (Prov. 7:21; 7:5; 2:16), and self-deception (Ps. 36:2). Yet so many body parts (of the body of Christ, that is) continually choose to indulge in this unsavory speech. "May the LORD cut off all flattering lips, and the tongue that speaks proud things" (Ps. 12:3, NKJV).

And how about gossip? Can a little gossip be so bad? We're just having a little fun. For whom? Check it out. How long has it been since you indulged in that faithless pastime that betrays close friends (Prov. 11:13), is forbidden by God (Lev. 19:16), and that inflicts mortal wounds (Prov. 18:8)? A gossip is a meddler exposing secrets in which he has no business (Prov. 20:19). Gossip is seen right smack dab in the middle of quarreling, jealousy, outbursts of anger, factions, slander … arrogance, and disorder (2 Cor. 12:20).

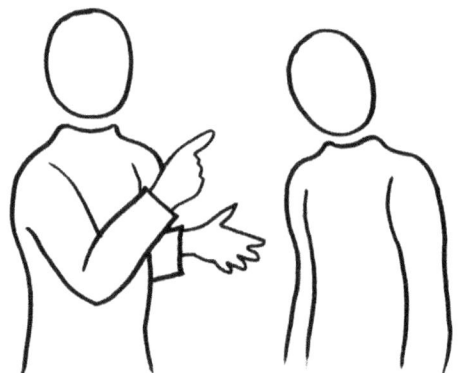

Hold it right there!
This gossip stops with you, not me!

These are not the set of companions we would choose for our children's playmates in the park. Who hasn't been the victim of a gossip? Who hasn't been cut by the serrated edges of smooth words uttered in malice (or fun)? Who has not uttered the words? Who has not thrown fuel on a fire already out of control (Prov. 26:20, 21)? Is there any question why God holds gossip in such abhorrence? There is only one recourse: repent, confess, and abstain without delay!

Once upon a time, close to forty years ago, Mirja and I were kayaking with some friends. As it happened, one of the friends had a brother with whom he was not on the best of terms. This brother, also one of my friends, was not with us that day. I cannot recall the details of the conversation but someone said something (gossip), and eventually this something was repeated to the absent brother. That was a lifetime ago; indeed, the serrated edges of smooth words uttered in fun can create long hurts.

Boasting? The Bible says quite a lot about boasting, and we can infer some guidelines about boasting. We learn from Paul that some boasting may be appropriate. However, when we boast of the exploits we plan to do tomorrow or next year, without acknowledging the Lord, we are clearly in the wrong (James 4:16). I think, with respect, that most of us are vulnerable to this evil. I will even go so far as to say that what we call speaking of our plans and dreams without acknowledging the Lord falls into the category of prohibited boasting: "Do not boast about tomorrow, for you do not know what a day may bring forth" (Prov. 27:1, NKJV).

We know that no one can redeem himself, or another for that matter, so of what value is it to boast in wealth, or position, or power (Ps. 49:6, 7)? Those who trust in themselves and amass great wealth with social and political status really are no better off than animals that perish. *They are destined for the grave, and death will feed on them* (Ps. 49:14). *He will take nothing with him when he goes down into the pit; his splendor will not descend with him* (Ps. 49:17). Not a happy ending for the boaster who ignores God.

But it need not be that way. Those who put their trust in God and, when they boast, boast in God, will be redeemed from the pit (Ps. 49:15)—though everyone goes there to rest for a little while (Eccles. 9:3, 5; 1 Thess. 4:14–16). Clearly, the boaster is trusting in his own power when, in humility, he needs to put total trust in the God of his salvation.[8] This trust must tie into our thanksgiving because, as our dear apostle Peter assures us, there is salvation in no other (Acts 4:12).

So many of our political animals seem to think that they have the answers to all our hopes, dreams, and ambitions. We elect them, and they serve us (or not) for a term or two. Some manage to stay in elected office long enough to collect a substantial pension. Fewer still become prime ministers or presidents and wield enormous power over the masses for a few years. Others make themselves presidents for life, a sorry myth of course, because most of these are rejected and ejected while they still breathe. Six months out of the headlines and we won't think of them; two years out of power or position and we'll have forgotten their names (Ps. 31:12; 88:5; Isa. 26:14). Same destiny for news anchors, television champions, hockey stars, and anyone else who boasts in his or her own glory. Your glory won't last (Ps. 49:16, 17). We need to learn a better language—a language of praise for our Maker and Sustainer, a language of trust in His ability and willingness to supply all our needs for this present journey and for our eternal destination (Phil. 4:19). No boasting needed.

Whining or self-pitying is usually not seen as the unsavory speech that it really is. It's

---

[8] Of the more than 150 texts in Scripture that refer directly to salvation, most speak to us of the "God of our salvation."

annoying, yes, but it is seldom recognized as an expression of self-centered, egotistical pride, as the grubby and smeared expression of the watch-me, pay-me-for-watching-me hubris of the movie stars and rock music bands. But that is exactly the nature of self-pity.

I suppose that in small doses we can handle it (and maybe have indulged it) and not suffer a whole lot as a body. However, we all know some who have taken this scurrilous habit to a fine art. Their lives are characterized by their chronic unhappiness, and their associates are made to suffer with them amid the added frustration of knowing that there is no remedy as long as the whiner is rewarded with attention.

Thankfully, this ultimately means that there is a ray of hope and a way to escape if we recognize our role in perpetuating the habit—a codependent relationship with the whiner in which we victims support her misery. Having recognized our role, we must absolutely refuse further to be a party to any of it, and a habit unrewarded might eventually become a habit of the past.

Grumbling is much like whining and self-pity but with some differences. One can grumble with a smile or lightly give voice to discontent. But grumbling can metamorphose into a deep-seated discontent with everything, a compulsion to see and express the worst in every situation. C. S. Lewis expresses this cleverly in *The Great Divorce* when MacDonald speculates on whether the harmless old lady was merely a grumbler or had actually become a grumble, in which case she was beyond hope.[9] The warning in *Divorce* is to recognize the potentially destructive tendency while it can be corrected and take every necessary and even painful step to make the change. Paul's assurance that we can do all things through Christ, the source of strength, shines great beams of hope on those of us who have developed destructive habits (Phil. 4:13).

We can't leave the topic of the flapping tongue without touching down on another aspect of unsavory speech: vocabulary. I'm not talking about just any vocabulary, but words in popular currency used to express sudden emotive outbursts of anger, joy, disgust, and fear. They are in such common use that frequently no spike of emotion is required to elicit an expression. (Most of us have encountered the person whose airtime would be halved by leaving out the expletives.) These words usually refer to persons or things holy or sacred, body parts or excretions, and heaven or the alternative. As Christians, we usually steer around the hard core expressions by adopting "sanitized" versions of the various words—not that they are considered in heaven as appropriate substitutes. If I read my Bible correctly, the *only* appropriate response to the urge to express in this way is to eradicate the desire to do so altogether.

I suppose you are now wondering about the identity of these so-called sanitized words. I'll identify a few of the more commonly used expressions, but this list is not exhaustive: George, Word, Gracious, Golly, Holy Smoke, Holy Cow, Gosh, Gum, Gee. Right about now, a conscious and persistent commitment to sanitizing our speech in order to hallow our Father's name in our lives would certainly be welcomed in heaven.

We've looked at some unsavory speech modes and habits. Let's finish up with a positive statement from the Bible: *Fact is, all your speech must be such that it will build up the body of Christ*

---

[9] C. S. Lewis, *The Great Divorce* (CS Lewis Pte. Ltd, 1946).

of which you are a member—as well as benefit all those who hear you. In all your speech and behavior, consider the needs of others (Eph. 4:29). If we take the time to internalize this principle, by the grace of our Father in heaven, it will be a guide to everything we say or do. When the world looks utterly hopeless, our words will express the sure hope that we have in God. They will express the joy only God gives when sorrow threatens to overwhelm like a tsunami, and they will comfort with the comfort of the Spirit in our unbearable sadness. While we live in a world that is threatening to implode or explode—simultaneously—we live always in the certainty that our lives are hidden with Christ in God (Col. 3:3). Do we need anything else to elicit praise, hope, and joy?

We might ask how we switch polarities? How can we transition from the sour-faced grump with the mouth perpetually turned down and dripping bitterness to the happy face of joy in the Lord? The answer is quite simple (though deeply rooted habits mightily resist any interference): because *you have been raised with Christ, set your hearts on things above, where Christ is seated at the right hand of God. Set your minds on things above, not on earthly things. For you died to these things, and your life is now hidden with Christ in God* (Col. 3:1–3). John adds to this assurance: we are children of God (imagine that for a while), and *we know that when he appears, we shall be like him, for we shall see him as he is* (1 John 3:1, 2).

We must consciously, deliberately, willfully, and persistently keep these thoughts uppermost and foremost in the consciousness. Old habits die hard. They will attempt to intrude and are persistent and tenacious agents of evil.

Only with ultimate good can we overcome evil (Rom. 12:21). Change will happen because, when we invite God in, He will do the changing.

Dump all your garbage in God's rubbish heap.

The choice is ours to make each moment of every day.

The Seal of Redemption—Paul tells us that *God's Holy Spirit is gentle and loving, and can be grieved by our thoughtless or irreverent actions* (Eph. 4:30). This may be a startling concept for those who traditionally have thought of the Holy Spirit as a force or power emanating from God but not really God. A careful reading of Paul teaches us that the Holy Spirit is a sentient being and is capable of emotions, including love and grief. Specifically, the actions of human beings bring Him joy or grief.

When we first believed, the Holy Spirit entered our lives and became the seal, or guarantee, of our inheritance until we experience redemption in its full reality (Eph. 1:13, 14). But we must stay away from careless indifference to the promise of life in Christ (2 Tim. 1:1); to the grace of God by which we are saved (Eph. 2:8); to the *riches of His glorious inheritance in the saints* (Eph. 1:18); to His *incomparable power for all those who believe* (Eph. 1:19); to His making us "alive with Christ" (Eph. 2:5); to His peace and reconciliation (Eph. 2:14, 16); to our solid "foundation of the apostles and prophets, with Christ Jesus himself as the chief cornerstone" (Eph. 2:20); to God's intent to express His manifold wisdom through the church to everyone in the cosmos (Eph. 3:10); to the indwelling of Christ in our hearts by faith (Eph. 3:17); and to God's ability "to do immeasurably more than all we ask or imagine, according to his power that is at work within us" (Eph. 3:20).

Careless indifference to any of these blessings will grieve the Spirit of God, our seal of redemption. Persistent grieving of the Holy Spirit is rebellion that can only end in our shutting Him out of our lives. Because only by the Spirit are we drawn to God, to salvation, and to repentance, persistent rejection of the Spirit will end in our inability to hear His voice calling us. This is the unpardonable sin because it is the sin for which we will *ask* no repentance.

One Solution Fits All—One solution does fit all: *get rid of all of it now* (Eph. 4:31). It's a simple, but not simplistic, solution because the One who commands the action also empowers the result. Get rid of all of it now! Turn all of it over to God, and He will throw it into the deepest canyon in the ocean—that's real deep. Listen to the voice of God's Holy Spirit pleading with you to end your dallying with sin. Don't grieve the Spirit by neglecting your immeasurable salvation through indifference to His pleas. If you can hear Him now, now is the time to wake up and take focused action (Rom. 13:11)!

Action can be rather simple. There are usually triggers that set off the wrong responses. Go for the triggers, such as the habits and attitudes of life that precipitate the outbursts of evil. This is where the Holy Spirit will meet the greatest resistance. Regretting the sad outcomes of rage and anger without giving up the attitudes that support them is not the answer. Recognizing that bitterness leads to alienation, physical illness, injury, or even death, without forgiving and giving up resentment is futile. Acknowledging that slander and malice are counterproductive to positive human relations without giving up the hatred that drives them accomplishes nothing good. This is where God's "incomparably great power for us who believe" (Eph. 1:19) is brought to bear on those who will receive it. This is the kind of power that brought Christ back from the dead (Eph. 1:20), and it will raise the dead in sin (Eph. 2:4, 5).

God will accept us, incapable of heart reform as we are, and transform us into the kind of people in the kind of church that will bring Him glory in all the cosmos (Eph. 3:10). He is the consummate Artist, the ultimate Craftsman. He will not reject any social outcast or princely derelict, but He will change them. He accepts us as we are and where we are, but He does not leave us there or in that condition. And this is where some of us err.

We like the idea of God's accepting us where we are. It gives us that warm and accepted feeling. We don't seem to be as ready to acknowledge that where we are is not the condition in which God intends for us to remain. And that's the rub. We like the way we dress; we like the things we eat; we like the things that entertain us; we like the way we spend our time; change is not always on our minds. But change in us is on God's mind. As Paul so powerfully wrote: *You must no longer be like [the Gentiles]* (Eph. 4:17). And so we go back to Ephesians to discover how the *manifold wisdom of God* (Eph. 3:10) will be broadcast throughout the cosmos through lives that are changed to glorify God.

I am a member of a congregation and a part of a church that God has raised up to glorify Himself through obedience. He has given us a mandate to share His grace with our neighbors throughout the world (Matt. 24:14; Mark 16:15). This is no light calling. We have put our hands to the plough, and we must not turn back (Luke 9:62). Yet, as Jesus sadly remarked, we are so "slow of heart to believe" (Luke 24:25, NKJV). We hear it in our after-church conversations; we detect it in the tone of the voice on the telephone; we see it in the lines in our faces and the postures we assume—yet our God is gracious.

Seeing all that we see, and so much more, you can still hear Him call out to us, *In the place where all this evil once ruled, set up kindness and compassion with forgiveness for everyone just as you have been forgiven by God* (Eph. 4:32)! The truth is, the evidence of our relation to our Father is not seen clearly in our dietary and clothing habits, in our infidelities unconsummated, or in the conversations we avoid. But it clearly is seen in kindness and compassion with forgiveness for everyone. Love for one another is the only clear identifier of discipleship (John 13:35).

Thank you, our Father, for being merciful and gracious with your forgiveness, truthful in your diagnosis of our sin, and patient with a slow and stubborn people. Do what You must to create in us clean hearts and transform us into living evidence to the cosmos of Your incomparably great power for us who believe. Show us the power like You exerted in Jesus when You raised Him from the grave (Eph. 1:19, 20). And do it quickly! Your honor is at stake in the way we live. Amen!

Chapter 5
Focusing the Light

More Living as Children of Light

We all know that children love to imitate. Those they love are the models they watch most closely and imitate most carefully. You are children of One who loves you intensely. The wonderful fact is this: Christ loved you to the point of offering up His eternal life so that you could have eternal life in exchange for your sordid, truncated, mortal life. His sacrifice to God was fragrant and beautiful. He is your role model in every human decision and relationship! Imitate Him!

Friends, listen to me, and listen well! The lives you lived in your former experience were not good or beautiful. They were shot through and riddled with sexual immorality, greed, and every kind of impurity. Your new lives in Christ must not retain even a hint of these shameful things. For God's holy people, all such thought and behavior is utterly unacceptable. Don't hurry away; I'm not through yet with prohibiting. Obscenity, foolish talk, and coarse joking don't belong among the behaviors of God's holy people. Replace all these shameful things with thanksgiving. If there is one thing of which you can be sure, this is it: no one who participates in these disgusting practices (such a person is practicing idolatry) will have any part in the eternal kingdom.

Satan will use every unholy tactic in his unholy arsenal to deceive you. His agents are fully equipped with empty words calculated to lead you back into your former way of life—which was actually the way of death. Keep your guard up. Don't be misled by mischievous blandishments. It is because of such things that God's wrath falls on the disobedient; don't participate with them in their folly.

Remember when you lived in spiritual darkness; remember the emptiness and despair you felt when the party was over and you were alone in the dark. But light has come into your soul and darkness has vanished before light. Therefore, live as the children of light that you are. (This is how you will recognize light: it is always expressed in goodness, righteousness, and truth.) You need to put a bit of focused effort into your experience in light. On the positive side, seek for and find out what pleases the Lord and follow that discovery by having nothing to do with the dead-ended deeds engendered by darkness; instead, you must expose them for what they are: utterly and eternally destructive to body and mind. The secret lives of the disobedient are shameful even to mention. On the other hand, the lives inspired by light are visible, open to view, engendering glory to God. Remember this scripture; fix it in your minds: "Awake thou that sleepest, and arise from the dead, and Christ shall give thee light" (KJV).

Life in the Light requires careful attention to the important things; wisdom and prudence are essential. Don't squander your time (time and life are equivalent concepts); use every opportunity to be in light because everything is evil outside in the dark. Because we live in evil times, we need to understand the will of the Lord. Anything willfully short of understanding the will of the Lord is utterly foolish and ultimately destructive.

There are many spirits out there vying with the Spirit of God for your attention and allegiance. Some you will find in a glass. These lead to debauchery; don't go down that drain. Instead follow the Light and be filled with the Spirit. When you meet one another, always be ready to share a psalm or a spiritual song or a hymn by which to cheer him on his way and encourage your own soul also. Go about your daily routines with songs to the Lord in your heart and share these songs with the birds if there is no one else there to be blessed by them. Give thanks to God, our Father, for everything, even for the temptations by which your faith is tested (though our Father doesn't bring the temptations). In fact, live in a continual attitude of thankfulness to God. I close this section with a command that will test the sincerity of your walk in the Light: out of your ardent love and reverence for Christ, submit to one another. (Eph. 5:1-21)

On the Imitation of Christ—In 1418, Thomas à Kempis, a German monk of the Brethren of the Common Life, published a devotional book that still today is read and appreciated by many Christians. *Imitatio Christi, The Imitation of Christ*,[1] presents the life of Christ as the highest study possible to human beings. Thirteen hundred years before Thomas, Paul also admonished us to imitate Christ—which means watch Him, study Him, spend quantity time with Him, and admire Him.

In the life and character of Christ, there are so many things to attract our attention and inspire admiration. We are astonished by His immeasurable love for broken-down, derelict humanity. He came into this world as the least of the weakest when society was almost at its lowest ebb. He lived with us, worked and played with us, laughed and wept with us, and carried our broken dereliction to the cross and to the grave just to redeem and reconcile a depraved race.

With nothing to recommend ourselves to Him, it was totally His doing and dying. And now—another astonishment—He has given us the ministry of reconciliation to assure broken humanity that God does not hold their brokenness against them. God is appealing to broken humanity through us: "Be reconciled to God" (2 Cor. 5:18-20).

This is the essence of imitating Christ. Be like children whose lives still revolve around their parents, whose parents are the only models they know; imitate Christ. Look to Him as the One who loves you intensely. He is your role model in every human decision and relationship. Imitate Him. Act as He acts; love as He loves; sacrifice as He sacrificed; live for the sake of others just as He lived. Your attitude should be the same as that of Jesus Christ: humble, serving, giving, obedient, totally honest with us—in fact, the essence of love (Phil. 2:5-8). Or, as Paul writes in Ephesians 4:2, *Be completely humble and gentle; be patient, bearing with one another in love.* Get to know Christ and imitate Him.

When I was a boy, my greatest desire was to be with my dad and do what my dad did. I hung out with him at every opportunity, observing the way he did his work. I always admired the way he used his tools, and I was really happy just to be near him whenever the opportunity presented itself, for I wanted to be the kind of man my dad was in my youthful eyes. My father and I had a bond that grew stronger as time went on. Our attitude toward Christ should be the same. *Imitate Him* in love and, assuredly, the humility, service, giving, obedience, and honesty will also be demonstrated *in every human decision and relationship.*

---

[1] Thomas à Kempis, *The Imitation of Christ* (Milwaukee, WI: The Bruce Publishing Company, 1940).

The Long Road to Grace

Hard-Nosed Paul Gets Specific Again

So we had better listen and listen well. Paul has no soft answer for those who yearn for or cling to habits of the former sordid, truncated, mortal way of life. We can't keep the old and ever experience the new; they are fundamentally, basically, utterly incompatible. The reconciled life has no room or sympathy for the ways of the old life. I've been on that road (even while attempting piety, which was only a show), and I know that everything on it leads eventually to physical dissolution and eternal death. Funny how we can deceive and be deceived.

The "good life" (with the beautiful body and all the perquisites) that so many of us want is neither good nor beautiful. If we thought of God at all at this time, it was, in effect, to say to Him: "I can do this myself. I'll try a little harder next time this temptation comes around. In fact, I'll create some small temptations, You know, just little ones to build up my resistance—sort of like an inoculation, to empower myself to handle them. Then I'll increase the dosage, so to speak, until I can handle the really big ones. Yes, that's what I'll do! I need to build up a bit of resistance. I'm excited!" Well, I have to say that's blasphemous. It's actually the wickedest thing we can say to God. Because of this hubristic attitude, as Paul reminds us, this imaginary good life is shot through and riddled with sexual immorality, with every kind of impurity, and with greed. Really? Is it that bad? It's worse!

Let's unpack Paul's assessment. We'll start with sexual immorality. Satan has worked overtime to refine and bait this trap to lure weak-willed humanity into it. Obviously, he recognizes its importance and power in advancing his kingdom of evil. How pervasive is sexual immorality? Maybe the term needs a definition. If we agree that anything that turns the mind, or is intended to turn the mind, to thoughts of wrong-headed, stupid, illicit sex should be classified as sexually immoral, then, even if no overtly sexual act is accomplished or undertaken, in the light of the magnificent law of liberty, guilt has been incurred (Matt. 5:28).

So with scriptural assurance we should conclude, for example, that the publishers and distributors of many of the books displayed at the check-out counters in most grocery stores have incurred the guilt of sexual immorality. It follows that those who willingly let their minds drift to the themes of the images flaunted on the covers and beneath also incur guilt (Matt. 5:28). The same can be said for much of the fare on popular television shows and movies frequently seen in the homes of many Christians.

These are probably the most basic examples and the easiest to see. However, men have their own displays calculated and designed to attract illegitimate attention: images of power, wealth, and status—thumping their chests like the grouse on the log in the spring. The fact is that men usually are the prime instigators of sexual sin. By their responses, they encourage; by their strength, they compel; by their greed, they create social and economic environments that force women and girls into impossible situations. Conversely, many women dress provocatively and entice the opposite sex to notice them. They attract inappropriate attention with their scantily clad bodies. Given this description of sexual immorality, we can see that the vice is rampantly pervasive. Riddled with guilt we can only take refuge in the assurance that Jesus came to save sinners from every hint of these shameful things.

But we live in a complex world in which we cannot drive, shop, work, or play blindfolded.

Living as hermits under tree stumps or on the tops of poles as St. Anthony, one of the first hermit monks, in the deserts of Egypt is not an option. We are social beings who, if deprived of the society of others, cannot achieve the potential our Creator intended for us. We are also sexual beings, and God created sex in Eden—with clear instructions on how to use, appreciate, and enjoy this gracious gift. In His compassionate encounters with human beings, Jesus also gave to us clear examples of how to treat the sinner—even when the sin is of a sexual nature (John 8:3–11). His purity and compassion for weak-willed, habituated sinners are astonishing. He expects (and empowers) us believers to express the same purity and compassion in every human encounter.

Our role as believers is to love sinners like He does, pray for them like He does, and work for their salvation like He does. We should not prey on them in compliance with the sexually perverted traps introduced by the devil. In all our encounters and in all our private musings, God intends that we keep ourselves unspotted by the world (James 1:27). It's a gracious order and, given our histories, ingrained inclinations, and humanity, it might seem on the surface to be impossible. It would be utterly impossible if we were alone in the dark, but we are never alone! We are with God, and all things are possible with God! He can take the camel through the eye of the needle—no problem at all (Matt. 19:26). He can even create in the camel the willingness to be taken through.

Clearly, we have missed the mark in our understanding of sexuality. Over the millennia the Platonist dichotomy of evil body and holy soul has clouded our thinking about many of the good things the Creator has given us. As a consequence we are too ignorant, afraid, or embarrassed to teach our children the rightness, pureness, purpose, and beauty of the gender differences. The Creator made us different for at least three purposes: to reproduce God's image by bringing new human beings into the world, to experience the unity of God through the intimate unity of two human beings, and to unite these two human beings with emotional bonds never to be broken while life lasts. We see that God created human sexuality to provide a lifelong experience in understanding our Creator and as a continual reminder of His presence in our lives.

To use this marvelous gift for personal gain or greedy pleasure outside of the closed circle of marriage has repercussions that cannot be removed on this earth. Through the destruction of a home and family, through distorting our understanding of the completeness of God's image, our children are marred beyond fixing in this world. When family unity has been shattered by infidelity, the sense of our unity with God cannot be fully appreciated, and the illicit emotional bonds, always created at the expense of legitimate bonds, weaken the sense of God's presence and impair our ability to bond with Him. Paul was right by insisting that our lives in Christ must not retain even a hint of sexual immorality.

How pervasive is sexual immorality? Paul said, *society is shot through and riddled by it* (Eph. 5:3): innuendoes, sly glances, lyrics of popular songs, jokes, and billboards that advertise cars all spread the lie that sexual immorality is acceptable in our society. How can we avoid being contaminated? Sadly, the church, the body of Christ, suffers almost as much as the rest of society from the ravages of rampant sexual immorality. What is the solution? A revival of true godliness both personal and corporate. God is gracious; He will do it when we ask Him. I am asking!

Mirja and I were at a mall on one of our excursions to the city. We were startled, dismayed, and not a little annoyed to see a life-sized display of an eight-year-old girl presenting herself in a sexually provocative fashion to sell clothes (50 percent off, at least) to little girls. Someone imagined that advertising; someone approved the idea; someone paid for it, and everyone who purchases a product in that department contributes to a little part of its cost. We were home again, 700 miles away, before we collected our wits enough to say to ourselves, "Why didn't we raise a riot? Why didn't we stage a sit in? Why didn't we find the manager and demand that she remove the degrading advertising or we would set up camp on the spot until she did?"

Are we complicit by quietly going about our business without a whimper of protest about these images that portray little girls, or anyone else, as objects to be sexually exploited? Do we have a responsibility to register our disgust and disapproval in a language that business understands? Should we "speak up for those who cannot speak for themselves, for the rights of all who are destitute" (Prov. 31:8)? Should we "defend the rights of the poor and needy" (Prov. 31:9)? If the answer is yes, then how would Jesus do it? He is our example, but do we take the example from John 8 or from Matthew 21 and John 2?

Perhaps the way we address these rampant, sexually immoral attacks on our characters and on our wallets will depend on whom we are addressing. A popular mall might require a metaphorical upsetting of their tills and cutting of their lines of communication to the banking establishments, which are certainly complicit in the sordid attempts to rake in sinners' hard-earned coin. However, the people in our midst might respond better to other approaches.

Paul speaks of *every kind of impurity*. What is included in this blanket prohibition against impurity? Things like the Walter Mitty syndrome,[2] habitual laziness, shoddy work on the job, half-hearted personal work, neglect of the needs of our animals, or carelessness with personal health and hygiene? Does it include reckless behavior, empty reading, immoral fantasizing, failure to protect personal assets, tossing garbage out the car window, neglect of family, hoarding, or even passing on a double line? Or do we restrict impurity to the overt practice of gross sins?

Actually, anything (like tossing a piece of garbage out the car window or passing on a double line) that tends to fray the moral fabric of our lives, anything that leads us to compromise our decision-making capacity, and anything that causes us to give in to the temptation to be satisfied with that which is simply "good enough" will contaminate the character. In the real lives of ordinary people, anything that tends to make us comfortable with the status quo fits within Paul's idea of *every kind of impurity* (Eph. 5:3). The status quo we choose to embrace will contaminate us to the core of our beings. And, really, the contamination can start with just a pinch of one kind of impurity that we previously considered insignificant. That little pinch, like yeast, works through all of the dough (Gal. 5:9). Those who trade the unseen realities of eternity to scratch

---

[2] The American Heritage Dictionary defines a "Walter Mitty" as a person who creates incredible daydreams of personal victories but never follows through. The character was created by James Thurber.

a few itches here in this world will find that, in the end, the itch remains, but to scratch it has become impossible.

And then Paul brings up greed for special attention. An internal, highly personalized vice, why is greed lumped with every kind of impurity? Without some measure of greed, wouldn't we all just sit back and enjoy the view—or give it all up under the pressure to scrape together a living? Not that we shouldn't go out and enjoy the view from time to time (Mark 6:31), and making a living is unambiguously commanded in the Bible (2 Thess. 3:10). The fact is this: spending time simply looking at creation has remarkable implications for our ability to think, reason, and feel well. Walking in creation, hearing, feeling, and seeing God's handiwork up close and intimately multiplies the endorphins coursing through our bodies and enhances their positive effects. Conversely, exposure to the raucous decibels and frenetic visual images of the city (where most of us live) adds to the physically and emotionally destructive stresses within the body. But let's return to greed.

Humanity does not need greed to propel it out the door to the job. Pure industry will do that just fine, and unmitigated reason will tell us when the day's work is done. Greed is the slave driver. Greed impels us to overreach, cheat, lie, and steal. Greed drives us to work extended days at the expense of family, friends, and God. We cheat God out of the pleasure of our society when we yield to the greedy impulse to spend overtime raking in the coin. God is pained by our neglect, and we are alienated from Him. In fact, greed makes money our god—the same god that was called mammon in ancient times (Matt. 6:24, KJV).

Whereas the Babylonians once were noted for worshiping their fishnets for the power and benefits they provided (Hab. 1:15, 16), modern humanity now worships the modern equivalent—position, power, money, and status. The only difference is that we don't make mammon into little silver images; we make him into bank statements, mortgage documents, jobs, credit cards, and savings portfolios. In this way we bow to the twenty-first century idols, and idolaters can never be content in a heaven where the pavement is made of gold.

More Specifics From Hard-Nosed Paul—There are more unholy practices that God's holy people have to shed: *obscenity, foolish talk, and coarse joking* next come under Paul's ban (Eph. 5:4). I think we all know the meaning of obscene, but here's a refresher: Webster defines obscene as that which wounds or offends the imagination in sexual matters, usually expressed in words or gestures.[3] Webster is right on the mark with its definition, and it doesn't move us very far from Paul's prohibition of any hint of sexual immorality and impurity. Coarse joking is partnered with obscenity to undermine the moral fabric of humanity. Related as they are to sexual immorality, can it be that these are two of the most prevalent and deadly sins of society?

The wounds inflicted on those who participate go deeper, fester more, and last longer than almost any other injury—with the danger of spiritual gangrene always present. Sadly, participation or exposure frequently starts very young. This lifetime is far too short to recover fully from the effects of obscenity and coarse joking encountered as a child. Many of the workers in

---

[3] *The New Lexicon Webster's Encyclopedic Dictionary of the English Language,* Canadian edition (New York, NY: Lexicon Publications, 1988).

The Long Road to Grace

my parents' bush sawmill were not above sharing the seamy side of their lives with us boys with a wink and a grin. Though we were forbidden access to the bunkhouses, we did not totally escape the Monday-morning coarse joking and obscene boasting of Saturday night exploits. Sixty years later unwanted thoughts still surface occasionally in my consciousness.

Certainly, our Father has forgiven me and has brought me into fellowship with Himself, and I have uncountable and infinitely better images upon which to dwell, but the early damage is still there today. It will remain there until this mortal puts on immortality and this corruption puts on incorruption, in an instant, at the glorious appearing of our Lord (1 Cor. 15:53, 54). Hey, let the appearing come! Soon!

I am guessing that most children today don't have the exposure to rough mill hands that I experienced as a child, but there is another perhaps more refined and certainly more sinister medium used to implant the seeds of moral decay in the minds of children and adults: TV. With its unending supply of sexually explicit visual images, sexual innuendoes, violence, unbelief, scorn, and coarse language, it is shaping the values of the family, the nation, and the world.

Wise are those who move the TV out of the house, but alas, they won't escape the obscene and coarse tentacles of the world without extreme measures. Our world is filled with little children who are stressed out by their perceived need to appear glamorous and sophisticated. They have such unwarranted concern for appearance and dress. They fear being shunned by their peers if they don't display the right labels on their sneakers. Vanity surgery for early teens and Botox injections for prepubescent girls are too common.

One day a young man came into Mirja's store while I was on customer service duty. "Do you have anything to remove stretch marks?" He exposed a muscular shoulder and showed me a little ripple in the skin—nothing that anyone but a self-absorbed hedonist would ever notice or care about. "That! You're worried about that!" I exclaim, astonished. (I suddenly forgot all I ever knew about selling.) "What are you going to do when you get these?" And I screwed up my face to emphasize seven decades of exposure to wind, sleet, hail, sun, heat, frost, time, and chance. "Botox," he declared flatly. I guess he didn't need his money. Sometimes I just can't perform as a serious customer service rep. I should be fired. I need to keep my mouth shut. Maybe.

The self-absorbed hedonist – he's got botox in his future.

Foolish talk is quite another field of study. We need to expand our minds a bit on this topic. Instead of moving outside the box, we'll discard the box entirely. With no fences to constrain our investigation, we'll first check with Webster for the meaning. Foolish talk lacks "evidence of common sense or judgment; [it is] witless, silly, irresponsible, thoughtless, lacking in good sense, imprudent."[4] This is an excellent perspective on the foolish talk that Paul absolutely rules out of the Christian lexicon.

Rather than stressing the definition of foolish talk, it might be more profitable to canvass the Bible for a divine perspective on talk that is appropriate for God's holy people. Paul is a

---

[4] Ibid.

major contributor to sound doctrine, and we look first to him. *Whatever is noble, right, pure, lovely, admirable, excellent, or praiseworthy—think about such things* (Phil. 4:8). That seems to rule out a whole lot of stuff. Personal experience has taught us that we talk about those things of which we think, and we think about those things of which we talk.

Thinking and talking tend to feed each other. They are complementary and mutually supportive elements of the human experience. Paul has given us here the formula for avoiding foolish talk, but there is so much more in the Holy Scriptures from which we can learn the type of speech that will honor our Creator and keep us out of trouble. Let's not be like the fool whose "mouth invites a beating" (Prov. 18:6) or like the fool whose voice is recognized by a multitude of words (Eccles. 5:3, NKJV).

Let's remember that *when words are many, sin is not absent, but he who holds his tongue is wise* (Prov. 10:19). Furthermore, a person of knowledge "uses words with restraint" (Prov. 17:27). My older brother taught me this bit of wisdom when I was about twelve: better to keep your mouth shut and be thought a fool than to open it and remove all doubt. But there are times when the mouth needs to be opened—with energy—and we will get to that in due time.

The Bible describes itself as a lamp and a light to guide our feet (Ps. 119:105). It gives us wise and gracious words from our Father in heaven that brighten our days and give light and understanding to the simple (Ps. 119:130)—those simple enough to take it as it is written (Matt. 4:4). If God's words are embedded in our hearts (Ps. 119:11), there is little chance that we will hurt Him or damage ourselves or others by foolish speech. If God's truth is in our minds, it will inspire, shield, and guide our thoughts and words. It will steer us around the snares too many people set for themselves by talking foolishly (Prov. 6:2). A gentle or soft answer is more likely to give us the immediate result we would like (Prov. 15:1).

In the longer term, the last judgment will assess our words with finality. Careless words will meet an accounting because by our words we will be acquitted, and by our words we will be condemned (Matt. 12:36, 37). "Before a word is on my tongue you, LORD, know it completely" (Ps. 139:4). There is so much wisdom in Scripture; there is no need to be unwise.

But what exactly is "foolish talk"? What are careless words? Remember, we have thrown the box away, so we are free to investigate in areas we might not have thought of before. Foolish talk covers a wider range of topics than we normally imagine. For example, take the man who is a chronic grumbler, who habitually demeans himself, whose face never reflects the sunshine. This sad person is a product of his own misery. His face and posture reflect the results of bad speaking habits gone horribly wrong. His self-centered, whiny, foolish talk has done a number on him that only a miracle of heavenly origin will change.

The opposite end of this spectrum of self-centeredness is recognized as pride. It is expressed in boasting of what we (imagine we) have and do, plan to do, or pretend we have done; all this talk originates in the evil one (1 John 2:15, 16). As the proverb says, "Do not boast about tomorrow, for you do not know what a day may bring forth" (Prov. 27:1, NKJV). "All such boasting is evil" (James 4:16). Instead we ought to give God glory for all His blessings, plan according to His will, and say so at every opportunity (James 4:15).

This failing to give God the praise for all our hopes, plans, and accomplishments is a pervasive failure among too many Christians. Surely, silence when we should speak in praise of God is as *foolish* as much talk.

We must all know someone whose mouth runs on and on with hardly a moment to breathe. And we know the topic—it's the talker talking about himself. (At least he is familiar with the topic.) Rarely does the talker give us a chance to talk about ourselves. Jesus was known for gracious words (Luke 4:22), and He spoke mainly about His Father. Can we learn from His example that if we focus our conversation on God, His love, and His plans for the world, as well as on others and their needs, hopes, and dreams, that our words also will be gracious and not foolish? We frequently make wrong choices and hurt others, often by gossip (Prov. 18:8), but *if any man does not offend in word (or by failing to speak up), the same is a perfect man, who is also able to bridle the whole body* (James 3:2, NKJV).

Other types of foolish talk include flattery, slander, and murmuring. This is not a happy trio, and in Scripture they are always associated with trouble, ruin, and death. The Bible seems to draw a distinction between legitimate complaining over a valid grievance and the whining behavior of the habitual complainer, who cannot see the sun for the shadows of the flowers. It's an ugly habit that won't die easily. But it will die—either by God's grace in the present experience or when it takes the whiner to the lake of fire. Lying also stands out as an obvious example of foolish talk that we all profess to abhor, as we should, yet lying has become deeply embedded in our systems from infancy. No liar will walk the streets of gold or splash in the river of life (Rev. 22:15). Lord, save us from foolish talk, for we cannot save ourselves!

The writer of Psalm 19:14 has given us a simple prayer that will serve as a wall that can never be breached between the soul and the hazards latent in our mouths: "Let the words of my mouth and the meditation of my heart be acceptable in Your sight, O Lord, my strength and my Redeemer" (NKJV). God will not leave us in ignorance if we are willing to honor Him with our words. Occasionally, He even uses other people to open our understanding. Many of those other people have been recorded in the Bible, and we do well to take heed to God's word (Ps. 119:9).

I have dropped several hints about the foolishness of not speaking when one should speak. We are commanded to "speak up for those who cannot speak for themselves, for the rights of all who are destitute. Speak up and judge fairly; defend the rights of the poor and needy" (Prov. 31:8, 9). To say nothing when one should speak is, in fact, to send a non-verbal message that may be just as clear as if these words were spoken: "We don't care; do what you want. God does not see; there is no penalty." One cannot escape the guilt of foolish talk through silence when articulate noise is demanded by the circumstance.

This is a pervasive theme in the writings and preaching of Bonhoeffer. He heard and powerfully answered the call to be the voice for those who had no voice. Ultimately, his shouting out against tyranny and brutality led him to the noose end of a Nazi rope at the tender age of thirty-nine. Let no one despise youth. Be an example to all of us "in speech, in [life], in love, in faith, and in purity" (1 Tim. 4:12). Don't worry that you are not getting the recognition by the world that you would like. Heaven will know and acknowledge you. *They will be mine, says the* Lord, *in the day when I make up my treasured possession. I will spare their lives ... And all will see the difference between those who serve and do not serve God* (Mal. 3:17, 18).

The Ubiquitous Expletive—Much foolish talk has no real meaning that cannot be expressed more graciously, powerfully, and effectively in other ways. Its meaning is almost exclusively restricted to emphasis and emotion. But the absence of the ubiquitous expletive would leave many people with not much to fill their airtime. Tough. Learn a few more words.

Christians should not really be troubled with this problem, as they have much praise to give to God for His manifold wisdom (Eph. 3:10), and surely they are familiar with the commandment that prohibits profanity (Exod. 20:7). Still, too many of them use too many words without knowledge of their meaning or their origin. Is it really important? It could be. If we have been commanded to refrain from taking God's name in vain, should we not obey? We should. Then why do Christians still thoughtlessly mouth expletives such as gosh, golly, and gee—all recognized as derivatives of divine names?[5] Mirja and I once learned a little lesson on the efficient Italian train system: ignorance is no excuse when knowledge is available (and knowledge was available). Now you have the knowledge, so you would be wise to be sparing in your words (Prov. 17:27).

Many common expletives refer to things holy, and we didn't even know it. It usually comes as a surprise to learn that "holy cow" and "holy smoke" most likely refer to the sacrifices and the smoke of the sacrifices described in the Bible. By George (you do the research on this one), heavenly days, good gracious—let's stop here.

Other expletives refer to body parts as well as functions of the body. These words are normally considered vulgar and even secular society tends to limit their use. So, where do these empty words belong in our ordinary speech? I submit that they do not at all belong in the speech of a Christian. "Let the word of Christ dwell in you richly in all wisdom; teaching and admonishing one another in psalms and hymns and spiritual songs, singing with grace in your hearts to the Lord. And whatever you do in word or deed, do all in the name of the Lord Jesus, giving thanks to God the Father through him" (Col. 3:16, 17, NKJV).

Indeed, let's hurry and be reminded once more of what Paul tells us: we should waste no time replacing all these shameful habits with thanksgiving. If there is one thing of which we can be sure, this is it: no one who knowingly, persistently, and ultimately participates in sexual immorality, impurity, greed, coarse joking, obscenity, and foolish talk will have any part in the eternal kingdom because such a person is practicing idolatry (Eph. 5:3–5).

Of this also we can be sure: God has begun a work in us. He will carry it through to a glorious completion that includes victory over every troubling sin—and all are troubling (Phil. 1:6). Just don't get in His way or, from another perspective, do get into His Way, and hurry. Let's not remain trapped a moment longer in the degenerate habits of our old experience when God is willing, able, ready, and eager to change us into beings that have overcome in His name (1 John 4:4; 5:4, 5; Rev. 21:7). And He has already begun His work—even when we were dead in our sins and following the ways of this world (Eph. 2:1, 2). However, we need to be clear on the division of

---

[5] See *The New Lexicon Webster's Encyclopedic Dictionary of the English Language* for meanings of gosh, golly, and gee.

labor in our lifelong sanctification, our growing up in Jesus. Our role is to stay connected with the Vine (John 15:4–8) and to fight the fight of faith (1 Tim. 6:12), by which we retain God's Holy Spirit in us.

Word Power!—We have heard of the wisdom that tells us that we will come to believe a lie to be truth if we repeat it often enough. We will have deceived ourselves and placed our minds under the rule of the most galling of masters—ourselves. It's true. Scoffing at truth to impress our peers, doubting for the sake of argument, arguing for the sake of dominating, these work their balefully certain effects on our minds until we are not sure of what we believe. Willingly listening to someone else lie can have a similar result.

There lived a man who was continually investigating every crank religious idea that came within his grasp. He spent so much time digesting the various fringe religious publications gratuitously distributed to the willing that he had no time to ingest the truth. Ultimately, this poor man knew naught of what he knew. The truth that would have been filling, nourishing, and life sustaining could no longer be swallowed, and his life ended in spiritual starvation. Without a doubt the pulpy productions of too many pamphleteers must be classified as foolish talk and come under the condemnation of the apostle.

We can be thankful that the opposite is also true and much more satisfying over time. Listening to gracious truth, telling truth, and loving truth will work its salubrious effects on our souls, on our characters, and on our peace of mind. We will find that the words of truth have power in our lives to bring us ultimate victory in every detail. As the Spirit revealed to John in the Revelation, we will have overcome the accuser and, I believe, our own inherited and cultivated tendencies to evil "by the blood of the Lamb, and by the word of [our] testimony" (Rev. 12:11). Word power!

Spoken words work their power on us. Choose wisely what you say and what you choose to hear. Every person who succeeds to wisdom will have eaten some words from time to time. It's part of the learning process. Nevertheless, choosing words carefully will reduce the risk of chronic indigestion. Archimedes is reputed to have boasted long ago: *Give me a lever long enough and a prop strong enough and I can single-handedly move the world.* Strong words. More recently, author Joseph Conrad responded to the ancient sage: *Do not talk to me of Archimedes' lever. He was an absent-minded old guy with a mathematical bent ... Give me the right word, spoken with conviction, and I will move the world.* A final word: if you want to speak with convicting power, eschew obfuscation! Where's Webster when we need him?

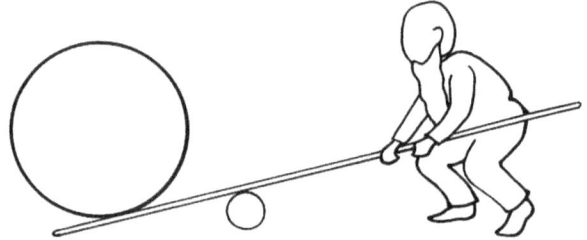

He was an absent-minded old guy with a big lever – but words are bigger.

Credulous and Foolish—We shouldn't leave the idea of avoiding foolish talk without a quick glance at the foolishness of believing everything that someone would like us to believe. This tendency of some was apparent way back in early antiquity. The Proverbs contain warnings against credulousness, or gullibility, the willingness to believe without sufficient evidence (proof) or without a known track history of reliability of the one who is delivering the message: "The simple believe anything, but the prudent give thought to their steps" (Prov. 14:15).

I think that many err by misunderstanding the nature of proof. Secular wisdom has us demanding so-called scientific *proof* for everything (of course, with the exception of the advertising industry in this age of persuasion, where mere repetition of sight and sound is all that is required—and it seems to work). This so-called scientific "proof" is conceited enough to suppose that the proofs are there to support their unbiblical positions on the origin and development of the earth and its life. Well, the *proof* just is not there.

Some evidence, yes, but all the evidence in the world is subject to interpretation and cannot be seen as proof. Ultimately, belief is based on a choice—as the advertising industry has discovered to its profit. The popular beliefs current today demonstrate popular gullibility and a desire to believe, without the proof or even the evidence, those things that make us comfortable in our alienation from the Creator.

No, there is no *proof* for creation either, nor can there be. We know that, and we don't mind admitting it. There is an abundance of evidence, certainly, but there is no *proof* as we define the results of the accepted scientific processes of "proving." Some things, like proof of beginnings, are way out of our short reach, and we have to interpret the evidence without even hoping to hold the *proof* in our finite, trembling, sweaty hands. So be it. We are content.

So we conclude that all the pompous talk of proof and proofs and proving our origins is *foolish talk*. The truly wise person, acknowledging the limits of reason unaided by revelation, will examine the evidence and come to conclusions consistent with revelation. The truly wise person will acknowledge that, as knowledge increases, present understandings of all evidence probably will have to be modified. Indeed, some understandings will have to be abandoned. Therefore, it is unwise to bind ourselves, our social standings, reputations, and academic biases too tightly to a popular belief that is rooted only in the unmitigated hubris of humanity. What is ultimately far wiser and infinitely more satisfying in every respect would be to bind ourselves to One whose track record of reliability is impeccably credible.

Shall we call this faith? Why not? Even the most calculating scientist steeped in the scientific method is unwillingly and unknowingly basing her premises on faith in the truth of something she can never see or prove. We don't apologize. In fact, we boldly acknowledge that we were *all* given a measure of faith to get us moving in the right direction (Rom. 12:3). This measure is increased by being carefully scrupulous in how and how often we apply the Word of God to our own lives and circumstances (2 Tim. 2:15; 2 Cor. 4:2). Now that I have brought these ideas to your attention, continue to nourish yourselves with the words of faith and good doctrine found in the Holy Scriptures—and, convenient or not, use every God-prompted opportunity to share the truth and the hope that inspires, motivates, and empowers you to get off the couch (2 Tim. 4:2).

On Your Guard!—We have spent considerable time discussing foolish talk. Why? Probably because foolish talk in one form or another is at the root of much of the sticky mess and trouble in which we frequently find ourselves. Even if you are fully committed in your soul to nourishing yourself daily with the Holy Scriptures in the presence of God, enter every day with caution.

Satan will use every tactic in his arsenal to deceive you. His agents are fully equipped with empty words [which are purposefully calculated] to lead you back into your former way of life—the way of death. Keep your guard up (Eph. 5:6), as they will not be mounting a frontal attack; their approach will be sly, insidious, and diversionary, so don't be sidetracked by flattery or a pretty face.

Ever notice that the defenses of the morning usually are set in place the night before? When I was little, my grandma taught me Ben Franklin's famous old maxim: *early to bed and early to rise makes a man healthy, wealthy, and wise*—and probably a woman, too, as well as all the little children. My grandma didn't have the ubiquitous TV, and now the Internet, to keep her up in the night. By mending socks in the light of an oil lamp, patiently demanding but hardly enervating or even exciting, she didn't overstimulate her brain with fantasies, and sleep could come soon after her head hit the pillow. My point (again): filling the evening mind with the fluff and buzz and fuzz of TV and the endless ranting of the Internet, even on the pretext of needing to unwind a bit, is not calculated to equip the morning mind to recognize and neutralize the snares that infest the day.

There is danger ahead on the road of life! There is a worldwide conspiracy to entrap every soul and the stuff that is beamed at our minds from satellite and communication tower is intended to penetrate every barrier against sin. *Keep your guard up!* Don't let the stuff inside. It's your move, your choice. You're holding the keys.

Because of such things God's wrath falls on the disobedient; don't participate with them in their folly (Eph. 5:6, 7). Did you ever consider that when you are entertained by the folly of others, you are participating in the folly? Do you realize that every time someone takes God's name in vain for a laugh and you don't protest, you are participating in the folly? Do you ever think that when you let the lyrics of the latest hit rattle through your brain, you are participating in the folly of the singer? That stand-up comedian isn't even a little bit funny; we laugh at the cost of our souls. It should be a sobering thought. At least it should get our attention, now! "The words of the LORD are pure words" (Ps. 12:6, NKJV), so must be ours!

Darkness, Emptiness, Despair—*Remember when you lived in spiritual darkness; remember the emptiness and despair you felt when the party was over and you were alone in the dark* (Eph. 5:8). I remember. We were all there at one time, *gratifying the cravings of our sinful nature and following its desires and thoughts* (Eph. 2:3). All of us were objects of wrath! Running scared with no place to hide. But! I like these "buts" in Paul's Ephesians; they introduce astonishing changes in our circumstances. *But* we don't have to dwell on our past broken experience. *But* God has forgiven, and we can forget. Our past is behind us, and our sins are crushed in the deepest sea! Gone! Light has come into our souls, and darkness cannot endure in the presence of light. Have you ever turned a flashlight on in the darkness of the night? Instantly light happens! Illumination follows the beam! We establish our coordinates again.

This reminds me of one night—a very dark night with a bit of a mist. The shorelines were precipitous and rocky. Safe landing places were rare. In the little boat we couldn't see a hand in front of our eyes. The quiet hum of the motor moved us slowly forward. But which way was forward? Somewhere out there in the dark blackness was a sandy beach and our work camp. It would gladly welcome us—if we found it before crashing our craft into the hostile shoreline. My crew and I strained our eyes in the darkness to see anything at all. Nothing. Why hadn't the lonely watchman in the camp left a fire burning to guide us in? We fired our rifle into the unrelenting blackness of the heavens. We fired again and again. And then we saw it. A single match strike across two miles of undulating water carried the light of deliverance. In minutes a blazing fire of driftwood was guiding our craft across the waves to safe landing on the sandy shore. "Thy word is a lamp unto my feet, and a light unto my path" (Ps. 119:105, KJV)—even across black waters of life.

God's word brings light into our darkness.

Ever try the reverse? Like, try to direct a beam of darkness into the light of the sun? Did the sun go out? Did the light vanish? What is a beam of darkness? Can one *project* darkness into light? The whole idea is ridiculous, oxymoronic, and preposterous! Since darkness always yields to light, since light is power and darkness is essentially nothing, and since we are children of light (1 Thess. 5:5), well, then, it follows naturally that we will live as children of light if, indeed, we remain in the light.

The choice is ours, of course, but why would we choose darkness, nothingness, over light and life? Why would we choose to muddle around, putter in dark and dangerous circles, grope helplessly, and grasp nothing, hoping for a saving beam from some sandy shore, when light is available, surrounding and embracing us? Why would we choose anything but the full-spectrum light of God's Spirit in our lives when He is free for the choosing?

Why, indeed?

We live in a confused world in confusing, ambiguous times. How can we be sure of anything? How can we recognize a safe and good landing? Is one option not just as good as another? Will I not be OK just trying to do the best I can to get through life without doing too much damage to the environment or to my neighbors? Live and let live? Maybe give a few coins to the pencil seller on the sidewalk and steer wide around some of the other street vendors.

There are some clues to help us concentrate on the Light of the world. That match flare across the miles of misty blackness to the bobbing boat gave us an immediate sense of correct direction. The driftwood fire, soon blazing on the shore, increased our confidence. We could now put full power to the prop without risk or fear of demolishing ourselves on some rocky headland. *This is how you will recognize light: Light is always expressed in goodness, righteousness, and truth* (Eph. 5:9). If these elements are missing, we can be certain that, however attractive it appears, what we see is not of God. But if we see goodness, righteousness, and truth can we be certain that, however daunting the circumstances, we are seeing light—that we are not being lured into the rocks by false appearances? We have heard that things that seem right and innocent (well, maybe not quite innocent; not totally good but not really *that* bad, either) might actually lead to death (Prov. 16:25). I think we might have discovered here a source of our uncertainty. If we are attempting to minimalize or quantify our works of righteousness, to get by with the least exposure to light, to have a little bit of both worlds, no, we will never recognize the Light.

It is wrong and futile to think of works of righteousness as a checklist of good things a good person will do—help the old lady across the street, keep food on the table for the kids, and all the hundreds of other things a reasonable person will naturally do. The only work of righteousness that is genuine is to retain Christ in your mind by faith through the indwelling of the Holy Spirit so that the life you live is Christ living out His life in you.

If, on the other hand, our intent is to walk in the light as it beams on us, well, the light will just keep on getting brighter. "The path of the righteous is like the morning sun [the first gleam of day], shining ever brighter till the full light of day [illuminates the way]. But the way of the wicked is like deep darkness; they do not know what makes them stumble" (Prov. 4:18, 19). The ordinary good girl or good boy (even good old boy) is so bitterly humiliated to acknowledge personal wickedness. But everyone who willingly, willfully, and ultimately refuses to choose the light is by default choosing darkness, is by default *dead in transgressions and sins* (Eph. 2:1)—that is, wicked by definition, no matter how punctual he or she is in paying the tax bill. You have read this idea before and now you see it again: you cannot be more God-defying, more wicked, more alienated from all that is good than to say to God, "I can do this myself. Please just stand aside and let me work out my own problems. Don't call me; I'll call You when I get in a real bind."

Focus the Effort—I think we can agree with Paul that we need to put some focused effort into our experience in light. But how do we focus our effort? Are we flirting with legalism? I think Scripture gives us some unmistakable clues to this mystery, so let's go there for our answers, starting with the familiar Psalm 119:11 in the King James Version: "Thy word have I hid in mine heart, that I might not sin against thee." Moving from the Psalms to the Gospels, we get a new perspective on "word." Again from the King James Version: "In the beginning was the Word … and the Word was made flesh, and dwelt among us" (John 1:1, 14). We thus understand from Scripture that the Word in our hearts is much more than the accumulation of a few memory texts.

For thirty-three years Jesus walked the dusty trails of Judea, Galilee, Samaria, and a bit of the surrounding landscapes. He boated on the placid-stormy waters of Galilee and, with no place to call His own (Luke 9:58), He warmed His hands at campfires along the Jordan and in the mountains of Syria, or He borrowed a place in the home or garden of a friend. This Man was no wimp!

When He was here, the scope of His work was limited only by His humanity. But Jesus is no longer bodily with us. We can't see His compassion-carved face or hear His voice in comfort or counsel. Even if He were still bodily on this planet, we could never be that blessed as to get an audience with Him; there would be too many people pressing about Him. Of course, He had the perfect solution to that dilemma, and He put it into effect 2,000 years ago: He left us. And because He left, He was able to send to us His Holy Spirit to be in each one of us forever (John 14:16–18)—or, stated another way, because He left us, we were in a position to receive His Holy Spirit (John 16:7). Whatever the reason the truth of the matter is this: Jesus now dwells in each believer in the person of His Holy Spirit (John 14:18).

Paul makes some bold, remarkable, encouraging, and empowering statements about the results of the indwelling of the Holy Spirit: *Live by the Spirit and you will not gratify the desires of the sinful nature* (Gal. 5:16) and from Romans 8:9, *You ... are controlled, not by the sinful nature but by the Spirit, if the Spirit of God lives in you*. As a result of this, we *live by faith in the Son of God who loves us and gave Himself for us* (Gal. 2:20). Wow! That's awesome! And how is the life of faith engaged?

David said it anciently, and we repeat: "Thy word have I hid in mine heart, that I might not sin against thee" (Ps. 119:11, KJV). If we understand "word" to be Jesus Christ in the person of His Holy Spirit then the verse actually says, *I have received Jesus Christ to live in my heart by faith, and I will not sin against Him*. Wow! That's awesome! The life of faith or the fight of faith is to retain Jesus in our hearts. And this will include getting to know Him through spending much time with Him in His word, in prayer, and in sharing what we know and experience with one another. The life of faith also involves our obedience to Jesus in the things we understand (Luke 17:5–10). Retaining Jesus in our hearts by faith (Eph. 3:17) is the good work that God prepared in advance for us to do (Eph. 2:10). Consequently, our focus now is not on doing this or that with a little help—or a lot of help—from God, but by faith to retain Jesus in our minds by His Spirit in us so that the lives we live are His life lived out in us. Wow! That's awesome!

Focus on Jesus. Spend quality and quantity time with Him, and your life will be lived in light. Seek for and find out what pleases the Lord and obey Him in the details. Faith will increase as Jesus told us in Luke 17. As our faith increases, the *manifold wisdom of God will be made known to all those in the heavenly realms through God's eternal purpose, which he successfully completed in our Lord Christ Jesus* (Eph. 3:10, 11). It's a done deal! All we need to do is sign in and remain in Christ (John 15:1–9)! Now!

Dead-Ended Deeds of Darkness—Having responded to and continuing to live in the light that God is shining on us in full-spectrum glory, the deeds of darkness, dead ended as they are, will appear to us as dark unholiness and vulgar emptiness. It should be a no-brainer to have nothing to do with them. Realistically, with the old nature still very much alive, if not well, and still salivating for our souls, the frailties of the human bodies in which we all live will frequently leave us vulnerable to the assaults of Satan.

But be warned, quiescent habits, defunct thought patterns, long-forgotten likes and dislikes, all the expressions of the old nature, dormant though still functional, will kick us when we're down with a cold or with a friend's betrayal or a pink slip. But we don't have to submit to their assaults. God is great, and through His grace and strength (Phil. 4:13), we can stand up and, controlled by the Spirit because He lives in us (Rom. 8:9), expose them for what they are—springs without water (2 Peter 2:17), "clouds without rain, ... autumn trees, without fruit and uprooted ... wandering stars, for whom blackest darkness has been reserved forever" (Jude 12, 13).

How do we expose these blots and blemishes for what they are? Just live in light, and light Himself will expose everything. Jesus said it in His sermon on the mount: *Let your light shine so that people around you may see your good deeds and praise (not you, but) your heavenly Father* (Matt. 5:16). Clearly, good lives are for God's vindication and glory, not for ours.

A few days ago, I participated in another

The Long Road to Grace

Adventure Race with the two partners in my team. We pushed our reluctant bodies up hill and down, through mud where even the patrolling quads got stuck, over boulders, across gullies, sometimes carrying our bicycles, sometimes pushing, and sometimes riding—for just short of nine hours. It was a time of bonding with friends, a time to pull together for the good of the body (of three). The two of us slow learners from last year's race had picked up a new partner who turned out to be a young man, twenty-two-year-old Travis, a co-worker with my original partner, Ron. Once, while Travis and I were alone together, he mentioned that he had never heard Ron say a bad word about anyone. It didn't surprise me. Ron's light was illuminating the path of a man forty years younger. At some point Travis may recognize the Source of Ron's light.

But in this world we might not only have to let our light shine, we might also have to confront and expose evil directly. Isaiah virtually shouted, "Cry aloud, spare not; lift up your voice like a trumpet; tell My people their transgression, and the house of Jacob their sins (Isa. 58:1, NKJV). Are there societal sins that should not be spared our anger, sins that should be confronted and condemned? Are there sins in the body that require radical surgery? Are some of us called to this ministry? Perhaps some are and some are not. But let us all live so close to our Father in heaven that He can guide us in every decision for every ministry and every action. Let us draw close to Him so that He may sustain us, as some of these potential confrontations could draw down severe repercussions on our heads.

Once upon a time the secret lives of the disobedient were shameful even to mention in public, but now it seems that everything once kept out of sight is flaunted brazenly for public display and discussion. Our very liberal CBC, the national radio and TV in Canada (also available through public radio in the United States), apparently has assumed the mission of opening every closet in the land to expose every deviant behavior and make it acceptable and familiar to this postmodern, secular, sophisticated, amoral society.

Because God is only a figment of tribal mythology, a creature of Bronze-Age barbarism, and we are the Brights, the progressive descendants of Darwin, there need be no secrets. Let's live and let live. Just stay out of my way. Well, the Bible tells us that only the fool thinks there is no God (Ps. 14:1). Those are hard words, and I am very reluctant to apply them to anyone. Yet given their prominence in Scripture, how much more foolish is the one who publishes these thoughts to draw others into his or her folly?

We can't move on without clarifying the identity of the disobedient. Everyone sins; that is a given; however, is everyone disobedient? I think the answer is a solid no. Disobedience happens when, knowing God, we deliberately choose to ignore Him. Speaking of the ancients, Paul writes: "Although they knew God, they neither glorified him as God nor gave thanks to him, but their thinking became futile and their foolish hearts were darkened. Although they claimed to be wise, they became fools" (Rom. 1:21, 22). These were disobedient. The result was the human descent into the maelstrom of wickedness.

We are the children of the ancients, but we do not need to follow their foolishly stupid ways in disobedience. No, we are disobedient only when we deliberately, knowingly, resolutely rebel and refuse to repent of our sin. Is sin inevitable in the life of the believer? I think not, but you will have to work out this question for yourself. However, we should be very cautious about thinking we have broken free of the power of sin.

Be more than cautious; don't think that way at all (1 Cor. 10:12). Besides, God has not asked us to fight against sin in our lives. He simply wants us to examine ourselves to see if we are in the faith (2 Cor. 13:5) and to continuously fight the fight of faith (1 Tim. 6:12). As we choose God and fight the fight of faith, our lives, inspired by His light will be visible, open to view, bringing glory to our Father. The warm wind of the Spirit has already brought you life. It's daylight now in your swamp; let the sleeper awake! Get up and the light of Christ will illuminate your way.

Life Specifics—*Life in Light requires careful attention to the important things; wisdom and prudence are essential* (Eph. 5:15). Scripture speaks of wisdom 222 times from Exodus to Revelation. In Exodus 28–36, God gives wisdom to those willing to commit themselves to the construction of the tabernacle under His direction. In these cases wisdom was given for what we would call manual work or perhaps artistry or artisanship. These willing individuals were endowed with the hand-eye coordination and the inner vision to produce works of beauty, function, and intricate design, to read and follow a blueprint actually laid out in heaven, and to visualize, design, and assemble these objects and structures. Scripture calls this endowment wisdom.

On a recent tour of a hospital (under construction), I was led by the master on-site builder through about seven acres of floor space under various stages of completion. I saw what looked like miles of piping for distribution of medical gasses, for heating and cooling; I was shown the intricate apparatus for temperature control and the control of pathogens. More miles of cabling to satisfy our modern appetite for information technology were laid out in mesh trays soon to be concealed above ceilings in the corridors. The heating center contained a dozen low-pressure boilers of the latest gleaming technology all activated by silicon chips in the master control room. The layout of the hospital can be expressed in one word: privacy. There is certainly privacy for the patient, who can be transported from surgery to recovery to convalescence through corridors never seen by the visiting public.

The designing and the construction of the facility elicits one thought: wisdom. Did the same God who endowed Bezaleel and Aholiab (Exod. 36:1, 2, KJV) with the wisdom to build the tabernacle in the wilderness endow the architects, engineers, and builders with wisdom to assemble the millions of pieces of metal, plastic, fiber, and mineral into an orderly array that will function as planned for the care of our injured and ailing citizens? My answer: a definite yes! Do we recognize and applaud the Source of our wisdom? My answer: sadly, seldom.

But wisdom is for more than building construction. We need to bring wisdom into all facets of our existence—building solid relationships, building healthy attitudes, building correct knowledge bases, and building ties with our Father. So important is God as the source of all wisdom that four times in Job through Proverbs, and written down over hundreds of years, we are told that the *fear of the Lord is wisdom's beginning* (Job 28:28; Ps. 111:10; Prov. 1:7; 9:10). A thousand years later we encounter New Testament writers speaking of wisdom: *All the treasures of wisdom can be found in Christ* (Col. 2:3), and if you find yourself *short on wisdom, ask for it. God will give it generously without criticizing you* (James 1:5). That is encouraging!

There is much in this world that is considered

wise, and the wise are revered for their flaunted wisdom. But don't be deceived by public opinion. If we measure ourselves by the standards of this fading world, we will be seen to be fools in the end (2 Cor. 10:12) because "the wisdom of this world is foolishness in God's sight" (1 Cor. 3:18, 19).

In keeping with the concepts of light and dark that we have been considering, we can see that wisdom is to folly as light is to darkness (Eccles. 2:12, 13). This can be shown to be true like a mathematical theorem. Just as darkness is the absence of light, so is folly the absence of wisdom. The poisonous fruit of folly is clearly articulated in James: "bitter envy and selfish ambition" (James 3:14). Where these elements are present, "there you find disorder and every evil practice. But the wisdom that comes from heaven is first of all pure; then peace-loving, considerate, submissive, full of mercy and good fruit, impartial and sincere. Peacemakers who sow in peace [raise] a harvest in righteousness" (James 3:16–18).

Paul speaks of wisdom and prudence. We have, I submit, correctly and adequately described the source, appearance, and results of wisdom. But what is prudence other than to choose wisdom? A life of prudence means being careful, very careful, to listen to the voice of wisdom among all the softly seductive or stridently rasping voices calling to us clamouring for and demanding our attention, time, money, and souls, every moment of every day. The voice that we should hear is the voice of God's Holy Spirit, by which all wisdom becomes ours to have, to hold, and in which to rejoice eternally—and obey in real time.

Life in this dizzily whirling global village is short, at best. Paul tells us not to squander our time and to use every opportunity to be in light because outside in the dark everything is evil. Living free and easy with our time is actually to squander our life. This idea reaches deeper into our pockets than we normally think or even want to think. The center of every village on this globe, the place where the people come most frequently, is not the church (surprised?), but the market, the place where we shell out our hard-come-by, hard-to-keep coin; the place where we drop our sweat-earned livings. In fact, it is the place where we give up large chunks of our lives. To give up a coin is to give up the portion of life represented by the time it took to earn that coin. To trade that coin for a bauble is to consider that bauble to be worth that bit of life that you gave up to have it around your neck, in your pocket, puffing out your nose, or even contributing to the adipose tissue around your liver. Is that thing really worth your life? I've honed this axe several times already, so you can guess where I would swing it, but I won't. It's time for you to swing that axe where you will.

Moving on with Paul, we learn that outside in the dark everything is evil, and we should be taking every opportunity to be in light. Is everything apart from Christ evil? Is there no good in the worst of us just as there is bad in the best of us? Let's go to Scripture to get the goods on this good-bad question that has stymied the best of minds for generations. Jesus said, "There is none good but one, that is, God" (Mark 10:18, KJV), and Paul speaking of us humans agrees: "There is none righteous, no, not one" (Rom. 3:10, KJV). That should settle the question of who's good, and we already know the answer: outside of Christ there is *no* good anywhere. In Christ, only in Christ, every believer is counted by God to be perfect (Col. 1:28). Would you say that if God makes the assessment, the argument is settled?

The opportunities to be in light are everywhere because light is there, everywhere, always—for now. The only thing that could possibly keep us away from God—or light out of us—is our own choice. Every new day is a new opportunity to embrace light. What comes first, God or the *Daily News and Gossip*? God or breakfast? God or our jobs? God or exercise? Every day is a new opportunity to immerse ourselves in light. What will I put first, the kingdom of God and His righteousness or something, anything, else?

This morning I woke at 5:30 to beams of sunshine after three days of rain, heavy at times. So what do I do first? I check the rain gauge (9.5 inches, 238 mm); I check the irrigation pump station at the lake (water's up on the pump base and still rising); I take the pump out and bring it to the shop; I also move the canoe to higher ground; I stop to pat the doggie who comes to greet me and then come into the house where I chat with Mirja before checking the weather report on the Internet. Only then do I turn to seeking God's kingdom. But that pump was in an emergency situation, right? It could have been flooded, and I would have suffered financial loss. Of course, I admit the emergency, but the emergency was created because I neglected to check the pump before going to bed. I could have read the signs then and recognized the need to remove it (Matt. 16:3, 4). Happily, I don't have a job. But what if I did? This is how I get into spiritual trouble. I don't know about you.

Evil Times and the Spirits That Surround Us

Paul said, *Because we live in evil times, we need to understand the will of the Lord. Anything wilfully short of understanding the will of the Lord is utterly foolish and ultimately destructive* of our relationship with Him—and of our salvation (Eph. 5:17). Are the times really that evil? Look about and listen: across the continents floods wreak enormous damage with loss of property and drowning of dreams (millions of dollars in damage and loss in my own town these last few days); monstrous wild fires turn our smoke and mirrors stuff to smoke and ashes; earth-shattering quakes reduce things that appeared solid to rubble; tsunamis rise up out of placid seas and without warning wash everything we valued away forever; hurricanes and tornadoes smash our things to bits. Then there are the wars, war mongers, rumors of wars, and the quasi, undeclared wars that kill, maim, and destroy just as effectively as real wars. At home we have the standard and regular murders, rapes, frauds, kidnappings, muggings, and drug-ravaged lives. And then we have the usual broken families, broken promises, and broken hearts. Did we mention disease, hunger, thirst, or poverty? Though we may never experience any of the above, in the end *six feet of earth makes us all of one size*—so many without hope of anything beyond. Is there any question that we are living in evil times?

But do we understand the will of the Lord for us in these evil times? Are we so caught up in slapping mosquitoes (wet weather this year means more of the poky critters) that we forget, for now, why we were left in the swamp? Our primary role is not to drain the smelly place but to point swamp dwellers to the Way out of its reeking mire.

Can't remember what I'm supposed to be doing here.

Our primary role is not to fight for social, political or economic justice, though some may be called to these roles. A few names come to mind: Wilberforce and the slave trade in Britain; Tom Dooley and health care needs in Laos; Mother Theresa and the poorest of the poor in Calcutta. These people did wonderful work but the slave trade goes on (yes, it does); health care is rudimentary at best for huge populations around this globe, even in enlightened North America where millions of people do not have medical insurance, and poverty really has not been touched—even in Theresa's Calcutta. The poor are still with us just as Jesus predicted (John 12:8). Certainly in the course of fulfilling our primary mandate, we may achieve some small political or social benefits for some of the people some of the time, but this is not our primary role.

All of the best intentions and efforts of politicians and judges piled together will not make a substantial difference in the pain this hurting world feels every day. The only solution is the promised divine intervention (John 14:1–3). Our primary role: to make sure that as many people as possible in our personal circles of influence know about the pending divine intervention and their opportunity to participate in the world to come—without neglecting the weightier matters: justice, mercy, and faithfulness (Matt. 23:23).

For believers, the will of the Lord is so basic. We are simply called "to love one another" (1 John 4:11). Is that it? Everything? Well, there is also the preceding command: love the Lord (Mark 12:30). It seems that all other good things that believers are expected to do, really do, or neglect to do are rooted in these two commandments (Matt. 22:40). And this love is poured out lavishly into our lives, the penstocks of God's grace to the world. The more of God's love we pass on to others, the more we receive to pass on. Let me illustrate.

As I sit here, a small drama is playing out about two and one-half miles down the highway. Because of the recent heavy rain, a lake has hugely expanded itself, rolling over its natural boundaries to the railway grade that parallels the highway and is now acting as a dam. Because the culverts are not passing sufficient water either under the railway (hence the lake perhaps now more than double its natural size) or under the highway, dangerous conditions are developing. The massive vortex created by the water rushing through the railway culverts and battering against the highway has already demobilized one of the three culverts and is eating away at the highway grade itself. This is only an illustration, but when we fail for any reason to pass on God's grace, His mercy, His compassion, His love, when the conduits are obstructed, we expose ourselves to serious personal spiritual damage and deny others the benefits they might have experienced.

Spirits and the Spirit—God's Holy Spirit will not cohabit or hobnob or do business with any other spirit whether found in a bottle, under a table, or in any other place or guise. Is He jealous? You bet He is, by His own admission (Exod. 20:3–5); in fact, His name is Jealous (Exod. 34:14)—bet you didn't remember that. Apparently, there is appropriate jealousy, a godly jealousy (2 Cor. 11:2), which motivates the believer to work hard for the salvation of others, to be proactive in sharing the gospel with unbelievers, and to point out danger spots to believers. Shall we venture into that territory?

What are some of those danger spots, those spirits vying for your attention and allegiance? I almost hesitate to mention some because they are so familiar and so intimately bound up in the lives of so many. No one on the way to the kingdom will knowingly be seduced by direct approaches of the enemy. (Pornography, for example, as is recognized by most societies, is utterly wicked, vile, evil, and no person with a hint of morality will continue to indulge.) However, there are subtler devices, the countless familiar spirits masquerading as quite innocent, that are more successfully used to mislead and entrap the unwary and the careless. Even those who imagine themselves to be sophisticated, wise, and most certainly not of the gutter sort who might resort to porn for their entertainment are not safe outside the protection afforded by wearing (not just storing or polishing) the full armor of God.

It goes without saying, one would think, but apparently it doesn't. Believe it or not, one of the *spirits* entrapping the souls of the kingdom is actually known as spirits. In reality: alcohol, drink, booze. I don't buy the current arguments for booze in some Christian circles. I've seen, too close and smelly, the consequences of the Saturday night wine glass or beer bottle at the beach. That delicate bouquet in the sparkling crystal of the high-end restaurant too often becomes cheap wine, shoe polish, and antifreeze with the dank, vomit-and-urine-soaked hallways of the flophouse. The smartly dressed sophisticate finds herself the harridan shuffling behind the grocery cart in the downtown east side of Everycity. This is not just poverty, but spirits-induced poverty—fully preventable. Too many people close to me died young with their boots on as a direct and immediate result of pretending that *it* wouldn't happen to them.

Sadly, foolishly, inexplicably, there is an element among those who claim to be waiting for the kingdom who apparently think that they are a cut above the rest of us. They apparently think they are smart enough, sophisticated enough, cool enough, spiritually advanced enough to indulge the alcoholic instinct without getting caught. Maybe. But then, maybe not. I don't know what they think, but I am going to suggest (rather strongly) that they are caught already, even without the hangover on Sunday morning. I am going to suggest also (rather more strongly) that their drinking is not an indication of the careful judgment of one saved by grace and experiencing salvation, one who is now free in Christ to indulge, but a symptom of a life that is already accelerating on the downhill run to the abyss. Paul clearly links wine drinking to drunkenness and debauchery. Wine (or any other alcohol) on the menu is not an option for end-time people. Don't go down that drain. Instead, stay in the light and be filled with the Spirit.

What about the countless other spirits? We've already mentioned some of the vehicles by which the spirits take over lives and destroy: pop entertainment, light reading, suggestive dressing, power displays, stuff and more stuff, pride of opinion, feeling sorry for ourselves, evil surmising … do we need to go on? Just reflect on the things in your own life that take your time and resources, your life. Are they Holy Spirit motivated? Holy Spirit motivation, guided by the clear Word, will answer any question of should I or should I not. Because we live in evil times, we need total submission to Jesus Christ in the person of the Holy Spirit, who desires to indwell our minds and steer us safely through the maze of other spirits all clamouring for our souls.

The Spirit-filled person will always be ready to share a psalm or a spiritual song or a hymn by which to cheer your way. This is genuine cheer and not the phony stuff from the bottle that leads to debauchery. This is the cheer that endures through tough breaks and good times. But to be ready we need a supply. We must have already stored in our minds with easy access the psalms and hymns—even if we have no one but the birds to hear our voices. Once again we are faced with the issues of time and choice for filling the files of the mind.

We'll never get away from time and choice in this life. Get used to it. Time and choice is inherent in the pain and pleasure the believer will feel until his or her mortal puts on immortality and *death is swallowed up in victory* (1 Cor. 15:53, 54). The tension the believer senses when deciding between the raucous clamours of the self and the still, small, and persistent voice of God's Holy Spirit is proof of God's serious interest in his or her salvation. The peace that suffuses the soul when the believer seizes the victory in Jesus is absolute proof of God's ability to save to the uttermost those who come to Him in Jesus (Heb. 7:25). Oh Lord, hurry the day when this faith becomes tangible and we feel the warm zephyrs of Eden restored to us. You have my permission to go to work on me.

Now We All Thank Our God—For everything we thank you, our Father. For everything? To the Ephesians that is exactly what Paul says: give thanks for *everything*. Give thanks for the tragedies that come into our lives? Give thanks for the betrayals that poison our days? Give thanks for the breakdown that nearly bankrupted me? Why should I give thanks for any of this? Why indeed? It doesn't seem to make much sense; except that is what God tells us in Paul's Ephesians to do. Should I obey without understanding? Because the Bible says so?

In 1 Thessalonians 5:18, also a letter of Paul, we find some clarity: "Give thanks in all circumstances, for this is God's will for you in Christ Jesus." Clearly, God wants our thanks, and for us to give thanks is good. Can we reconcile the "for everything" of Ephesians with the "all circumstances" of 1 Thessalonians? Let's try.

If we look at every bad experience, every temptation, every hurt—even every joy and every profitable day (yes, we humans tend to take our good things for granted and forget to give God thanks for the unexpected bonus)—as opportunities to give glory to our Creator Father, then in these circumstances we should recognize personalized opportunities to take our faithful God at His word and seize the way of escape He has provided for the occasion (1 Cor. 10:13). It could be quite exciting!

So, in reality, we are not thanking God that our friends deserted us or that the contract was voided to my financial loss; we are thanking Him for the opportunity to honor Him by the way we react to our changed circumstances. We are thanking Him for His promise to work out every bad experience for our eternal good if we only give Him the chance, and we are asking for the grace to accept the good times without becoming smug or complacent (Rom. 8:28). We are thanking Him for new opportunities, fresh every day like bread from the village bakery in France that Mirja and I enjoyed so much—even the morning walks to the bakery and the chats with the baker. After all, Jesus is the Bread of Life. He, too, enjoys the morning conversation; He is fresh every day.

In retrospect, I can dredge out of my mind the memories of many occasions (happy and sad) when I should have thanked God for the opportunity to grow in His care. When I was young I partnered once with my brother-in-law to chainsaw clear several miles of power line right-of-way through high mountains just south of the Alaskan Panhandle. In the lower sections, we contended with thick stands of massive hemlock trees. They had to be felled, cut into man-sized sections, and all the limbs and smaller pieces burned. There was no other form of machinery, as our only access was by helicopter. We started on the north end and slowly worked our way south into high country where only the rare shrub interrupted our progress—that and the rain.

Because of the miles of big timber, we were able to negotiate a higher rate for the entire contract, and we felt very good about the job. When finally we cut down the last hemlock giant and disposed of it according to the contract, we were satisfied with a job well done. Ahead of us were miles of alpine meadow at the same price. My partner and I left our good French crew in camp and caught a helicopter to the end of the road. We needed showers—several of them.

Two days later we returned to find our entire camp dumped in a heap at the end of the road and our workers needing their pay. Our contract had been voided by the company. Reason: company maintained we had abandoned the contract by our absence. Really? Hardly! But we were young, inexperienced, without resources to fight a corrupt company, so the company made thousands at our expense. It hurt—rain-soaked, wind-battered, and separated from our families as we had been for months! Did I see this as an opportunity? Not really. Actually, not at all! Not then. Plans for university receded another year. Did I thank God in or for this experience? Not that I recall. I grumbled; I complained. Perhaps that is why I was given other opportunities. Once I—oh, I'll spare you the tale of that learning experience.

These temptations come to us every sunny day and starlit night in one guise or another. All of them are unexpected. The moose materializes in the beams of the setting sun and ends up in the passenger seat; the service mechanic is distracted and forgets to tighten the drain plug in the crank case; the Internet goes down just when I need to send my document. Out of the blue we learn that the landlord has other plans for his commercial space. With every temptation comes a way of escape direct from our Father in heaven. Cool, eh? As we go through life we learn to trust our Father in every circumstance. That is why we can thank Him *in* and *for* everything. We grow the attitude of thankfulness so slowly, but it is God's continuing gift to us through the long or short lifetime of our sanctification, and it governs our response to every temptation.

The Test of Sincerity—And now, finally, the test of the sincerity of our walk in the light! One question: *out of our ardent love and reverence for Christ, [do we] submit to one another* (Eph. 5:21)? How else could we submit to one another if not out of love and reverence for Christ? Submission would be impossible outside of Christ. That's the way it is, folks. Love and reverence for Christ is a sham, a delusion, a misnomer, a charade, a hypocritical front if we refuse to submit to one another. Submit? Really? What does it mean to submit? Does it mean to let people walk all over us? Does it mean to let others hold us hostage by their ever-changing moods? Does it mean to let the loudest voice determine the vote at church board? What is mutual submission? Is submission different in the family of God than in the market place?

Following a good biblical principle, the last question will be the first addressed: yes, submission is different both in degree and in order in the family of God than in the market place. In the market place, we have the same obligations as all other players, only more so. Our obligation to play fair, negotiate openly, and give honest returns to our investors is, if anything, much greater than that of the unbeliever. We have God's reputation to uphold as well as our own. (And like it or not, as a congregation we have an obligation to ensure that members of the body who come up short in the honesty of their dealings are disciplined and seen to be disciplined for the sake of God's reputation.)

Within the family we have the same obligation for fairness, openness, and honesty as we have in the market place, but we need to take our relations to the next level. Out of our ardent love and reverence for Christ, we need to ensure as far as possible that there is mutual satisfaction and benefit and that our actions glorify God. In the church board, we might have to show, with firmness, gentleness, compassion, and full integrity (1 Tim. 5:1, 20) that the loudest voice doesn't always communicate the best solution and, in fact, it might be blocking the voice of God's Spirit—even if he or she is right. The grace of God teaches us to say *No* to passionate outbursts and to *live self-controlled, pure, and godly lives every single day, while we wait for our greatest hope—the glorious appearing of our great God and Savior, Jesus Christ* (Titus 2:12, 13).

The member who attempts to hold the congregation hostage by moody outbursts cannot be allowed to do so. However, in rebuking the behavior, we are not repudiating him. We need to have compassion for his feelings, and we need to attempt to understand the reasons behind the moods. The outbursts may be the cries of pain that others cannot feel. It will take more time to work through the real problem that he is trying to express.

Because some dear saints have not learned in childhood and youth how to deal with differences of opinion, disappointment, and even good times, they are "more-grace-required" people. We submit to this saint by holding on in love through his underdeveloped communication attempts without allowing him to control the outcome. It might even be necessary occasionally to say goodbye and hang up the phone. Be sure that some of these exercises in submission will take more than one walk around the block and more than one cursory prayer for grace.

Genuine submission in the congregation is to approach potential differences with the intent to find out what pleases the Lord (Eph. 5:17)—we might find that the Lord is not pleased by either of our wants. Ultimately, mutual submission requires that we submit to God as a first step. Remember Moses, the man who has come down through history as the meekest of men? Watch as he rebukes the Pharaoh, leads to freedom and nationhood the ragtag mob of erstwhile slaves, stands between the people and the sea, receives the commandments from the hands of God, orders the execution of thousands of unrepentant rebels, intervenes with God for the lives of the penitents, and finally, is barred from entering the Promised Land! Moses was called meek because he bowed to God, not because he let king or slave stand on his neck. Because he bowed to God, he was empowered to endure four decades of abuse from the people he loved more than he loved his life (Exod. 32:32)—his eternal life. Now that is real submission! That is the type of submission that God is looking for in every believer. Are we up to it? It's impossible, of course, unless by the

Wives and Husbands

Wives, husbands, I'm talking directly to you now about submission. This is a delicate topic, especially for women; I am sure that you would like me just to skip over it. I can't do that. The Spirit has spoken plainly: Wives, submit to your husbands as if you were submitting to the Lord. There's a good reason to do so: in God's economy He has designated the husband as the head of the wife, just as Christ was appointed to be head and Savior of His body, the church. It is no secret (and we all fully agree) that the church is to submit to Christ, its Head. Just so, wives are to submit to their husbands.

But this is not a one-way relationship. Husbands have a God-mandated responsibility to love their wives. After all, Christ loved the church. It just follows that husbands ought to love their wives in the same manner. Christ gave Himself up for the church, His body. (I have written elsewhere of how He did not cling to His divinity, His right, but descended to earth as the poorest of poor children and submitted even to the extent of giving up His eternal life on the cross for the church. Husbands, did you know this?) His intent was to make the church holy, cleansing her with water and word and then to present her to Himself spotlessly clean, radiantly shining, wrinkle free, and without a single blemish. His church will be holy, blameless, faultless, undefiled by His own will and action. (Husbands, are you hearing this?)

Apply the principles to your relationship with your wife. In loving her as you love your own body, you will truly love yourself. Certainly you must know that no one hates his own body. It doesn't make sense to do so. You live in your body. You feed your body; you care for your body. Christ cares for the church in the same way, and we are members of His body. This is why you left your parents' home and set up a new home with your wife. You were united to her and became one flesh with her. What a mystery! However, though I speak about Christ and the church, husbands must love their wives and wives must respect their husbands. (Eph. 5:22–33)

Wives and Husbands—When we venture to speak or write of husband-wife relationships, especially if we even remotely suggest or vaguely imply that the wife should be submissive, we are very soon in very deep water. It's swirling around our noses; it's turbid, it smells, and it's rising fast. Prudence could recommend that we back paddle really vigorously. But Prudence is an old-fashioned girl with old-fashioned values, and she advises us to listen to Paul. Do we look for interpretation of Paul in the postmodern values of present society? Probably not.

Scripture must be its own interpreter, and it must be consistent with itself. We learned a bit ago the reason that we remember Moses as the meekest of men: he submitted to God with reverence and obedience in everything, not to a pharaoh or to a squalling mob of discontents. He is our example in submission.

In working our way through this *delicate topic*, we would not be smart to read the first paragraph without reading the second and third paragraphs in immediate context. When we read the entire passage, we learn that the wife's submission is not to a domineering, overbearing brute; instead, the wife is to submit to a guy who willingly would give his eternal life for her just as Christ did for the church.

Husbands and wives own a mutual interest in the peace, prosperity, and happiness of the union they have established. Having left their parents' homes and established a home of their own, why would they undermine or compromise their hope of earthly happiness in the oneness of their union by needless and vain attempts to dominate each other? Scripture requires submission on the part of the wife; it does *not* sanction domination on the part of the husband. In fact, by citing Christ's care for the church as the example for the husband's care for his wife, the Word of God absolutely *forbids* domination by the husband. We will take our understanding one more vital step: it is congenitally impossible for a wife to be submissive to a domineering husband. It can't happen because submission, by scriptural definition, is a willing and eager response to love, not mere compliance with demands enforced by strength.

Thoughtful writer that Paul is and ever conscious of the value of ink, parchment, and time, he uses the vehicle of his discussion of husband-wife relationships to teach other important spiritual truths. You noticed above that submission is impossible in a violent and domineering relationship. The analogy of a husband-wife relationship in which submission and love are the governing principles teaches us of the relationship Christ desires to have with His church. He has already poured out His *agape* love in quantities that cannot be measured. The response of the church that He can rightfully expect would be willing and eager submission, of course.

What does this type of submission look like? Paul has gone to great lengths to describe the life of the believer in relationship with other believers—that is, in the church. Believers' lives will be characterized by the life that Jesus Christ demonstrated for us while He walked this sod. They will be empowered by the indwelling Spirit of Jesus Christ, which He gave us in rich abundance.

The character of Jesus will be expressed in every aspect of our lives: in the way we use our resources to ease the passage of those who have nothing, in the way we share the good news with as many as we can reach in the least time possible, in the way we dress with modesty and simplicity, in the way we speak in purity, honesty, reverence, and humility; in short, His character is expressed in how we believers love one another in submission to Christ, the Head of the church. All these and more describe in grubby, real life meaning the willing submission of the church to Christ, of the wife to the husband.

Describing the submission of Christ to the will of His Father, Paul tells us that He gave Himself up for the church, His body (Phil. 2). He assures us that our *attitude should be the same as that of Christ Jesus* (Phil. 2:5). Of course, having an attitude that is the same as that of Christ Jesus is a gift of God to those who will receive it. How could it be self-generated? Here again the concept of willing submission (there can be no other) is unambiguously taught. Jesus gave up His divine prerogatives. Having made himself nothing, He descended to this earth as a human being (Phil. 2:7).

Well, what's so bad about being human? Did we say it was bad? It's certainly not divine! His incarnation was so infinitely humbling that we cannot find an analogy adequate to describe it. Would it be like Prince Caspian becoming a toad to save the toads? Hardly close. Every prince and every toad are the handiwork of the same Creator. Was it this Creator who became a human being to save us? Exactly. And this Creator will retain His humanity for all eternity. He was given (He was not here on loan) to the human race (John 3:16) so that we could form some concept of divinity that even begins to approach reality—and for other reasons as we well know.

But He descended much further. When He found Himself to be "in appearance as a man, he humbled himself by becoming obedient to death—even death on a cross!" (Phil. 2:8). Death is horrifying and horrible enough, but what is death on a cross? Jesus could have been stoned to death—or drowned, a much faster and cleaner processes. In the Jewish tradition, malefactors were typically stoned. Remember that Deacon Stephen suffered stoning for virtually the same offense as Jesus was crucified (Acts 7:59).

The rabbis in their mercy could have spared Jesus the agony of a prolonged death exposed to public scorn but, no, they wanted Him *crucified*. What they really wanted was to ensure that He would never rise from the grave: they believed that crucifixion ensured that the everlasting curse of God would be upon Him (Deut. 21:22, 23). And the curse of God was upon Jesus (Gal. 3:13). He was made a curse for us so that we would not have to suffer eternal separation (the curse) from God. Don't pretend to understand the hows or even the whys of the mystery of salvation. Just accept that because Jesus was made to be sin for you, because He willingly took your curse (2 Cor. 5:21) and died with your sins on His record, you do not have to die eternally.

But you will have to accept your death in Him. As Paul assures us in 2 Corinthians: "We are convinced that one died for all, and therefore all died. And he died for all, that those who live should no longer live for themselves but for him who died for them and was raised again" (2 Cor. 5:14, 15). And from the Romans we learn that *if we have been united with him like this in his death, we will certainly also be united with him in his resurrection* (Rom. 6:5). And being united with Jesus in His resurrection, the lives we live will be new, submissive, honoring to Him (Rom. 6:4). In Him we have *become the righteousness of God* (2 Cor. 5:21). Here is the only and entire example, power, and motivation for love and submission in the family and in the family of God.

God's intent in bringing us to salvation in Christ is to *make the church holy, cleansing her with water and word and then to present her to Himself spotlessly clean, radiantly shining, wrinkle free, and without a single blemish* (Eph. 5:25–27). Notice who is doing the cleansing; notice who presents *her to Himself*; notice that I don't iron out the wrinkles or remove the spots and blemishes; I don't polish to a high shine. This is the work that Christ does through the indwelling Holy Spirit in those who submit to Him.

The husband-wife analogy is a masterful instrument for teaching us the Christ-church relationship that changes our lives, replaces our urge to dominate with a submissive spirit, and enables us to experience the full measure of the love of Christ. Christ loved the church and gave Himself for it. As members of the body, we are now positioned to love and submit. This concept is no longer a thorny issue of women's rights and patriarchal domineering. What a mystery—solved! Though Paul speaks about Christ and the church, husbands can now love their wives and wives can now respect their husbands. There is no need to work out who is superior to or independent from whom. In Christ all this has been solved already. In submitting to Christ, the Head, we submit to one another; we respect one another; we love one another. May it be so in all of us!

Chapter 6
In Submitting Conquer

Other Relationships

Remember the principle we stated earlier? How could we forget? Out of our ardent love and reverence for Christ, submit one to another. We learned that submission cannot be compelled; it can only be inspired and motivated by agape love. Parents, you must especially remember this in dealing with the smaller members of the family. And children, the Lord wants you to obey and honor your parents (for this is right) and especially so if they love and revere Christ. So important to Christ is your obedience of and honor for your parents that He has actually promised you good things and the enjoyment of long life for obeying Him in your obedience to your parents.

Now fathers, a special word of counsel for you. Don't exasperate your children. As a man, you may naturally expect too much of your offspring too soon. Focus on training them gently and on instructing them in the love of God. And be sure of this: no instruction that is not demonstrated in your daily life and work will stick to your children. (Eph. 6:1–4)

Submit to Your Children?—Parents, have you ever thought of submitting to your children? Does it not make sense for you to give in to your children's whims, to let them have their own ways, to facilitate their immature desires—for peace sake? Does this principle only apply between peers? *Out of your ardent love and reverence for Christ, submit one to another* (Eph. 5:21). We don't see age or relationship caveats in this statement, do we? Do you see anything here that admonishes mutual submission when dealing with your kids who are getting on your nerves?

I am sure we all have been unwilling witnesses to the plight of the poor parent in the grocery store who has been taken hostage by a three-year-old tyrant demanding a box of *Super Sugar Snaps Modified Breakfast Cereal Fortified with 30 Vitamins and Minerals Specially Balanced for Tiny Tyrants*—guaranteed to stiffen the neck and provide the essential energy required by small children to pick their parents' heads up from the floor and bang them down again. What a travesty

Hey, Mom! Who's in charge here?

of the parental role! What a travesty of truth in advertising! Yet so many generations of parents have succumbed to the false concept of children's rights that we are now into the third or fourth generation of those parents who have no realistic concept of the true parental role. They are clueless about how to communicate with their kids, how to discipline them, how to restrain their powerful in-born urges to restrain their parents.

Real parental effectiveness starts with an ardent love and reverence for Christ. Christ's classic teaching and example of how to treat children: *He was much displeased when His disciples tried to shield Him from the children; He said to them, Allow the little children to come to me; get out of their way and help them come for of such is the kingdom of God* (Mark 10:14). Our love and reverence for Christ will translate into how we teach, care for, and role model for our children.

Real parental effectiveness is rooted in the principle of mutual submission. This does not mean caving in to Tiny Tantrum. It does mean respecting the child enough as a child of God, as are you, to prevent this child from ever reaching the status of tyrant. It doesn't mean that a rebellious child (most of us were) should never feel the consequences of rebellion. It does mean that the parent has no right to punish in anger or frustration or to throw a tantrum for the child to emulate. And it certainly means that the child must have the assurance of parental love even when experiencing the punishment.

I was a rebellious four-year-old cowboy. We lived not too far from the river, but I was banned from ever approaching the bank without my parents' immediate presence—so great was the danger. Freddy came over to play one day, and before long we had encouraged each other in the forbidden act. Wandering nonchalantly about the yard we were soon out of sight and heading for the riverbank. Once at the river, we had a great time getting our pants wet as we threw sticks into the current to watch them sail to far-off lands

Time to stop pretending? This Mom holds the power.

unknown. That was bad enough. Worse was the deception we practiced when Mom called.

Pretend you didn't hear, Freddy hissed. We pretended. It was not so easy to pretend we didn't see when Mom appeared on the riverbank equipped with a supple willow switch. It was harder still to pretend we didn't feel as Mom, with appropriate vigor, applied the willow switch to our wet trousers. Mom was simply respecting our rights as mutual children of God to experience the natural results of rebellion (perhaps the *natural* result of this act of disobedience was averted by the timely arrival of my mother on the riverbank).

Did I resent my mother for cutting short our play in the river? Did I think that she had no right to cut long the supple willow and apply it to my wet pants? Not at all. She was simply using body language to communicate through my backside the message that words had failed to impress on my rebellious four-year-old ears. Her message was simple, consistent, and understandable: "Stay away from the river!" I had no reason to misunderstand either her love for me or the limits she set on my wanderings.

Out of her ardent love and reverence for Christ, my mother was effectively parenting me through this stage in my life. If she had neglected to share with me her displeasure in my disobedience, she would have given me an entirely different message: "I really don't care that much about you. In fact, stay out of my way most of the time, and we will both be happier." Did the punishment compel my submission? It certainly encouraged it. However, as the one who felt the sting of the supple willow through my wet pants, I am confident that subsequent submission was not solely from fear of consequences; it was also motivated by the assurance that my mother cared about me. I wanted to obey (of course, there were other lessons still to be learned).

True *submission* is mutual, and it cannot be compelled; it can only be inspired and motivated by *agape* love. My parents knew this intuitively, and in dealing with their smaller members of the family of God, they practiced the principle of mutual submission to the best of their ability. The Lord also practices this principal in His dealings with His erring children. He respects the young ones enough to address them directly; He respects them enough to make them role models for adults in their humility (Matt. 18:3, 4). Obedience is the greatest evidence of honor that a child can give. Knowing from experience that a child will obey is the greatest assurance a parent can have as the child moves toward maturity.

So important to Christ is your obedience and honor for your parents that He has actually promised you good things and the enjoyment of long life for obeying Him in your obedience to your parents (Eph. 6:3). As children mature into adulthood, the act of obedience becomes less of an issue. Most parents by this stage in life have become reconciled to the fact that the child will be making her own decisions. In fact, wise parents will have been grooming that child for many years to make good decisions and will take pride in a child who is able to handle wisely the choices that life presents. Most wise children will not spurn good advice of older members of their families, but the wise parent will wait for an invitation to give advice. Honor is another matter.

There is no time limit to honor and the promise of enjoyment of long life goes to the one who continues to honor his parents while they live and beyond. Do we have to explain or describe honor? Most expressions of honor should be obvious: kindness, support in old age, communication, sharing memories, looking together at old pictures of times and people seldom brought to mind. One expression may not come so readily: ask parents for advice from time to time; make them genuinely useful as they age.

My mother was able to age in the home in which she had lived (at least on the same property) since her children were small. From her garden she supplied tons of fresh vegetables every year. (One year I hauled a truckload of gorgeous squash from her garden in September.) She baked bread for the entire family; it was virtually impossible to visit her without bringing home a loaf of bread loaded with good stuff from her garden. Though she has been gone for seven years, I still feel the occasional impulse to pick up the phone and share an idea or ask for her opinion. I suppose this will pass if I enjoy a life long enough. My dad has been gone for forty-five years and my memories of him have faded somewhat though I still recall his integrity and strength.

Fathers, Your Turn—Fathers, I realize that you are busy people with untold and escalating pressures. If you have a job, you need to perform it well. Your bosses frequently are not the most forgiving of people. These days work opportunities are known to vanish into the stock exchange or they might have already disappeared in the aftermath of the great housing crisis or some other scandalous financial debacle. Moneylenders, in their greed, seduced you into overestimating your capacity to repay. To give your children better experiences than you think you had, you mortgaged your roofs to pile stuff on top of stuff until your garage could contain no more, and you had not even the time to use your stuff (like the fancy camping gear and travel trailers that don't get used from season to season).

Too many of you have had no option but to abandon your hopes and all the stuff that represented your now-fading optimism. It's a sad and tragic finale to the American dream that now keeps far too many in North America awake in the night waiting for the morning as their aching bodies shiver on the cramped seats of their cars. And morning brings only another dreary day that ends in night still with no place to park.

But not all of you are there yet. You want to stickhandle yourselves and your kids through the potential traps. You want to salvage what is left of your hopes. You want to believe that there is still some reason to believe. (There is! There really is a reason, but it will not be found in the stuff of this disintegrating world.) Some of you are not even touched by the cares that infest the days of thousands of your neighbors. Life sails on. Life is good, and you feel it. Shall we go sailing today or take a run on the slopes? Maybe we'll go golfing? Shopping? And some of us are somewhere between these extremes.

But fathers, no matter your financial or social status, you are still very busy men and, as men, busy or not (but probably busy), *you may naturally expect too much of your offspring too soon* (Eph. 6:4). Fathers tend to exasperate their children. Don't. Do train them gently being always conscious of their need for example and opportunity to practice; they need that more than they need a lecture or a kick. Example, fathers, example! They need your example more than anything else. I saw two fathers demonstrating two sets of values today. (Oops! It's 4:20 in the morning; let's make that yesterday.)

I already mentioned a flood. It's been only two weeks, and we already have a repeat. The same bridges, roads, and buildings are being threatened and fears and tensions are surfacing revealing the substance of the soul beneath. We came out of church (now yesterday) to discover that an ugly stream of brown-muddy water had escaped the streambed where it belongs and was already tearing up our driveway and parking lot. There was no use calling an emergency response team because every machine operator and every piece of equipment was already fully engaged in saving the bridges on the main roads. We members of the body had to go to work with our own chain saws, backhoe, and shovels. One fetched his dump truck, a load of sand, and a supply of sand bags, and we began to confine the stream within its designated boundaries.

The volume of water increased until it exceeded the capacity of the culvert to contain it. It gushed over the road and down a ditch toward the neighbors' houses, rapidly seeking the lowest level. One man was particularly upset and cursed us for the threat to his property. In the bigger flood of two weeks ago no water came down this ditch. No water appeared until the backhoe came, so this crisis was clearly our fault.

We needed all hands to sandbag the properties, even the angry man's hands could have been helpful. However, we found that he could not reason. He would not help; he would only watch—and rant and curse and threaten. Watching daddy intently, his little son was learning his lessons well. With the church property secured, we moved down the road with the dump truck, sand bags, and backhoe. We cleared out the streambed and sandbagged the edge of his property. Success. The water was confined in the main stream. Without the owner's help. The cursing continued anyway. Someone will be paying for something. Not sure who or what. Lessons given; lessons learned.

This lesson I also saw: one of the fathers (the mother was also there and working, but this is about fathers) had his three young children with him as he worked in the rain and the mud to save the neighbors' properties. These young children, without grumbling (they hadn't eaten their lunches either, such was the emergency), even joining us in a laugh at a joke or two, filled sand bags like reservist soldiers. Good lessons given; good lessons learned.

Did I mention that fathers may exhibit a tendency to exasperate their children? I believe I did. This is not because we are inherently mean and ornery, though some of us are. Maybe we are just better pushers than leaders. In spiritual matters we have expectations of how we want our kids to behave. We tend to measure spirituality by behavior, but we fail to see that we don't achieve spiritual growth by demanding and measuring correct behavior. We overlook the second and more important part of the directive: we need to *instruct* them in the love of God. If we were to put our energies into leading our children to Jesus rather than into pushing them to act and look in a certain way, I believe we would, in the end and perhaps before the end, have children who both love the Lord and honor Him by the way they live.

Fathers, do you expect success or even dream of success in bringing up your children to love and serve God? Your example will have to match your words. Hey, don't go away; I am still talking to you, fathers. This is one principle of which you can be sure: no instruction that is not demonstrated in your daily walk in the Light is likely to stick to your children past puberty. Fathers, we gotta examine ourselves every day to see whether we are in the faith or not (2 Cor. 13:5) because faith, not police work, is the victory that overcomes the world—for us oldies and for our children (1 John 5:4). Of course, a little pushing of the right kind is OK from time to time to achieve some ends, but too much pushing in the spiritual realm really will exasperate the kids, and that is not good for them or for us. When Christ is our leader and we confidently follow Him, our kids are more likely to see the good reasons to follow us. In this ambiguous, confused, confusing world, they need to see many good reasons every day.

Slaves and Masters

Slaves, Christ commands you to obey, respect, and fear your masters sincerely on this earth, just as if you were obeying Christ Himself. (You are also slaves of Christ, as I am.) Serve your masters honestly. Just as you serve Christ, obey them from the heart, even when they are not watching you. You owe your masters wholehearted service, as to the Lord. And remember this, my fellow slaves: you will not go unrewarded for the good you do in obeying this command. Your masters also will be rewarded for the good they do.

Slave masters, you share the same Master with your slaves, and He doesn't play favorites. From heaven He observes the master-slave relationship. He wants you to treat your slaves with respect, with honesty, and without threats. On the day He hands out His rewards for the good you do, you will share equally with your slaves (Eph. 6:5–9).

Slaves and Masters, Then and Now—Though slavery in various forms is still rampant around this world, most of us reading this book do not live in slave societies. Because we don't want to see the misery, we easily close our eyes to much of the tragedy caused by the callous greed and abject need of broken humanity. Just this morning I listened to a CBC interview with author Scott Carney. Topic: his recently published book, *The Red Market*,[1] in which the author takes us inside the misty world of organ brokers, bone thieves, and blood farmers, as they supply the global trade in human recycled body parts. Among the plethora of appallingly awful atrocities daily perpetrated on helpless children, women, and even strong men, the one that I hadn't encountered earlier and wouldn't have imagined is blood farming. In the case reported, an entrepreneurial type kidnaps, in this case men, holds them captive in disgusting conditions for years in a dairy shed, and *milks* them of their blood for sale (at just $25 per pint) to the blood banks.

(We don't approve, do we?) But before we succumb to a severe case of smugness, pause a moment and consider: where is the primary market for *milked* blood, black market kidneys, bones, and hearts? Whose blood components are you receiving as you lie on the gurney hooked to the little plastic bag on the post beside you? To what extent are we all complicit in the wretched agony of others? What are we condoning just to have the mere hope of a few more days of mortal life?

Does God's injunction through Paul to the Roman slaves apply in postmodern times to slaves caught in a system that is tacitly condoned while internationally condemned? Should the trapped men in the milking shed sincerely obey and respect the criminal who stole their bodies to *milk* their blood for the benefit of the guy from Montreal who just flew into Mumbai for a cheap kidney transplant (discount the profit motive as you ponder your answer)? *Slaves, Christ commands you to obey, respect, and fear your masters sincerely on this earth, just as if you were obeying Christ Himself* (Eph. 6:5).

Although ancient slavery was cruel, harsh, and brutal, it was recognized as legitimate, even by the slaves. Were the circumstances reversed, they quickly and happily would have enslaved their masters. Paul's work as a Christian apostle and evangelist was not to change society by upheaval and insurrection. His goal was to make believers of masters and slaves, to bring Christ into their lives by the Holy Spirit. Their new relationship, now motivated and empowered by Christ, would provide an argument without answer for the power of the gospel. So to answer our questions with the least ink: no!

The principle of loving our enemies never changes, but I have failed to find a command in Scripture that says we should remain in these present-day, degrading circumstances or allow them to continue or be complicit in their continuing. Our moral outrage should be hurled against every evil that destroys the dignity of God's human creation.

Just what is the principle in Paul's command to slaves and masters that is applicable in present-day relationships? We can try to apply it to the boss-employee relationship. There might be some validity in this application, but there is no common reference point to be found in the master-slave, boss-employee circumstances; they are from different worlds. I think it would be easier

---

[1] Scott Carney, *The Red Market: On the Trail of the World's Organ Brokers, Bone Thieves, Blood Farmers, and Child Traffickers* (New York, NY: HarperCollins, 2011).

to compare masters and slaves with parents and children.

If we consider certain key words in the passage, we might see the key to a principle: sincerity, honesty, and respect. Our human relationships, whatever they are, should be characterized by sincerity, honesty, and respect and be without coercion of any kind. It's really quite simple. Mutual sincerity, mutual honesty, mutual respect. We have here the translation of the command Paul gave us at the beginning of his instruction on human relationships: *out of our ardent love and reverence for Christ, by His grace submit one to another* (Eph. 5:21), or in other words, treat each other with sincerity, honesty, and respect.

Reward and Punishment—What about the rewards of which Paul writes? In the judgment, will good be rewarded? And if good is rewarded, will evil be punished? Are punishment and reward in the plan of God? Some people have trouble reconciling the concepts of punishment and reward with the idea of grace that the Bible also strongly teaches. Yes, the Bible does teach reward and punishment, but the conflict vanishes when we understand reward and punishment correctly.

Salvation, that is our justification, our sanctification, and our glorification, is entirely by grace. We were saved by grace when we were God's ungodly, sinning enemies (Rom. 5:6–10)—this is our justification. We were saved by grace through faith and not by works from the old habits and ways of life (Eph. 2:8–10). This began our earthly lifelong (or short) experience in cooperating with God in our character development; this is our sanctification by grace ongoing. The good things we do by God's grace as we cooperate in developing our characters, honor him in this life, and for these acts we will be rewarded in the kingdom. By God's grace we will be taken to live eternally in the kingdom (John 14:1–3)—this is our glorification. "Come, Lord Jesus" (Rev. 22:20)! Soon!

Sadly, some people, far too many people, apathetic, indifferent, careless, or rebellious, choose to go it alone through this life, as they hope for the best and trust in themselves. Refusing God's grace, rejecting His love, denying His sacrifice, ignoring His blessings, scorning His existence, they really are on their own. The tragically fatal choices they have made will incur the punishment intended only for the devil and his angels (Matt. 25:41; Rev. 20:15).

God's Armor
My final instruction to you points you straight to the Lord. His mighty power is totally sufficient for all your needs; be strong in Him! God has provided armor that is able to shield the wearer from every sly or frontal attack of the devil. You must wear every piece of it. Neglecting to put on even one piece will leave you fatally exposed. Don't ever forget that you are not engaged with human foes. Your enemy is the devil and his cohorts, evil spiritual authorities whose powers govern this dark world and have the conceit to suppose they can threaten even heavenly realms. This is every motivation you need to put on every piece of God-provided armor. Evil days are coming, but if you are safely shielded in the armor of God (nothing else is required), you will be able to stand firmly in your appointed place.

So wrap that belt of truth around your waist and buckle it securely. Strap on the breastplate of righteousness over your heart. No spiritual warrior is ready to face the enemy without the well-fitted shoes of the gospel of peace. But there is more! You will be facing a blizzard of fiery enemy arrows that can be extinguished only by the shield of faith. The helmet of your assurance of salvation has been crafted at Calvary for your head. One size fits all with total comfort; never take it off. Take the sword of the Spirit in your hands! Keep it polished; keep it sharp; practice it daily!

You might think that your armor is now complete. Think again. Every warrior must have clear communication lines direct to the Commander. As spiritual soldiers you communicate through prayer. Don't let any situation cut your links with your Commander. Talk continually with Him about every detail of the battles. Your strength to stand is provided moment by moment as you pray. Don't just pray for yourself. Pray for all the warriors whose battles are unique though not unlike your own. And be alert to all the signals that the Commander sends.

I need your prayers, too. The devil attacks me constantly and, without prayer, I am in danger of saying the wrong thing as I face him in the persons of human enemies and difficult circumstances. However, I must fearlessly preach the mystery of the gospel and not be distracted by these incidental issues of little importance. Though I am God's ambassador in chains, the gospel will not be chained as long as you continue to pray that I fearlessly declare it to the world, as I should. (Eph. 6:10–20)

Fatal Exposure? Never!—Whatever our circumstances in this world, Paul points us straight to the Lord. Where else could we go but to the Lord? Where else that makes a modicum of sense? Though we still work for the dollar or yen or ruble or colon or lempira or some other flimsy currency, our confidence in any currency is somewhat tenuous, and rightly so. Some of us have put money in property and other investment opportunities hoping to put ourselves on easy street for a few short days only to see the bubble burst and yesterday's imagined profits blowing like confetti in the wind. This is how I mastered Economics 101.

Where should we go but to the Lord? Where should we have gone before blowing our resources on imaginary dreams? Paul was in chains for the Lord, yet his confidence in Him was rock solid and unshaken. Raising his shackled hands, he points us post moderns to the Lord, the only stable anchor point in these or any other troubled times. He shouts above the raucous din of every hectic life: *God's mighty power is totally sufficient for all your needs; be strong in Him* (Eph. 6:10)!

Now Paul turns our attention to the immediate and pressing need to be prepared to meet every sly or frontal attack of the devil. The need is pressing because though the preacher may go away for a few days in the sun, the devil takes no holidays. He's always on patrol; he's always hunting for food and the tastiest morsels are the hearts of Christians who thought they were standing firm and tall (1 Cor. 10:12). You may have some personal stories to verify the devil's intent. I know I do. The good news is that God's armor is freely provided and only the foolhardy would neglect any piece of it. Would you go about fatally exposed?

In the hazardous gas fields around the world, technicians understand the vital necessity of preparation when working with sour gas. Would a power engineer attend a leaking gas well without complete and functioning protective gear? Hardly likely. The death wish is not that strong. So why would a Christian face one day, one hour, even one moment of this world without complete protective gear? Is the death wish so strong?

We are not engaged with human foes (don't ever forget it). Know your enemy, but know better your sure defense (Ps. 91). *Let us fix our eyes on Jesus, the author and perfecter of our faith, who for the joy set before him, endured the cross, scorning its shame* (Heb. 12:2). There is our example and our strong defense; there is the One who has proved Himself in battle (Ps. 24:8).

Just as Moses assured Joshua, his successor, that the Lord would go before him, so we can be assured that He will go before us (Deut. 31:8); just as the prophet assured Jehoshaphat that the battle belonged to the Lord, so we can be assured that our battles are also His, not ours (2 Chron. 20:15). Satan is a defeated, eviscerated, emasculated enemy; nevertheless, he is a dangerous enemy. He lost his chance against the Son of Man at Calvary and, like a toothless lion without claws (which is what he is, remember), can do us no harm unless we stupidly, knowingly, rebelliously walk into his mouth. How, then, can he be the governor of this dark world?

The answer should really be quite obvious to anyone who has plowed this far in a study of Paul's Ephesians: the devil can have no power over anyone who has not yielded him the power willingly. End of excuses. Every piece of God-provided armor is there for us to wear. A stupid, willful, careless, sleepy, arrogant neglect to put the armor on does not absolve anyone from the responsibility of facing the enemy or the consequences of facing him unprepared (though God still forgives and continues to hold His armor out to anyone who will take it). The answer: the wily devil governs only with the consent of the governed—with your consent and with my consent. Funny, we didn't think of him as a democrat. What a clever deceiver! This is every motivation we need to put on every piece of God-built, God-provided armor.

Let's put on every piece (in reality, neglecting one piece effectively negates all the rest). *Evil days are coming, but if you are safely shielded in the armor of God (nothing else is required), you will be able to stand firmly in your appointed place* (Eph. 6:13). It is good to be assured that God has an appointed place in which every one of us is to stand for Him and, I think, places for every family, group, and congregation. Because He knew each of us from the beginning of the world, this should be no surprise to us at this late date in the course of this deluded world's allotted time. Let's armor up immediately and stand tall for orders.

In the coming evil days (we have only the faintest idea of how the evil will present itself), God's armor is crucial and complete for our overcoming. Financial troubles are looming, (certainly anyone with Economics 101 between the ears should recognize the signs), and we can't get out of the world just yet. We can take steps to shield ourselves from some of the fallout (buy gold?—naw, probably not; however, downsizing and shedding personal debt will relieve much unnecessary stress). Sickness could strike at any time, and we know social upheaval certainly will be one of the consequences of the coming economic disintegration.

Wars and rumors of wars all over the planet keep us tense and nationally broke and disrupt the distribution mechanisms for food and other essentials; floods, hurricanes, earthquakes, and other earth-based catastrophic events sap our resources, destroy crops, and prevent harvests. Fully armored, we will stand firm. Abandon now any false confidence in the stuff of this life; our bread and water in the crisis is assured (Isa. 33:16), but now, before the real hurricane begins to blow (Rev. 7:1–3), we must trust our God and buckle on His armor. It is not necessarily harder to trust in easy times, just easier to cruise along, forgetting the need to put everything in the hands of our sustainer God.

Buckle It On!—All of it! Leave no straps hanging.

The Belt: *So wrap that belt of truth around your waist and buckle it securely* (Eph. 6:14). Knowing what is truth seems to puzzle most people these days. Even caring that there is truth escapes most people. We are all but inured to the advertising beamed into our houses, through our car radios, flashing on billboards, and popping uninvited into our faces on our computer screen. Promoting everything from *abaca* to *zoris* (these words have real meaning), with sensuous sales tricks inviting us to trade our money (and even our morality) for vacation fantasies or the latest concoction guaranteeing our return to lost youth with only three applications or triple our money back, we have all but lost the concept of truth. What is truth? How would I recognize Truth if He stood in front of me?

Let's turn to the Bible for help in recognizing truth: "Your word is truth" (John 17:17); *I am the truth* (John 14:6); "you will know the truth, and the truth will set you free" (John 8:32); *God cannot lie* (Titus 1:2). Furthermore, truth is the essence of God (Exod. 34:6, NKJV). Clearly, our Father places high value on truth, and His children must do the same. Because we believe and accept that the Holy Scriptures are the clearest revelation of God to humanity, we turn frequently to the Word for truth in its purest form. We get to know God mainly through the Bible, the source of truth, and to know God is to recognize truth. God's Holy Spirit is our guide into all truth as we dig into the Scriptures (John 16:13). He will not speak of Himself but of Christ, the way and the truth (John 14:6). But not only do we find truth in Scripture! We find the gospel coming to us *not simply with words but also with power, with the Holy Spirit and with deep conviction* of its absolute truth (1 Thess. 1:5). In the gospel we also encounter the awesome *power of God that gives salvation to all who believe* (Rom. 1:16). How true!

So dally no longer with indecision—that sorry, unhappy, unpleasant agent of Satan! Wrap that belt of truth around your waist without delay! There is no other way than to search the Scriptures daily, filling our minds with the Word, hiding the Word in our hearts where, readily accessible to us, it cannot be lost or stolen. We have to receive the Holy Spirit, who is the representative of Jesus Christ, the Word. *For the Word of God is living, active, and sharper than any double-edged sword* (Heb. 4:12).

Minus the belt of truth, our armor is flawed, incomplete, and ineffective; minus the belt of truth, our characters are flawed and incomplete; minus the belt of truth, we have no answers for the postmodern embedded in her certainty of relativity; minus the belt of truth, there is no place to secure the bottom straps of the breastplate of righteousness. Minus the belt of truth, we can only display our failure to receive Jesus Christ.

The Breastplate: *Strap on the breastplate of righteousness over your heart* (Eph. 6:14). With truth securely fastened, we can protect our hearts with the breastplate of Christ's righteousness. This vital preparation to stand in the face of unrelenting foes was well-known in antiquity. Proverbs 4:23 assures us that *the most important thing you can do is to guard your heart because it is the wellspring of life*. Jesus Himself warned us that *the mouth speaks from the overflow of the heart* (Matt. 12:34).

Jesus further emphasized the vital truth that only an impure heart produces evil thoughts, "sexual immorality, theft, murder, adultery, greed, malice, deceit, lewdness, envy, slander, arrogance, [fear] and folly. All these evils come from inside and defile a person" (Mark 7:21–23).

Wow! That seems to be all inclusive of the evil of which we are capable when the heart is not guarded or protected by the breastplate of Christ's righteousness! Our recent iteration of human depravity during the Boston Marathon bombing, with its horrifying slaughter and maiming of the innocents, reinforces the warning. Guard well the avenues of the soul! It's the same thing.

How do I guard the way to my soul? How do I guard my heart? How do I fasten on the breastplate? The answer lies in the breastplate itself, the breastplate of righteousness. I have no inherent righteousness (Rom. 3:10). In fact, anything in me that I might imagine to be *my* righteousness resembles filthy rags (Isa. 64:6). It follows that the breastplate cannot be of my making or doing. It must be supplied, a gift of God's grace. Because this is so, the height of arrogance is to suppose that I can guard myself against the artillery of the devil without the righteousness of God. I've tried that folly—practicing on the little temptations to build up strength for the big ones. It's a pretty standard procedure for us do-it-ourselves human beings.

There are enough breastplates in God's armory for every person who asks for one. The secret is to ask. Ask and receive. That simple? That simple! Having received the breastplate, there are a few things we can do. (But notice what comes first—the breastplate. Our efforts are worthless without the breastplate.) We must block the avenues of the soul to the three devices by which Satan seduces all those who will be seduced: "the cravings of sinful man, the lust of his eyes and the boasting of what he has and does" (1 John 2:16, NIV84). The entire arsenal of the enemy contains only these three worn out weapons. As grateful recipients of the breastplate, we are now enabled to repudiate, distance from, and shun every means by which the devil formerly gained access to our minds. We are also powerfully motivated.

But, while secure in Christ's righteousness and experiencing the real joy of victory in Christ, don't be complacent. The heart of a human, that wonderful thing, is the seat of the emotions, and it can still deceive (Jer. 17:9). Though we have experienced the new birth, the old nature doesn't go away easily. Knock it down hard (Paul calls this a crucifixion) and the old self will still rise up at the slightest provocation or inducement. Many things out there (and within) can trigger old feelings for the once familiar. Our only recourse is to run immediately to Christ for refuge in Him. Better yet, never stray from His side. This is why well-fitted shoes (on our feet, not in the closet) are an essential part of the armor of God.

The Shoes: *No spiritual warrior is ready to face the enemy without the well-fitted shoes of the gospel of peace* (Eph. 6:15). Years ago I did a lot of logging during my downtime from university. Hobnailed Kodiak boots were the prescribed footwear intended to prevent slipping and falling as we walked the massive felled trees. Heavy and hard, they didn't mold well to my feet. In fact, they hurt my feet, and I didn't like them much.

One day I opted for my comfortable, flexible boots, perfect for most jobs and most surfaces. I was walking a tree and preparing to jump with my chainsaw to a parallel tree about four feet distant and about four feet above ground. Another tree lay parallel to it a few feet beyond. Follow me closely, but stay safe. I jumped—almost far enough. The ball of my right foot contacted the target tree. It slipped, and I dove nose first into the next parallel tree. Contact! Splat! That tree couldn't have been positioned more precisely to present my nose with a more solid landing pad. My poor nose now knows personally the

For fight or flight the boots gotta be on the feet.

crushing end of a fall, and my whole body suffered intensely.

When a bad choice of shoes results in a spiritual fall, it is not just the nose that suffers. The whole body suffers; the body of believers suffers; Jesus Christ suffers. Let's pray with Paul that our "whole spirit, soul and body be kept blameless at the coming of our Lord Jesus Christ. The one who calls you is faithful, and he will do it" (1 Thess. 5:23, 24). Let's go fully shielded in His armor.

You've now heard my story of the shoes. What's your story? We know that the gospel is the story of the birth, life, death, and resurrection of Jesus Christ. That's it in its simplicity, beauty, purity, and peace—and totality. Everything else we love about the old, old story, its application, its affect on sinners' lives, and our blessed hope and confidence in the *glorious appearing of our great God and Savior, Jesus Christ* (Titus 2:13) is the result of the gospel. Without the gospel every good thing we do would be disgusting (Isa. 64:6). Jesus Christ "gave himself for us to redeem us from all wickedness and to purify for himself a people that are his very own, eager to do what is good" (Titus 2:14). As we remain shod with the gospel of peace in our day-to-day activities, the lives we exhibit will bring glory to God, our Father in heaven (Matt. 5:16).

Shoes are worn for safe movement as well as for secure standing. "How beautiful are the feet of those who preach the gospel of peace, who bring glad tidings of good things" (Rom. 10:15, NKJV)! As Isaiah puts the same thought: "How beautiful upon the mountains are the feet of him who brings good news, who proclaims peace, who brings glad tidings of good things, who proclaims salvation, who says to Zion, 'Your God reigns'" (Isa. 52:7, NKJV)! And my God does reign. In His good time even the enemy will bow to Him and acknowledge His sovereign glory (Isa. 45:23; Phil. 2:10). In the meantime, our role as believers, fitted out in the total armor of God, is to carry the gospel with sure-footed, committed assurance to every person who will hear it, always alert to signs of the enemy within or without.

Emergencies will come—every day; well-fitted shoes are absolutely essential for flight or fight. The fully grounded assurance of our salvation is our only and certain escape from every slyly disguised danger. Of course, some emergencies call for immediate flight: fornication (1 Cor. 6:18), idolatry (1 Cor. 10:14), and a whole ragtag army of others (1 Tim. 6:11). The direction of flight is as important as the speed. It does little good o escape the lion and the bear only to fall under the curses of Goliath. In fact, if not *to* the Lord, running in any direction is futile because only the Lord can deliver us from our enemies. At the first hint of danger, flee to the Lord to escape fornication; at the first hint of danger, flee to the Lord to escape idolatry; at the first hint of danger, flee to the Lord to escape the entire ragtag army of assorted ruffians (Ps. 143:9). He is our sure defense, our fortress, the only defense and fortress, and in Him alone can we find rest (Ps. 62:6). But what about shoes for the fight?

What fight? Shall we take on Satan? Shall we fight the enemies of the truth? Shall we war with the saints who disagree with us? Shall we battle the secret enemies within? Paul told Timothy that he had fought a good fight (2 Tim. 4:7). Was he doing more than beating the air (1 Cor. 9:26)? Was he doing something we will never do? Paul answers our questions in his first letter to Timothy. Said Paul: "Fight the good fight of faith" (1 Tim. 6:12). The "good fight" to which he refers in his second letter to Timothy must be the same good fight of faith (2 Tim. 4:7).

Our entire saving relationship with God is based on faith alone. We are saved through faith in Christ (Luke 7:50; 18:42), and we live by faith in Christ (Rom. 1:17). To engage in the fight of faith we do no more and no less than put our complete confidence in Jesus Christ. To engage in the fight of faith we have to pay close attention to the Word of God. To engage in the fight of faith we obey the Word of God. When Satan brings his armies against us, our sure and only defense is our hope of glory, Christ in us, by faith. Shod with the gospel of peace, we are equipped for flight to Jesus and for the fight of faith. Fight or flight or both, if we are shielded by faith in Christ, we are always ready!

The Shield: *You will be facing a blizzard of fiery enemy arrows that can be extinguished only by the shield of faith* (Eph. 6:16). In this life crises will come onetwothreefour and then bring on fivesix. Frequently, they come in pairs or multiples. We just get the Kenworth truck back on the road with a repaired fuel injector when the newly licensed driver in the family totals the Windstar (thankfully with only a few bruises on his own teen body). Then the rains come with fury just as the spring breakup is ending and shut down the log haul for weeks. During this time the finance company is not excited about a missing payment due on the new Freightliner. To add to the misery, a mudslide generated by the 200-year rains destroys the shop and buries thousands of dollars in tools. It's enough to make a grown man cry—and throw in the towel because it's too small to absorb the tears!

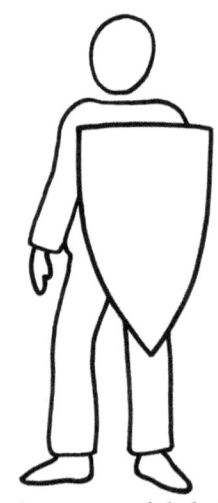

Arrows punch lethal holes! Keep that shield in place!

Is this just the beginning of sorrows? When we look at the sorrows of Somalia or Sudan or Bangladesh or Congo, or Boston, or almost any place on earth, our own sorrows come into perspective, and we marvel at the obstinate, continuing, universal will to live. How many more arrows can we dodge before taking one in the heart?

How many arrows does the devil have? Is he responsible for our pain? Do we foolishly or stupidly set ourselves up for attack? Do all arrows look like trouble or are some of them more subtle, coy, deceptive, attractive, inviting, fun, and even more destructive? Arrows can come as an offer of a promotion that will require some compromises to offset the huge salary increase. Others are disguised as coworkers, casual acquaintances, or longtime friends.

That blizzard of fiery enemy arrows, custom designed for every personality by a master of human psychology, are already stringed. The bows are tensioned and ready to launch the missiles whenever our guards are down. With no inherent human defense (in fact, the natural human is quite willing to be shot through by many of these arrows), we have been given a sure defense: the shield of faith. Every human being has been given a shield of faith (Rom. 12:3) sufficient to extinguish every enemy arrow. With the shield in place, not one of the fiery arrows can get through to our vitals. However, if we take no steps to augment this faith, as we know very well, it will ultimately become ineffective against the enemy, and we could find ourselves even cooperating with him as he aims his deadly missiles at our inward parts. Strange things go on in the unprotected head!

The Helmet: *The helmet of your assurance of salvation has been crafted at Calvary for your head. One size fits all with total comfort; never take it off* (Eph. 6:17). In the primitive forest-based economy in which I grew up, the limbs and snags that broke from a falling tree forty or eighty feet above the logger's head were respectfully known as "widow makers" for their capacity to break the skull of the unwary. Eventually, hard hats became mandatory equipment at any job site with the potential to drop a hammer or a piece of board or an innocent-appearing limb from a tree. Fast forward sixty years. To go into my private forest today, minus my hard hat, for a quad load of selectively harvested beetle-killed-pine firewood seems almost to be a violation of morality. I feel naked and exposed! To have my skull penetrated by the sharp end of a broken limb silently falling could irreparably spoil an otherwise really nice day. Ergo, I continue to wear my shiny green hard hat—which doesn't absolve me from the need for eternal vigilance and the responsibility to know and respect the hazards around and above. The same applies in the spiritual realm in which we all live.

Hazards abound around, above, and within. Know them and respect their ability to penetrate the unwary mind. Any one of them is quite enough to crack open an unprotected head. Hence, we desperately need the helmet of our assurance of salvation, the one crafted at Calvary for every head on earth. Wear it with confidence; *never take it off!*

We've already discussed the hazards within and otherwise in enough detail (too much description risks giving a false sense that anything not mentioned is OK) and, in any case, to know the feel of the helmet is much more profitable. At Calvary, Jesus Christ bought our salvation at the price of His own life—fully paid, now fully ours. Our assurance is the promise of eternal life made by God, Himself, before time began. Because God does not die (1 Tim. 1:17) and cannot lie (Titus 1:2), this assurance of salvation is rock solid. Those who believe in the One who paid the price are already in life (John 5:24), a guarantee that God cannot break without violating the essence of who He is.

Sadly, so many still go out among the potential dangers of this life without the helmet, with no assurance of salvation, exposed to all the hazards flying about, continually hoping but never rejoicing. For some inexplicable reason they cling to the fantasy that if they provide for themselves a cowboy hat or a bandanna or a sombrero, or some other flimsy head covering—maybe with just a bit of *Son* screen on the nose—that God will look at their best efforts and make up the difference. God has already made up the difference at Calvary, and we should do nothing but accept the helmet of our assurance of salvation and wear it with confidence, not in our own futile efforts but in the completed sacrifice of Jesus Christ.

One size fits all with total comfort. Never take it off. A hard hat offers some protection from certain hazards on industrial sites, but it can't protect the worker from all hazards. However, the helmet of assurance of salvation is totally adequate for all spiritual attacks. As we hold to the sacrifice of Jesus Christ for all our sin, we have no need to jerry-build any other contrivance to assist Him in the work of saving us from our sin. Just as the angel assured Joseph, *He [not you] will save us from our sins* (Matt. 1:21).

I can't save you or even myself; you can't save me or even yourself. Jesus has already saved us both and our role is to receive the helmet and wear it with full confidence in the saving life and death of Jesus Christ. That's it! Nothing more! Don't be like the guy who was too proud to wear the helmet, thinking he was fast enough on his feet to dodge the widow-makers. Actually, the poor guy was still clinging to the fatally flawed idea that he somehow had to provide some sort of covering for his own head to supplement the already-provided helmet of assurance of salvation. Clearly, he had not taken up the sword with any serious intent.

The Sword: *Take the sword of the Spirit in your hands! Keep it polished; keep it sharp; practice it daily* (Eph. 6:17)! I've put up a few fences in my brief span. For some fences I would find the positions of the end posts, line the route with two construction cords, and manually dig the holes, ensuring a result that is straight and pleasing to the eye with no outliers. For other fences I would find the positions of the end posts and then, with the help of my neighbor's expertise on the Caterpillar, I would push each post into the earth with the weight of the machine. The result would be a satisfactorily straight fence for

The sword of the Spirit cuts to your own soul. Don't use it on me.

pasturelands and fields. That's my experience with fencing. What's yours?

But didn't we start to discuss the sword, which implies an entirely unrelated type of fencing? In fact, we might be leaning radically out of line. This is not about fencing at all, any kind of fencing! With eternal implications, our swordplay is much more serious than that. Paul tells us to take the sword of the Spirit. The *sword of the Spirit*? Of course, the Word of God (Eph. 6:17)! With the sword of the Spirit, we hold the cutting edge of all truth (John 17:17), all comfort (Rom. 15:4, NKJV; Ps. 119:50), and all instruction in righteousness, reproof, doctrine, and correction (2 Tim. 3:16). The devil cannot reach us while we wield the sword of the Spirit with faith-grounded knowledge, perseverance, and humility under the divine mentoring of the Holy Spirit (John 16:13).

No sword, least of all the sword of the Spirit, is fully useful unless it fits well and comfortably in the hand. Comfort and confidence in handling the sword come through daily use under expert tutelage. The haft must be natural in the hand; the balance a familiar feel. Time! Time! Correct practice! Willing to be taught! Welcoming correction! More time! Apparently it takes 10,000 hours to become a master in most skill areas. The Beetles did their hard time in Berlin plucking their strings and stressing their vocals twelve hours every day in the coffee houses. Only then were they ready for big time in the United States. We don't let the greenhorn doctor diagnose a runny nose before he has put in his 10,000 hours of grueling preparation, and even with that behind him, he has to do a lot more time before he is able to remove my gall bladder.

My class one license is a legal document giving me the right to meet you at 100 kilometers per hour in my Super B Train (thirty rubbers meeting the road), but no employer still with his wits intact would put me behind the wheel of his rig given that my driver's abstract doesn't show any heavy-duty activity during the last thirty-two years (nor would I have the foolish conceit to climb behind the wheel).[2]

If I had wanted to remain a truck driver, I would have kept up the skill practice day after long day pounding over the roads (brake checks, circle checks, fuel checks, binding checks, air checks, bounced checks). I would have kept up with the changing laws of the road and maintained my contacts with clients and fellow truckers. Time! Commitment! It wasn't there for me.

Just so, we should take the sword of the Spirit in our hands; keep it polished and keep it sharp! Time! Commitment! There is no other way to become proficient in the use of the sword. Unlike the result of correctly practicing with a steel blade (which increases the confidence in our own ability to thrust and parry), correct daily practice with the sword *of the Spirit* will enhance our confidence, not in ourselves, but in the sword itself and in our tutor, the Holy Spirit, to whom it belongs.

Actually, the sword of the Spirit is, and always will be, sharp. "For the word of God is living and powerful, and sharper than any two edged sword, piercing even to the division of soul and spirit, and of joints and marrow, and is a discerner of the thoughts and intents of the heart" (Heb. 4:12, NKJV). Unlike the steel blades, this sword is not for mutilating and killing our enemies. Its purpose is to cut to our own hearts revealing our own thoughts and intents, exposing to ourselves our own duplicity, avarice, malice, laziness, lust, and every other sin, and to excise these malignancies for our own healing.

The more time we spend becoming familiar with the sword, squirreling away the Word in our hearts (Ps. 119:11), the more we will trust in the Lord to keep us upright in this battle to end all battles. After all, the battle is the Lord's, as shepherd David shouted through the mounting tension on the field of Elah (1 Sam. 17:47), as is the armor, and the victory, just like king David acknowledged at the end of his prosperous reign (1 Chron. 29:11).

Yet, while time spent with the Master is important, in fact crucial, time is not everything; profound knowledge is not everything. Simple, willing, obedience is what Jesus expects of everyone. Said Jesus to the renewed man fresh and happy in his sanity: *Go home to your family and tell them how much the Lord has done for you and the mercy He has given you* (Mark 5:19). While this man gladly would have remained at the side of Jesus, his present role was to go to his family with a simple, candid message: "Look and see. You are seeing the work of Jesus! Believe!"

This role has been assigned to all of us. Look and see; believe! *Give all glory to God* (Matt. 5:16)! Simply, willingly obey the command: take the sword of the Spirit in your hands. You see, God never leaves us. He is with us while we obey Him in the humdrum routines of our lives, including in becoming familiar with His Word. We are with Him, in fact and in reality. With His Word in our hearts, we have power-loaded motivation to resist the devil. Coward that he is, the devil will not face us as we stand firm in the armor of God. Put it on now; never take it off!

For every circumstance that we encounter on the battlefield, the protocol has been clearly

---

[2] Since this writing because of the loss of vision in my right eye, I have traded in my class one for a class five that still allows me to drive my pickup and pull a trailer.

The Long Road to Grace

written in the Manual. As spiritual warriors we are expected to become totally familiar with every word of truth available to us. To do less is to devalue the work of the Commander and of all His lieutenants who have labored unsparingly to record His words for our benefit and instruction. To become totally familiar with every word of truth is the established way of transferring it from paper to our hearts. Jeremiah recorded God's promise of a covenant with us: "This is the covenant that I will make with the house of Israel after those days, says the Lord: I will put My law in their minds, and write it on their hearts; and I will be their God, and they shall be My people" (Jer. 31:33, NKJV).

Among many other statements from the Word, two passages describe the intimacy with which we must willfully associate with God's Word to us: "Bind them continually upon your heart; tie them around your neck" (Prov. 6:21, NKJV) and "Let not mercy and truth forsake you; bind them around your neck; write them on the tablet of your heart" (Prov. 3:3, NKJV). Clearly, there is a connection between God's writing His law on our hearts and our writing His word on our hearts. It is a work of mutual cooperation. God's doing is only with our active cooperation. Warriors, read your Manuals! Daily!

Keep Talking: You might think that now with your armor complete the matter has come to its conclusion. There's more. *Every warrior must have clear*

Listening for direction from the Supreme Commander. Keep the channel clear.

communication lines direct to the Commander and use them often (Eph. 6:18). When I feel an attack is imminent, I put in a call to the Commander immediately (there's no hold button at headquarters). Sometimes the attack is well under way before I realize that I am in mortal danger. My mind has betrayed me to the enemy, and he is already within the fortress. One quick, simple prayer for me is actually a song that goes something like this: "Lord Jesus, I long to be perfectly whole. I want you forever to rule in my soul." Words, volume, and melody can be changed to suit the circumstances, but it never fails to bring in the reinforcements in full battle readiness (the battle is the Lord's, remember, as is the victory). The enemy is usually in rapid retreat if not in total rout before I've finished the song. Of course, I don't stop until he's been driven off the field.

As spiritual warriors we must recognize that to let any situation cut our links with our Commander is fatal. I am sure that anyone would call the Commander if he is up to his navel in hungry alligators. It's a no brainer that these situations require an immediate call for help. But what about the good times when the sun shines all day, the job is giving full satisfaction, the bills get paid, the crisis of the past weeks is a fading memory, and no one in the family is waiting in the line up to see the doctor—or the probation officer? When the sailing is smooth and the sun is warm, do you forget to pray? (As I write this, an old song is teasing me. I recall only these words: *Don't forget to pray.* But maybe that's all I need to remember.)

Prayer in the good times is as crucial as prayer in the bad times—maybe more so because, we imagine, surely the enemy can't be very close when the sun shines and everything's going my way (and my guard begins to relax just a little).

Doesn't he lurk in the dens of iniquity where I never go? Then wham! I've just been blindsided.

The enemy within has opened the gates to the enemy without. From ancient times Scripture has warned us about the tenacity of the enemy and the need to, as Paul unmistakably put it, "pray without ceasing" (1 Thess. 5:17, NKJV). He describes his own practice in other language: continually (Eph. 1:3; 2:13), at all times (Rom. 1:9, 19), on all occasions (Eph. 6:18), always (Col. 1:3), and night and day (2 Tim. 1:3). This clear statement has generated a lot of discussion as people try to rationalize their lapses. How can I pray ceaselessly when there are so many details on my mind? That might have been OK for Paul when times were simple but in the postmodern world it's just not practical. We feel it's easier to ask for post-fall forgiveness than to maintain a constant alert. I would suggest (strongly) that Paul was teaching exactly what the Commander expects of ever warrior—continual, unceasing communication with Himself.

Granted, there are many things we might have to cut out of our lives to achieve this level of contact, but the price is cheap enough at any cost. We are told to talk to our Commander about every single detail of our battles—our victories, defeats, near misses, joys, and sorrows. The Commander is interested in knowing our fears, our weariness, and our longing for victory, especially over the things that interfere with prayer. Always give thanks to God for everything (Eph. 5:20)—don't forget that the victory belongs to the Lord, and He will give it to us when He sees that we are ready to receive it. Just keep on praying—continually, at all times, on all occasions, always, night and day, without ceasing, and the grace of the Commander will be with us without intermission.

Our strength to stand is given to us when we pray. From this we could learn, if we would, the crucial nature of continuing, uninterrupted vigilance maintained through uninterrupted prayer. Our victory is worth the price. Lord, grant us this grace: to pray without ceasing in the name of Jesus, our Brother in the battle. We need nothing else.

Pray for all the warriors whose battles are unique though not unlike your own (Eph. 6:18). Might we learn from this command that our own standing in the battle is somehow related to our interest in the standing of our fellow warriors? Notice, too, that the command is to pray for all the warriors, not just those we like, who do not irritate us, or those who appear to pull their weight in the battle or who happen to be members of our platoon. We neglect or ignore this command at our own peril. Paul reminded his Ephesians that for three years he "did not cease to warn everyone night and day with tears" (Acts 20:31, NKJV). When we look at Paul's prayer life, we can be sure that he was praying night and day for them as well.

And be alert to all the signals that the Commander sends (Eph. 6:18). In this battle for our souls, we need to be careful not to limit the avenues by which God chooses to communicate with us. He is the Commander, after all, before all, and in spite of all—in spite of how important we are tempted to think we are. In past ages He spoke through prophets, priests, and kings. He spoke through a little girl (2 Kings 5:3) and through a little boy (1 Sam. 3:18). He spoke through wind, fire, earthquake, and a still small voice (1 Kings 19:11, 12). He spoke through rain (Gen. 7:12; 1 Kings 18:45) and the absence of rain (1 Kings 17:1), and when His stubborn people obstinately refused to open their ears, He spoke with the sword of metal (Ezek. 5:17).

Has God changed (Mal. 3:6)? Where should we direct our antennae for authoritative messages in the twenty-first century? Looking about this sad earth today, we can see horrifying destruction by fire, water, and wind, by heat and cold, by earthquake and tsunami, by war and social tumult. People try to get public attention by bloody acts of slaughter of the innocents as in Norway, Finland, Britain, Spain, the United States, Pakistan, and Iraq. Do these events have meaning? Does God attach messages to these "natural" and human-instigated disasters? How should we interpret them? Thankfully, we have the Written Word and the Holy Spirit to assist us as we try to make sense of senseless destruction.

Jesus, in teaching His disciples of times to come (including our time), used a word with eternal significance: watch. *Keep watch, because no one knows the day or the hour I will return* (Matt. 25:13). Keep alert; guard the avenues of your soul. Put on the full armor of God; fill your mind with the Word of God; ask for and receive the gift of the Holy Spirit (Luke 11:13), and cry out for God while He is near (Isa. 55:6). Paul tells us that we must endure hardships as good soldiers in the Lord's army (2 Tim. 2:3). *You've enlisted in God's army and put on the full armor, don't be distracted now by civilian affairs* (2 Tim. 2:4). Keep alert to all the signals that the Commander sends!

The Pastor Needs Our Prayers—Paul, called and commissioned by God to share the gospel with Gentiles and kings (Acts 9:15), felt a most compelling need for the prayers of the congregations of believers he had raised up and nurtured across Asia Minor and parts of Europe. In the vanguard of the army of believers, he was continuously exposed to the threats and assaults of the devil—as we are, though he was probably more acutely aware of the source of his trials.

I believe that because of his unswerving obedience to the divine commission Paul was more savagely targeted by the enemy than is the nominal Christian. He experienced his own dictum that "everyone who wants to live a godly life in Christ Jesus will be persecuted" (2 Tim. 3:12). After reminding Timothy of the persecutions and sufferings he had endured, he went on to encourage the young man: Continue in what you have learned. Don't let the threat of persecution and even death deter you from following my example and teaching. Persecution and death are to be scorned; we should only fear separation from God. However, know this: God has promised never to leave us (Heb. 13:5).

If God will never leave us, our prayer has to be to remain in His presence, to retain the Holy Spirit in our minds, to have the presence of Jesus in our hearts through faith, and to take hold of His grace and obey. Paul experienced continuous attacks from Satan. Because of his ministry, he was exposed and vulnerable. He was a popular and hated man. Those who hated him did so passionately; his friends loved him with equal and opposite passion. Poor, vulnerable Paul! He had no earthly escape, no retreat from friend or enemy. He could hide only in Christ.

Paul cherished his friends deeply, but the love and admiration of his friends was perfect camouflage for the enemy. The many revelations from God also appealed to his pride; hence, God gave him the thorn in his flesh (2 Cor. 12:7). We need to be careful about fretting over trials in our lives; they could be messengers of God to keep our hubris in check. As for our pastors, though not usually in metal chains and stone dungeons in North America, they really are exposed and vulnerable.

Upfront people are sometimes popular and sometimes simply tolerated; few are hated. They daily face the devil in the guise of human enemies, friends, and difficult circumstances. Sadly, in the houses of friends our pastors receive the greatest abuse (Zech. 13:6) and are in the greatest danger. They need our prayers. We need to pray for them that they will *fearlessly preach the mystery of the gospel and not be distracted by these incidental issues of little importance* (Eph. 6:19). We would pray for them if we were obedient to our own calling.

I am simultaneously excited at the prospect of a congregation united in prayer and saddened at the apparent indifference of so many members. We go through the motions of church (I can still talk about me in these terms) without the power of the promised Spirit. Pray! Pray! Don't give up so near our blessed home!

A weak example is all I can muster at 4:00 a.m. I'm riding my bicycle in the race. The hill is steep (15 percent), long (300 meters), and the gravel resembles boulders. My whole body wants to throw myself off the bicycle, and my mind is almost convinced to obey. I gauge the distance to the horizon at which incline disappears into sky. Don't give up now! You've come this far; this is not where you want to give up! But I do want to give up! I do! Desperately! That's the problem! The horizon gets slowly, painfully (very painfully) closer. Don't give up here! I'm wobbly! I hurt! My body *wants* to quit! My mind *wants* to quit. Not here! This is not the place. Don't quit here. Push on! Push on! Don't stop!

This is not the place to quit. We have infinitely more and stronger resources than the weak will of an exhausted peddler. We have every resource of heaven! Just ask! This is the time to pray without ceasing. This is the time for all of us to pray for our pastors, for ourselves, for each other, for submission, for the promised gift of the Holy Spirit (Gal. 3:14). Pray! Now! Don't stop here! Paul, God's ambassador in chains, was totally confident that the gospel could not be chained as long as the believers continued to pray for him to preach it fearlessly. The gospel cannot forever be chained by its enemies … though it can be obstructed by its friends.

We are well aware that the gospel has been virtually obliterated in many areas at many times. Jesus was rejected and crucified. The "falling away" (2 Thess. 2:3, NKJV) obscured the gospel for centuries. Rationalism tried in the eighteenth century. Official atheism in the Soviet Union, China, Albania, and elsewhere made heroic efforts to stamp out any vestiges of the knowledge of God. Unofficial atheism (secular humanism in all its forms) today is rendering the gospel a curiosity to some, if they ever think of it, and a thing to scorn by those who imagine themselves to be wise. Non-Christian religions are rising up to reject with violence the threat of the gospel.

Still, the gospel cannot be chained forever. God's purpose knows no haste and no delay. Time means nothing to Him because He lives outside time. When earth time is right, He will intervene in our lives, our societies, our affairs (we actually imagine these things are ours); we will know then that He is in charge.

That being so our prayer must be to remain in Him (John 15:4). Our prayer for our pastors must be for their continuing faithfulness in fearlessly preaching the gospel and in rebuking sin, as they should; our prayer for ourselves must be for grace to uphold the pastors in their work. Our prayer for the congregation must be for unity in the Spirit of God. We must pray for fearlessness for ourselves in sharing the gospel. When He comes, will Jesus Christ find faith on the earth? I believe He will. There will be a congregation of believers waiting to welcome Him. Who will be among that congregation? I believe it will be those who have continued in prayer, in trust, and in confidence in the One who cannot lie, who has promised never to leave us nor forsake us (Heb. 13:5). It will be those who wore the armor through hot and cold and who would not, did not give up even when the pain of continuing was too hard to endure.

The pastor needs the prayers of the members. The congregation needs the experience of never-ending prayer for the pastor—and for each other in this soon-ending battle of the Lord; His fight; His victory. We are not pawns. We are the prize. And we get to choose between the One who will take us home—or the one who will take us to the other place, the place prepared for him and his angels (Matt. 25:41). Pray without ceasing!

Grace and Peace to All

I am sending Tychicus, my dear and faithful brother in the service of the Lord, to you dear saints in Ephesus so that he can tell you all the news about me and encourage you in the Lord.

Peace, love, and faith from God the Father and our Lord, Jesus Christ. May God's grace continue to bless you because you love our Lord with a love that will not die. (Eph. 6:21–24)

Blessings on You, Dear Friends; I Remain, Paul—Paul is in prison for the Lord and for the sake of the gospel to the Gentiles. His wrists are manacled and rubbed raw by the iron cuffs. He is cold and his old bones ache. Yet, true to his calling, he is thinking of the congregation he left behind so long ago in Ephesus. How are they faring? How is their courage? Are they faithful in the Lord? Ah, Tychicus! He will send Tychicus whom he trusts not only to give an accurate picture of his own love for the Ephesians and of his strong and enduring confidence in God but also to faithfully encourage them in the Lord. Of utmost importance is the message of the true nature of his captivity: he is a prisoner of the Lord, not of the Romans (Eph. 3:1). As a prisoner of the Lord, he is there for his love for the gospel and the people whom he has led to Christ. Paul the apostle, Paul the prophet, Paul the evangelist, Paul the consummate pastor and teacher is consistently and passionately leading his people, always concerned for their continuing commitment to Christ, always ready to suffer for them. Can we take him as our role model in these things? Is he an example for believers in this generation?

Paul is a worthy role model and example for us as we approach the end of temporality and the beginning of the age to come. It is so easy to argue that Paul was this or that and, because we are not this or that, his life and work are largely irrelevant. Having read Ephesians scores of times in the course of this study, I have formed my short and decisive answer to this argument: Paul is writing under divine inspiration, he *is* writing for our time, and we would do well to follow his example in word and in behavior.

Paul signs off with a flourish. Just as he opened his letter with a prayer for "grace and peace to [the church] from God our Father and the Lord Jesus Christ" (Eph. 1:2), so he closes: *Peace, love, and faith from God the Father and our Lord, Jesus Christ. May God's grace continue to bless those who love our Lord with a love that will not die* (Eph. 6:23, 24). With full confidence in the Ephesians, Paul delivers his completed work to the care of trusty Tychicus for the dangerous journey to Ephesus. Little might he realize that 2,000 years later, congregations of believers and companies of warriors around the world, in digging into the Ephesians for nuggets of truth, will joyfully discover that they have unearthed not just a few nuggets but the mother lode.

Epilogue

Thank You, Jesus, for sending Your Spirit to revive my soul. This two-year ride through Ephesians on the shoulders of Paul is actually the story of my rescue from my delusional, faithless experience—from deadness in sin to life in Christ. This story of God's grace for a little part of the dying race, this story of what God is able, willing, eager, and ready to do for each one of His self-deceived children is my story.

I have not written a detailed account of my growth in grace, but as I rode the shoulders of Paul through Ephesians, I continually discovered viewpoints from which I was able to observe grace at work in my life. I have recounted this working of grace in the hope that my experience might in some way encourage another traveler on the way to the eternal kingdom of light, music, color, laughter, joy—through grace to glory.

Growth in grace does lead to growth in obedience. Obedience in the details of daily life is important to our Father as an indicator of the level of faith we possess and the grace we have been willing to receive. Before this world ends in the fire and holy smoke and royal glory of the second coming of Jesus, God will have been vindicated in those who take His name. Their lives of obedience will have honored Him; their love for all the saints will have brought Him glory—and will continue to do so throughout eternity.

Finally, I now understand that our Father is facing judgment in *us*. Our lives are going to vindicate Him in the judgment—what an awesome assignment! He has, so to speak, stuck His neck out with the irrevocable promise that His grace is sufficient in power and sufficient in scope to cover all our deficiencies (2 Cor. 12:9). Clearly this includes our need for peace in the congregation, our need for obedience in the details, our need for love for all the saints, our need to worship Him in memory of His creative and redemptive acts, and our need to rejoice and be thankful under all circumstances. Not only does He cover our spiritual deficiencies, He removes them and gives us the character of His Son, Jesus.

Thank You, Lord, for taking a man who was trying to atone for his own sins and showing him the folly of his attempts. Thank You for taking this silly, obstinate, obtuse slow learner and gently, and sometimes not so gently, leading him to ultimate full victory in Jesus.

Am I there yet? I would never claim to be. The closer I come to Jesus, the more wicked I seem to myself. The more I study Ephesians, the more hypocritical I appear in my own eyes. I am daily seeing other flaws that I have given God permission in advance to remove. I am willing for Him to work on me until the last flaw is gone. Because He is the One pressing me to the sanding wheel, He gets all the glory, the full vindication in the finished product of His grace. May God be honored in me forever—and in you, too! Lord, thank You again!

That's my story. What's yours? By the way, I did memorize the entire letter of Paul to the Ephesians in the NIV. Try it; you'll like it.

We invite you to view the complete
selection of titles we publish at:

www.TEACHServices.com

Scan with your mobile
device to go directly
to our website.

Please write or email us your praises, reactions, or
thoughts about this or any other book we publish at:

P.O. Box 954
Ringgold, GA 30736

info@TEACHServices.com

TEACH Services, Inc., titles may be purchased in bulk for
educational, business, fund-raising, or sales promotional use.
For information, please e-mail:

BulkSales@TEACHServices.com

Finally, if you are interested in seeing
your own book in print, please contact us at

publishing@TEACHServices.com

We would be happy to review your manuscript for free.

www.ingramcontent.com/pod-product-compliance
Lightning Source LLC
Chambersburg PA
CBHW081838170426
43199CB00017B/2769